Installing, Configuring, and Administering Microsoft® Windows® XP Professional

Student Lab Manual

Exam 70-270

Installing, Configuring, and Administering Microsoft® Windows® XP Professional

Student Lab Manual

Exam 70-270

First Edition

Kenneth C. Laudon, Series Designer
Stacey McBrine, MCSE, MCSA

The Azimuth Interactive MCSE/MCSA Team
Carol G. Traver, Series Editor
Kenneth Rosenblatt
Robin L. Pickering
Russell Polo
David Langley
Barbara W. Ryan
Mark A. Maxwell
Brian Hill, MCSE, MCSA
Richard Watson, MCSE, MCSA

PEARSON
Prentice Hall

Upper Saddle River, New Jersey, 07458

Senior Vice President/Publisher: Natalie Anderson
Executive Editor: Steven Elliot
Senior Marketing Manager: Steven Rutberg
Assistant Editor: Allison Marcus
Manager, Print Production: Christy Mahon
Production Editor & Buyer: Carol O'Rourke
Manager, Multimedia: Christy Mahon
Composition: Azimuth Interactive, Inc.
Quality Assurance: Digital Content Factory, Ltd.
Printer/Binder: Courier, Stoughton

10 9 8 7 6 5 4
ISBN 0-13-144450-6

*To our families,
for their love, patience,
and inspiration.*

Brief Contents

Preface xiii

Lesson 1   Introducing Windows XP Professional 1.2

Lesson 2   Installing Windows XP Professional 2.2

Lesson 3   Managing Hardware Devices 3.2

Lesson 4   Working with the Control Panel 4.2

Lesson 5   Managing Data Storage 5.2

Lesson 6   Installing and Configuring Network Protocols 6.2

Lesson 7   Performing Administrative Tasks 7.2

Lesson 8   Administering User Accounts and Groups 8.2

Lesson 9   Working with Shared Folders 9.2

Lesson 10   Setting Up, Configuring, and Administering Network Printers 10.2

Lesson 11   Working with NTFS Permissions 11.2

Lesson 12   Configuring Local Security Policies 12.2

Lesson 13   Monitoring Events and Resources 13.2

Lesson 14   Backing Up and Restoring Data 14.2

Lesson 15   Working with the Registry and Boot Process 15.2

Lesson 16   Configuring Remote Access and Dial-up Networking 16.2

Lesson 17   Introducing DNS and Web Server Resources 17.2

Contents

Preface xiii

Lesson 1   **Introducing Windows XP Professional** 1.2

1.1   Identifying the Key Features of Windows XP Professional 1.4
1.2   Introducing Windows XP Security Features 1.6
1.3   Introducing Workgroups and Domains 1.10

Lesson 2   **Installing Windows XP Professional** 2.2

2.1   Identifying Pre-Installation Tasks 2.4
2.2   Installing Windows XP Professional Using a CD-ROM .2.6
2.3   Upgrading a Previous Version of Windows to Windows XP Professional 2.10
2.4   Using the Windows XP Setup Manager 2.14
2.5   Installing Windows XP Professional Using an Unattended Setup 2.20
2.6   Using the System Preparation Tool 2.24
2.7   Resolving Problems Encountered During Setup 2.28
2.8   Installing Service Packs and Automatic Updates 2.32

Lesson 3   **Managing Hardware Devices** 3.2

3.1   Configuring I/O Devices 3.4
3.2   Configuring Mass Storage Devices 3.6
3.3   Adding a Modem 3.8
3.4   Configuring Fax Devices 3.10
3.5   Upgrading Device Drivers 3.12
3.6   Managing Driver Signing 3.14
3.7   Managing Universal Serial Bus and Multimedia Devices .3.16

Lesson 4   **Working with the Control Panel** 4.2

4.1   Tuning System Performance 4.4
4.2   Configuring Internet Settings 4.6
4.3   Configuring Scheduled Tasks 4.10
4.4   Setting Display Properties 4.12
4.5   Configuring Multiple Displays 4.14
4.6   Configuring Power Options 4.16

Lesson 5   Managing Data Storage 5.2

5.1   Upgrading a Basic Disk to a Dynamic Disk 5.4

5.2   Creating Volumes 5.6

5.3   Converting File Systems 5.10

5.4   Introducing Disk Quotas 5.12

5.5   Copying and Moving Compressed Files and Folders 5.16

5.6   Using Disk Defragmenter 5.20

Lesson 6   Installing and Configuring Network Protocols 6.2

6.1   Configuring TCP/IP to Use a Static IP Address 6.4

6.2   Troubleshooting TCP/IP Problems 6.6

6.3   Installing NWLink on a System 6.8

6.4   Configuring Network Bindings 6.12

6.5   Configuring Network Bridge 6.14

Lesson 7   Performing Administrative Tasks 7.2

7.1   Viewing Preconfigured Microsoft Management Consoles 7.4

7.2   Creating Custom Consoles 7.6

7.3   Creating Taskpad Views 7.10

7.4   Adding Extensions to Snap-ins 7.14

7.5   Configuring Logon/Logoff Scripts 7.16

Lesson 8   Administering User Accounts and Groups 8.2

8.1   Creating a Local User Account 8.4

8.2   The User Accounts Utility 8.8

8.3   Managing User Accounts 8.10

8.4   Creating and Using a Password Reset Disk 8.14

8.5   Creating Local Groups 8.18

8.6   Adding Members to a Group 8.20

Lesson 9   Working with Shared Folders 9.2

9.1   Sharing a Folder 9.4

9.2   Introducing Types of Permissions for Shared Folders 9.10

9.3   Monitoring Access to Shared Folders 9.14

9.4   Configuring and Managing Offline Files and Folders 9.18

Lesson 10 Setting Up, Configuring, and Administering Network Printers 10.2

10.1 Adding and Sharing a Local Printer 10.4

10.2 Connecting to a Network Printer 10.8

10.3 Assigning Printer Permissions 10.12

10.4 Configuring and Managing Printers 10.16

Lesson 11 Working with NTFS Permissions 11.2

11.1 Identifying Types of NTFS Permissions 11.4

11.2 Assigning NTFS Permissions 11.8

11.3 Using Special Permissions 11.12

Lesson 12 Configuring Local Security Policies 12.2

12.1 Configuring Password Policy 12.4

12.2 Enhancing Computer Security Using Account Lockout Policy 12.8

12.3 Configuring Security Options 12.10

12.4 Increasing Security Using EFS (Encrypting File System) 12.14

12.5 Recovering Encrypted Files Using Recovery Agents 12.18

12.6 Securing Data on a Network Using IPSec Policies 12.22

12.7 Working with Security Templates 12.26

Lesson 13 Monitoring Events and Resources 13.2

13.1 Introducing Auditing 13.4

13.2 Auditing Access to Files and Folders 13.8

13.3 Managing Auditing 13.12

13.4 Monitoring System Performance 13.16

13.5 Configuring Alerts 13.18

Lesson 14 Backing Up and Restoring Data 14.2

14.1 Backing Up Data 14.4

14.2 Restoring Data from a Backup 14.8

14.3 Changing the Default Backup and Restore Options 14.12

14.4 Performing an Automated System Recovery Backup 14.16

14.5 Using System Restore to Revert to a Previous Configuration 14.20

Lesson 15 Working with the Registry and Boot Process ..15.2

15.1 Working with the Registry Editor 15.4

15.2 Modifying the boot.ini File 15.8

15.3 Identifying Advanced Boot Options 15.10

15.4 Using the Recovery Console 15.14

Lesson 16 Configuring Remote Access and Dial-up Networking 16.2

16.1 Creating a Dial-Up Connection to a Remote Access Server 16.4

16.2 Connecting to the Internet by Using a Dial-Up Connection 16.8

16.3 Setting Up a VPN Connection 16.12

16.4 Configuring Inbound Connections 16.16

16.5 Configuring Internet Connection Sharing 16.20

16.6 Setting Up a Firewall 16.24

16.7 Configuring Remote Desktop and Remote Assistance 16.30

Lesson 17 Introducing DNS and Web Server Resources ..17.2

17.1 Configuring Windows XP as a DNS Client 17.4

17.2 Managing Web Server Resources 17.6

The purpose of this Student Lab Manual is to provide you, the student, with another opportunity to review Windows XP Professional concepts and skills, and to apply them to situations that you are likely to encounter on the job. The Laudon Certification Series textbooks contain a great deal of conceptual and hands-on material. The Laudon Certification Series Student Lab Manuals are designed to give you an opportunity to put those concepts and skills to work in a variety of different real-world on-the-job situations, and to understand the textbook contents in greater depth.

The Student Lab Manuals are organized in the same two-page highly illustrated format with conceptual material and instructions on the left-hand page, and screenshots and conceptual diagrams on the right-hand page. The Lessons in the Student Lab Manuals follow the Lessons in the textbook. Each Lab Manual Lesson is composed of a number of projects that reinforce the concepts and skills taught in the accompanying textbooks.

Lab Manual Lesson Contents

The Lab Manual Lessons have a number of elements designed to speed your learning and help you understand key concepts and skills.

Introductory Page: Each Lesson begins with an introductory page that reviews the key concepts and skills that you will be asked to apply in the lesson.

Scenario: Each Lesson has a brief scenario that describes the setting in which the projects take place. These scenarios provide you with a sense of how the concepts and skills that you have learned in the book are used in realistic business settings.

Project/Objective Table: Each Lesson includes a table that lists the Lesson projects and the corresponding exam objective supported. Where the project relates to a basic understanding of the subject matter, this is referred to as "Basic knowledge." You will always know how a project relates to MCSE/MCSA exam requirements.

General Requirements: At the beginning of each Lesson, there is a description of the hardware and software that you will need to complete the projects in the Lesson.

Project's Exam Objective: For each project there is a description of the specific MCSA/MCSE exam objective supported by the project.

Overview: Each project presents a specific assignment that builds on the Lesson's main scenario.

Learning Objective: Each project includes a specific learning objective that describes what you will be able to do after completing the project.

Specific Requirements: A list of specific requirements for each project is provided.

Estimated Completion Time: For each project, there is an estimated time for completion based on the experience of MCSE/MCSA professionals and instructors in colleges and training institutes. You should use these estimates only as a guide because your actual completion times will depend on your prior experience with Windows XP Professional.

Project Steps: Each project includes a set of step-by-step instructions for completing the project. These instructions are similar to those in the main textbook, but often differ because new options and pathways may be explored in the Lab Manuals.

Tips: Throughout the Student Lab Manuals you will find Tips and Cautions that offer you suggestions or comments about completing the project and working with Windows XP Professional.

Graphics and Illustrations: As you can expect from the Laudon Certification Series, there are many screenshots and conceptual graphics provided that show you how the software should look at various points in the project. These are intended to familiarize you with the Windows XP Professional environment and assure you that you are on the right track.

Quality Assurance

We have made every effort to ensure that the Student Lab Manuals are written to the same quality standards as the main text-book and the Laudon MCSE/MCSA Interactive Solutions CD-ROM. The Student Lab Manuals are written by MCSE and MCSA professionals with many years of real-world experience. The initial instructions and scenarios are then reviewed by independent technical editors who test each project, and each step. These results are then verified by the MCSE/MCSA team at Azimuth and the Series Designer and Editor. The end result is a product that students and instructors can understand and trust.

Notice

The projects in the Student Lab Manuals have been built using the most recent release of Windows XP Professional and Windows 2000 Server software. Your school or other institution may be using an earlier release of the software, or its environment may differ in some respects from the environment in which the projects were built. At times, these variations in environment and service packs can cause variations in the progression of steps and screenshots so that a screenshot in the book does not precisely match the screen you may be looking at. If this should occur, please report this to the authors at the Web site for this book.

Introducing Windows XP Professional

The features and enhancements in Windows XP Professional include:

- **Reduced total cost of ownership:** Microsoft claims that Windows XP lowers the total cost of ownership (sometimes referred to as TCO) of corporate networks by using technologies that enable automatic installation and upgrading of the operating system and applications.
- **Security:** The Windows XP operating system incorporates a variety of enhanced security features. When used in a network running the Active Directory, the Kerberos authentication protocol provides a very secure method for authenticating users. Files and folders can be encrypted using the Encrypting File System (EFS). Internet Protocol Security (IPSec) and Layer 2 Tunneling Protocol (L2TP) allow for more secure VPN connections. Internet Connection Firewall blocks unauthorized connection attempts. Windows XP also has the ability to perform system audits and impose secure access to files, directories, printers, and other resources.
- **Multiprocessing, multitasking, and multithreading:** The Windows XP operating system supports multiprocessing, multitasking, and multithreading.
- **Connectivity:** Windows XP Professional supports a variety of network protocols, such as TCP/IP (Transmission Control Protocol/Internet Protocol) and NWLink, as well as providing connectivity with UNIX systems. Windows XP also supports dial-up networking.
- **Hardware support:** Windows XP Professional supports Plug and Play, which allows a computer to automatically detect and configure a hardware device and install the appropriate device drivers. Windows XP also supports the Universal Serial Bus (USB) standard, which allows a single port to support up to 127 peripheral devices and enables you to connect and disconnect devices without shutting down or restarting your computer. The IEEE 1394 high-performance serial bus, also known as FireWire, is also supported. DVDs, digital scanners, hand-held devices, and cameras are supported as well.
- **Greater Ease of Use:** Windows XP features an enhanced user interface that makes the operating system easier to use and control.
- **Manageability:** Windows XP Professional can participate in either a workgroup or a domain. Many of the best manageability features are only available in an Active Directory domain. When used in a network running the Active Directory, Windows XP Professional can be centrally managed through the use of Group Policies. Active Directory provides a centralized method for managing workstation configuration, security rules, application installation, network resources, and network access. Windows XP computers also have the ability to automatically assign themselves IP addresses even if a network server is offline.

Scenario

You are working as an Administrator at Pyramid Inc. The company currently has 8 employees but there are plans to hire an additional 5 employees within the next six months. You want to upgrade the operating systems of the computers in your network from older versions of Windows to Windows XP Professional. In order to do this, you must prepare a presentation to convince the CEO of your company that the various new and enhanced features of Windows XP Professional, make it a vast improvement over earlier Windows versions. You also want to consider whether to switch from your current peer-to-peer workgroup environment to a domain-based network.

Lesson 1   Introducing Windows XP Professional

Project	Exam 70-270 Objective
1.1 Identifying the Key Features of Windows XP Professional	Basic knowledge
1.2 Introducing Windows XP Security Features	Basic knowledge
1.3 Introducing Workgroups and Domains	Basic knowledge

General Requirements

There are no special requirements for this lesson.

project 1.1 | *Identifying the Key Features of Windows XP Professional*

exam objective

Basic knowledge

overview

In order to convince the CEO of your company of the benefits of Windows XP Professional, you will prepare a presentation that describes the features and advantages of Windows XP Professional.

learning objective

After completing this project, you will be able to identify the benefits of Windows XP Professional.

specific requirements

None

estimated completion time

15 minutes

project steps

1. Describe the features and advantages of the Windows XP Professional operating system (**Figure 1-1**).
2. Describe the enhanced features of Windows XP Professional and explain its benefits compared to earlier versions of the operating system.
3. Explain the ways Windows XP Professional can be used in a network environment.

Figure 1-1 Windows XP features and enhancements

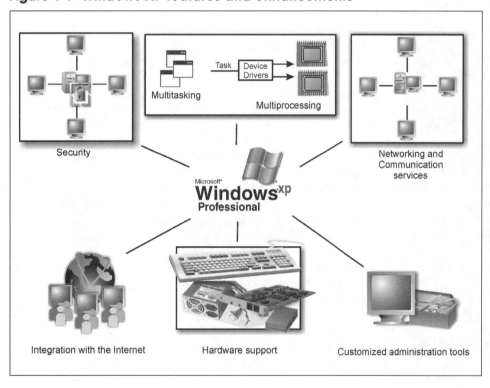

project 1.2

Introducing Windows XP Security Features

exam objective

Basic knowledge

overview

In your presentation, you also want to describe the benefits of using Windows XP Professional as a secure network operating system. This will convince the CEO of your company that using Windows XP Professional in a network environment is superior to using earlier versions of the operating system. The features of Windows XP Professional relating to system security include **(Figure 1-2)**:

♦ **Kerberos V5:** This is an Internet standard authentication protocol for handling the authentication of user or system identity. Kerberos V5 is the primary authentication protocol for the Windows XP operating system in an Active Directory domain. With Kerberos V5, the user's password is used to generate an encryption key that is then used to encrypt a series of messages that are sent between the client and a Kerberos Authentication Server. The Authentication Server along with the Ticket Granting Server act as a third-party that distributes tickets used to authenticate network communications. The user's password never crosses the network connection and all messages that are exchanged, are protected from capture and replay through time stamps stored in the messages.

♦ **Encrypting File System (EFS):** Using Windows XP Professional, users can encrypt files on a hard disk as long as it has been formatted with NTFS. Data in an encrypted file is scrambled using a symmetric encryption key. This means that the same key that is used to encrypt the file is also used to decrypt it. Symmetric encryption is very efficient; however, if the file encryption key (FEK) is compromised, the file will no longer be secure. For this reason, EFS also uses asymmetric encryption in the form of a public/private key pair. EFS encrypts the FEK using the user's public key. The user's private key, which is normally stored in a secure area of the user's profile, is used to decrypt the FEK which in turn decrypts the contents of the file. Either the user that encrypted the file or a user account that has been designated as a recovery agent for the file can simply log on in order to transparently decrypt the file.

♦ **Internet Protocol Security (IPSec):** IPSec is used to encrypt Transmission Control Protocol/Internet Protocol (TCP/IP) traffic to ensure that communications within an intranet or the Internet are more secure. Typically used to support VPNs (Virtual Private Networks), IPSec provides the highest level of Internet security currently possible. IPSec is a security addition to the IP protocol that, when enabled, protects communications so that no one except the receiver can read what is sent over the network.

♦ **Smart card support:** Smart cards are credit-card-sized devices that are used to store passwords, public and private keys, and other types of identifying data. You can attach a smart card reader to a Windows XP computer to enable a secure two-factor authentication scheme. To log on to Windows XP Professional, a user inserts the smart card into a smart card reader and enters a personal identification number (PIN). The smart card then uses certificate-based authentication to securely log the user onto the system.

caution

If for any reason all private keys associated with an encrypted file are lost, it will be practically impossible to recover the contents of the file.

tip

You can improve the performance of IPSec by using IPSec Enabled network adapter cards.

Figure 1-2 Windows XP security features

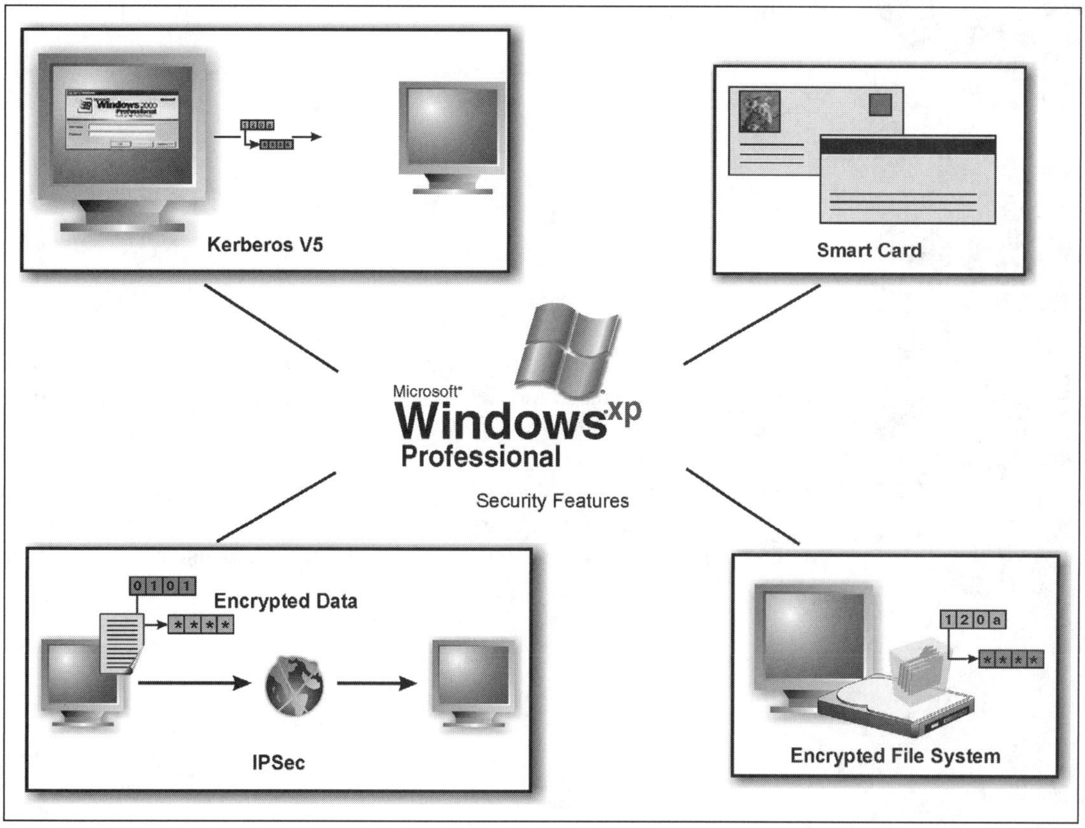

project 1.2

Introducing Windows XP Security Features (cont'd)

exam objective	Basic knowledge
learning objective	After completion of this project, you will be able to describe the new security features of Windows XP Professional.
specific requirements	None
estimated completion time	15 minutes
project steps	Using Windows XP Help and Support, create a presentation describing the following points:

1. Explain the features of the Kerberos V5 protocol that support network security.
2. Define the concept of Virtual Private Network support (VPN) and list the protocols used to create a VPN.
3. Explain what EFS is (**Figure 1-3**), what file system(s) supports it, and how will it help to keep network resources secure.
4. Describe smart cards and explain how they are used to enhance network security.

Figure 1-3 Using EFS to encrypt a folder on an NTFS disk

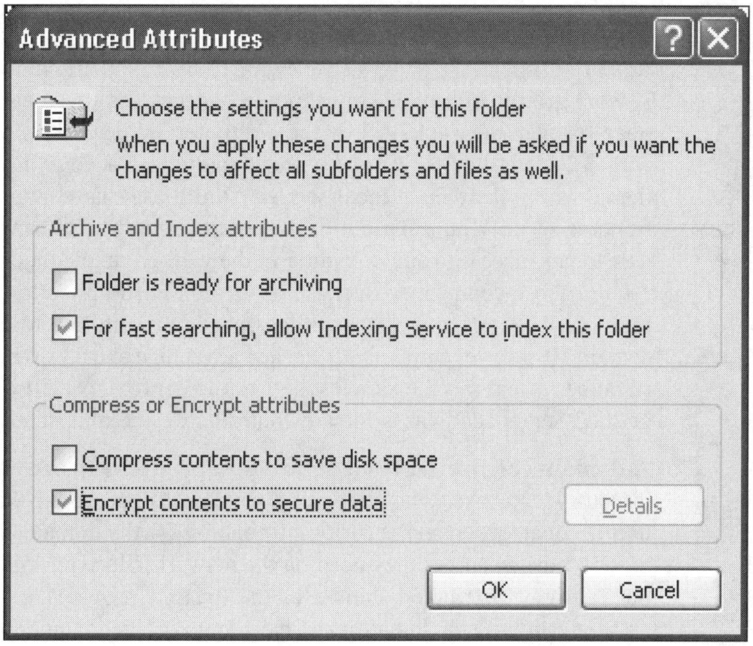

project 1.3

Introducing Workgroups and Domains

exam objective

Basic knowledge

overview

Your current network uses a workgroup network structure. You are aware that the Windows XP operating system supports both workgroups and domains, and you wonder whether it might be more advantageous to switch to a domain-based network structure. You decide to investigate the advantages and disadvantages of both types.

A **workgroup (Figure 1-4)** is an interconnected group of computers often referred to as a **peer-to-peer network**. All of the computers in a workgroup share resources as equals, without a dedicated server and without centralized account management. Each computer on the network maintains a **local security database** that contains user accounts, groups, and resource security information for the computer on which the database resides. In order for a user to gain access to any computer in the workgroup, he or she must have a user account on each of those computers. Because of the administrative effort to maintain user accounts in multiple locations, a workgroup does not scale well and Microsoft recommends that they contain 10 or fewer computers. One key advantage to using Windows XP workgroups to share resources is that it is the simplest network to configure and does not require a Windows 2000 or 2003 Server acting as a domain controller to store information.

A **domain (Figure 1-5)** is a logical grouping of network computers that share a central directory database. The **directory database**, known as Active Directory, contains all user account, group and security information for the domain. Users can search the directory to locate the resources they need on the network. Since the entire network directory is stored on a single distributed database, the system provides centralized administration and authentication. Each domain must have at least one domain controller where the contents of Active Directory are stored. A Windows 2000 or 2003 server is required to provide Active Directory. Active Directory is very scalable and can support the largest of organizations.

learning objective

After completing this project, you will be able to identify the advantages and disadvantages of a workgroup vs. a domain-based network structure.

specific requirements

None

estimated completion time

15 minutes

project steps

Prepare a memo that reports your findings on the following topics:
1. The main features, as well as advantages and disadvantages of the workgroup network structure.
2. The main features, as well as advantages and disadvantages of the domain network structure.
3. Your recommendation regarding switching from a peer-to-peer workgroup structure to a domain structure.

Figure 1-4 Windows XP in a workgroup environment

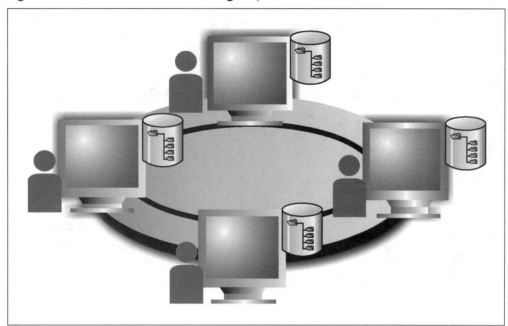

Figure 1-5 Windows XP in a domain environment

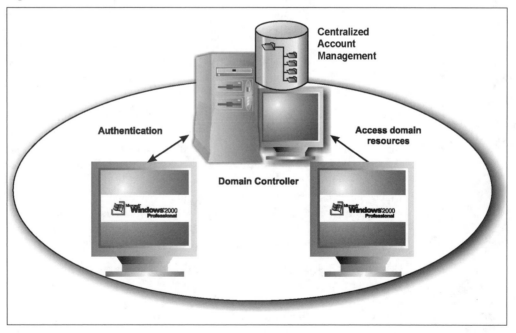

Installing Windows XP Professional

Before you install Windows XP Professional, you should perform certain pre-installation tasks, such as checking that the computer on which the operating system will be installed meets minimum hardware requirements and that all hardware devices are compatible with Windows XP. You must also decide if you want to perform a clean installation of Windows XP or just upgrade from a previously installed version of Windows. If you are currently using Windows 98, ME, NT 4.0 SP5, or 2000 Professional, you can upgrade the existing operating system to Windows XP. You can use the Windows XP Upgrade Advisor to generate a compatibility report about the current hardware and software on a system. The Windows XP Upgrade Advisor can be found at:

http://www.microsoft.com/windowsxp/pro/howtobuy/upgrading/advisor.asp

Once you have completed the pre-installation checklist, you will be ready to actually install Windows XP Professional. There are several different methods from which you can choose. Windows XP Professional can be installed using the Windows XP Professional installation CD-ROM if the computer supports booting from the CD-ROM drive, with floppy boot disks in conjunction with the installation CD-ROM (if your CD-ROM drive is not a bootable drive), or over a network.

Manually installing Windows XP Professional on multiple computers can be a tedious and time-consuming task. To maximize the efficiency of this process, you can use the Windows XP Setup Manager Wizard to create answer files that contain information about the settings that will be used in the installation process. This type of installation is called an unattended installation. The computer is set up with Windows XP Professional, and other applications if desired, with little or no user intervention.

To install Windows XP Professional on multiple computers that have identical hardware configurations, you can create a disk image of the Windows XP Professional installation and copy this image to the other computers. A utility called Sysprep is used to prepare the system for duplication, also referred to as cloning. Sysprep makes sure that the security identifiers (SIDs) are unique on each of the target computers. It also initiates a Mini-Setup Wizard, which can be used on each of the targets to enter computer-specific information such as the user name, domain name, and time zone. Sysprep is included on the Windows XP Professional installation CD in the \Support\Tools\Deploy.cab folder. A third-party utility is used to duplicate the master disk image onto the target computers.

Despite your best efforts, you may still encounter problems during the installation process. If you do, you can look at log files called the action log and the error log to obtain information that can help you diagnose the problem. Once you have successfully installed Windows XP Professional, you should be aware that Microsoft periodically releases utilities and patches that contain error correction or improvements to the operating system and other applications, in the form of service packs.

Scenario

You are a Network Administrator. Your company has decided to switch to Windows XP for their standard desktop operating system. The current network is configured as a workgroup with 5 computers (two with Windows NT 4.0, one withWindows 95, two with Windows 98), and has also purchased 5 new computers with identical hardware configurations. Your company's management would like the switch-over to occur with minimal disruption to the ongoing activities of the business. Also, some employees are concerned that they will not be able to continue to use an application that can run only on the Windows 98 computers.

You are in charge of installing Windows XP Professional on these computers.

Lesson 2   Installing Windows XP Professional

Project	Exam 70-270 Objective
2.1 Identifying Pre-installation Tasks	Prepare a computer to meet upgrade requirements.
2.2 Installing Windows XP Professional Using a CD-ROM	Perform and troubleshoot an attended installation of Windows XP Professional.
2.3 Upgrading a Previous Version of Windows to Windows XP Professional	Upgrade from a previous version of Windows to Windows XP Professional.
2.4 Using the Windows XP Setup Manager	Perform and troubleshoot an unattended installation of Windows XP Professional. Create unattended answer files by using Setup Manager to automate the installation of Windows XP Professional.
2.5 Installing Windows XP Professional Using an Unattended Setup	Perform and troubleshoot an unattended installation of Windows XP Professional. Create unattended answer files by using Setup Manager to automate the installation of Windows XP Professional.
2.6 Using the System Preparation Tool	Perform and troubleshoot an unattended installation of Windows XP Professional. Install Windows XP Professional by using the System Preparation Tool.
2.7 Resolving Problems Encountered During Setup	Troubleshoot failed installations.
2.8 Installing Service Packs and Automatic Updates	Perform post-installation updates and product activation.

General Requirements

In order to complete the projects in this lesson, you should have a computer that meets the minimum hardware requirements needed to support a Windows XP Professional installation and the Windows XP Professional installation CD-ROM. Project 2.4 requires a computer with a previous version of Windows that can be upgraded to Windows XP Professional.

project 2.1

Identifying Pre-Installation Tasks

exam objective

Prepare a computer to meet upgrade requirements.

overview

Before you begin to install Windows XP Professional on the existing computers, you need to assess whether they are capable of running Windows XP, and whether user requirements can be satisfied, decide how you will minimize disruption to the business during the process, and also gather certain information that is needed for installation. Prior to installation, you should also decide whether the existing network structure will suffice for the future needs of the business, or whether this also needs to be changed.

learning objective

After you have completed this project, you will know how to prepare a computer to meet upgrade requirements and plan for an installation of Windows XP Professional.

specific requirements

◆   A Windows XP Professional CD-ROM.
◆   A computer with an existing Windows operating system and a connection to the Internet.

estimated completion time

15 minutes

project steps

Verify that the target computer has compatible hardware and software.

1. Make sure that the target computer meets the minimum requirements to run the Windows XP Professional (**Table 2-1**).
2. Boot the target computer and log on.
3. Insert the Windows XP Professional CD-ROM into the CD-ROM drive.
4. The **Welcome to Microsoft Windows XP** screen will appear (**Figure 2-1**). Click **Check System Compatibility**.
5. On the following screen click **Check My System Automatically**.
6. The **Upgrade Advisor** window will appear (**Figure 2-2**). Make sure that **Yes, download the updated Setup files (Recommended)** is selected. Click **Next**. The Dynamic Update process will attempt to connect to Microsoft's site and download the latest updates for the **Upgrade advisor**.
7. If any updates are found, the next window provides the option of either downloading the updates or skipping to the next step. Make sure that **Yes, download the updated Setup files (Recommended)** is selected and click **Next**.
8. The **Upgrade Advisor** will analyze your hardware and software for compatibility with Windows XP Professional and display a list of any items that are not compatible (**Figure 2-3**).
9. Select each item from the list and click **Details** to see more information regarding Compatibility for that item (**Figure 2-4**).
10. Close the **Compatibility Details** window, and then click **Finish** to exit the **Windows Upgrade Advisor**.

caution

If the CD-ROM does not auto-play, use Windows Explorer to browse to the root of the CD-ROM and double click on setup.exe.

tip

The Upgrade Advisor can also be accessed by running \I386\winnt32 /checkupgradeonly from the Windows XP Professional CD-ROM.

Table 2-1   Hardware requirements for Installing Windows XP Professional

Component	Requirement
CPU	Intel Pentium/Celeron, AMD K6/Athlon/Duron or compatible processor;233 MHz supported, 300 MHz recommended
Memory	64 MB RAM supported, 128 MB recommended
Hard disk space	1.5 GB available
Networking	Appropriate network adapter card
Display	Super VGA (800 x 600) resolution or higher Video Display Adapter (VDA) and monitor
Other devices	Recommended: CD-ROM or DVD drive 12x or faster, unless you are installing Windows XP Professional over a network
Accessories	Keyboard and mouse or other pointing devices; 14.4 Kbps or higher modem for Internet access (33.6 or higher for voice and videoconferencing)

Figure 2-1   The Welcome to Microsoft Windows XP screen

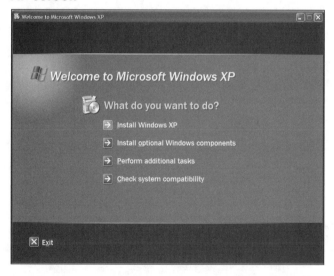

Figure 2-2   The Microsoft Windows Upgrade Advisor Update Setup Files screen

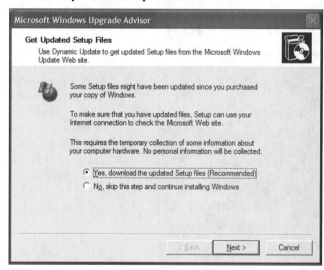

Figure 2-3   The Microsoft Windows Upgrade Advisor Report System Compatibility screen

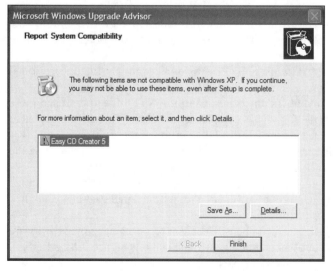

Figure 2-4   Compatibility Details

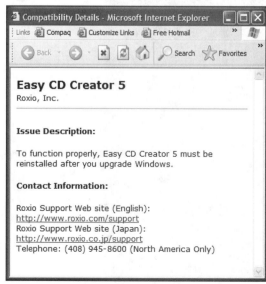

project 2.2 | *Installing Windows XP Professional Using a CD-ROM*

exam objective

Perform and troubleshoot an attended installation of Windows XP Professional.

overview

You decide to start with a clean installation of Windows XP Professional on the computer that is currently running Windows 95 because it is not a candidate for an upgrade. You also want to test Windows XP in your current workgroup environment before upgrading to an Active Directory domain. During the setup process, the current partition on your fixed disk along with the Windows 95 operating system will be removed. Since the computer has a bootable CD-ROM drive, you will begin the installation of Windows XP Professional by booting the system from the Windows XP professional installation CD-ROM.

caution

This project will **delete all data** and the current operating system from the target computer.

learning objective

After you have completed this project, you will know how to install Windows XP Professional using a CD-ROM.

specific requirements

◆ A computer that meets the minimum hardware requirements for Windows XP Professional with a minimum of a 2 GB hard disk, 64 MB RAM, and a bootable CD-ROM drive.
◆ Note that although the project scenario describes a computer currently running Windows 95, this is not necessary. Any computer with or without a previous version of Windows that meets the minimum hardware requirements for Windows XP Professional can be used for this project.
◆ A Windows XP Professional installation CD-ROM.
◆ Make sure that you have any updated software drivers or new hardware that the Upgrade Advisor identified as required. (See Project 1)

estimated completion time

45 minutes

project steps

1. Insert the **Windows XP Professional CD-ROM** in the CD-ROM drive of your computer.
2. Boot the computer.
3. The **Windows Setup** screen will begin loading files and drivers necessary to complete the setup process.
4. Press **[ENTER]** at the **Welcome to Setup** screen to continue the installation (**Figure 2-5**).
5. Read the **Windows Licensing Agreement** and then press **F8** to accept it.
6. The next step is to partition the drive that will contain **Windows XP Professional**. On the partitioning screen (**Figure 2-6**) select the partition containing your previous operating system and press **D** to delete it. To confirm the deletion press **L**.
7. To create a new partition for **Windows XP Professional**, highlight the unpartitioned space and press **[ENTER]**.
8. On the next screen select **Format the partition using the NTFS file system** and press **[ENTER]** to continue. Once the format has completed, installation files will be copied to the partition and the system will reboot into the GUI portion of the setup.
9. Setup will continue copying installation files, including those for devices such as the keyboard and mouse (**Figure 2-7**). The screen may flicker during this process.
10. Next, the Regional and Language Options screen opens. Here, you can customize **Windows XP** for different regions and languages. Accept the default settings and click **Next**.
11. The **Personalize Your Software** screen opens. Here you can personalize your software by providing information about yourself and your organization (**Figure 2-8**). After you have entered the required information click **Next**.

caution

If the computer does not boot from the CD-ROM, reboot it and enter the BIOS configuration for the system. Set the computer to boot from the CD-ROM.

Figure 2-5 Windows XP Welcome to Setup screen

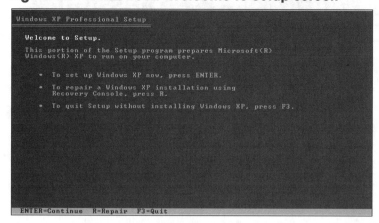

Figure 2-6 Managing partitions during setup

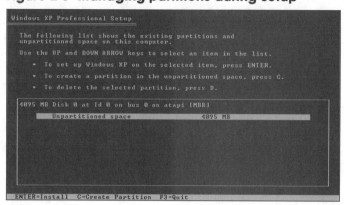

Figure 2-7 Installing Windows XP components

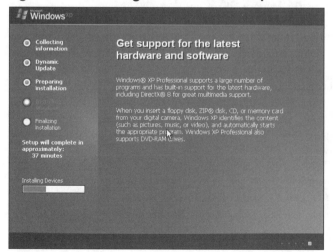

Figure 2-8 Software personalization

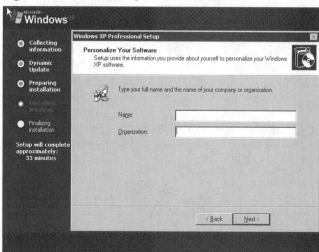

project 2.2

Installing Windows XP Professional Using a CD-ROM (cont'd)

exam objective

Perform and troubleshoot an attended installation of Windows XP Professional.

project steps

tip

If Windows XP is installed to an existing partition formatted with FAT or FAT32, you will have the option to convert it to NTFS. The actual conversion will happen after the computer restarts.

tip

The NetBIOS computer name cannot contain more than 15 characters.

tip

To ensure the security of your computer systems always use complex passwords.

tip

If the computer is not on a network choose to join a workgroup.

tip

Windows XP must be activated within 30 days or it will cease to function. It will also require re-activation after any major hardware changes.

12. Enter the 25-character product key number for Windows XP Professional on the **Your Product Key** screen (**Figure 2-9**). The product key is provided with the Windows XP Professional CD. Click **Next** to go to the next screen.

13. The **Computer Name and Administrator Password** screen opens. Type the computer name, for example, **comp1**, in the **Computer name** text box. The computer name will be entered in all capital letters. This is the NetBIOS name for the computer. It cannot be the same as the name given to any other computer, workgroup, or domain. This computer name will appear as an object in Active Directory on a domain-based network.

14. Type a password, for example, **aDm!npa33**, in the Administrator password and Confirm password text boxes. You will need to remember this password in order to have administrative rights on the computer.

15. Click **Next**. The **Date and Time Settings** dialog box opens. Set the correct **Date & Time** and **Time Zone**. If daylight savings is used in your area, make sure that the **Automatically adjust clock for daylight saving changes** check box is selected and then click **Next**.

16. Setup now installs the network software that enables you to communicate with other computers, networks, and the Internet.

17. When the **Networking Settings** screen opens, you can select typical or custom settings for configuring the networking settings. When you select the **Typical settings**, you will create network connections using Client for Microsoft Networks, File and Printer Sharing for Microsoft Networks, and the TCP/IP protocol with automatic addressing. If you choose **Custom settings**, you can manually configure the networking components. Click the **Custom settings** option button and click **Next**. The **Networking Components** dialog box opens (**Figure 2-10**). You can add or remove networking components to match the requirements for your network. Accept the default components and click **Next**.

18. The **Workgroup or Computer Domain** dialog box will open (**Figure 2-11**). Here you must specify whether your computer will join a workgroup or a domain. Select **Make this computer a member of the following workgroup** and enter **WORKGROUP** for the workgroup name and then click **Next**.

19. Setup continues copying files to complete the installation (**Figure 2-12**). The final tasks include installing the Start menu items, registering the components, saving the settings, and removing any temporary files. When these tasks are completed, the computer restarts.

20. The Welcome to Microsoft Windows screen appears with the message **Let's spend a few minutes setting up your computer**. Click the **Next** icon in the lower-right corner of the screen. The **Checking your Internet connectivity** screen appears.

21. Leave the default **Yes** option button selected and click **Next**.

22. On the **Ready to activate Windows?** screen, select **No, remind me every few days** and click **Next**. You will learn about activating Windows later in this project.

23. On the **Who will use this computer?** screen, enter the user names **user1** and **user2** in the first two text boxes and click **Next**.

24. A thank you message appears. Click **Finish** in the lower-right corner of the screen to complete the installation and configuration.

25. The **Windows logon** screen appears. Click **user1** on the right half of the screen to begin using Windows XP Professional. Windows applies **user1's** personal settings and the default desktop appears with the Start menu open.

Figure 2-9 Entering Your Product Key

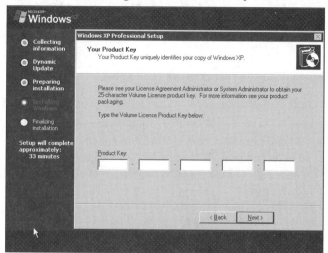

Figure 2-10 Selecting Networking Components

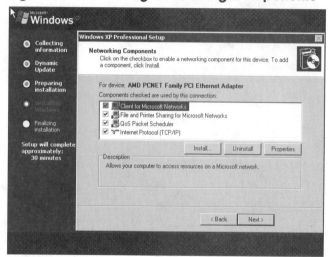

Figure 2-11 Choosing to join a network

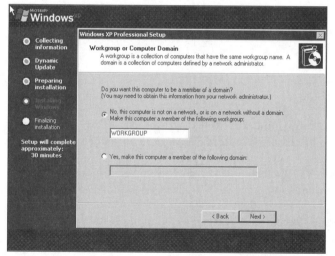

Figure 2-12 Final Installation tasks

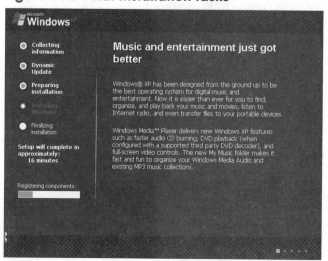

project 2.3

Upgrading a Previous Version of Windows to Windows XP Professional

exam objective

Upgrade from a previous version of Windows to Windows XP Professional.

overview

You decide to upgrade the computers in your company that are running Windows 98 instead of performing a new installation. When upgrading from a previous version of windows to Windows XP Professional you need to be sure that all existing hardware and software on the system are compatible with Windows XP. There are certain applications that should be removed before you upgrade. Among those are antivirus applications and disk quota software, because the upgrade from NTFS 4 to NTFS 5 has instituted changes that may cause problems. Any custom power management software and tools should also be removed because they are now irrelevant. In many cases third-party software for writing to CD-RW drives is also incompatible and should be removed.

When the upgrade is started, the **Windows XP Upgrade** Advisor is automatically run first to identify any components that need to be removed or upgraded before proceeding.

caution

Third-party network protocols and client software that do not have an updated version in the \i386\Winntupg folder on the Windows XP CD-ROM should also be removed.

learning objective

After you have completed this project, you will know how to upgrade a computer from a previous version of Windows to Windows XP Professional.

specific requirements

◆ A Windows XP Professional CD-ROM.
◆ A computer with a CD-ROM drive and an existing Windows operating system that is upgradeable to Windows XP Professional.

estimated completion time

45 minutes

project steps

1. Insert the **Windows XP Professional CD-ROM** into the CD-ROM drive of your computer. The **Welcome to Microsoft Windows XP** screen asks you what you want to do (**Figure 2-13**).
2. Click **Install Windows XP**. The **Welcome to Windows Setup** screen opens. Here you can specify whether you want to upgrade to Windows XP or install a new copy of Windows XP.
3. Make sure that the **Upgrade (Recommended)** is selected in the **Installation Type** list box (**Figure 2-14**), and click Next to open the **License Agreement**.

tip

An upgrade to Windows XP Professional can also be started by running **\i386\winnt32.exe** from the Windows XP Professional installation CD-ROM.

Figure 2-13 The Welcome to Microsoft Windows XP Screen

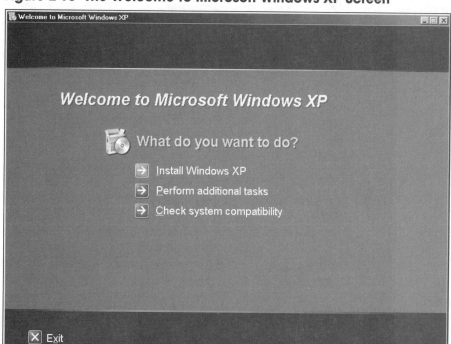

Figure 2-14 The Welcome to Windows Setup screen

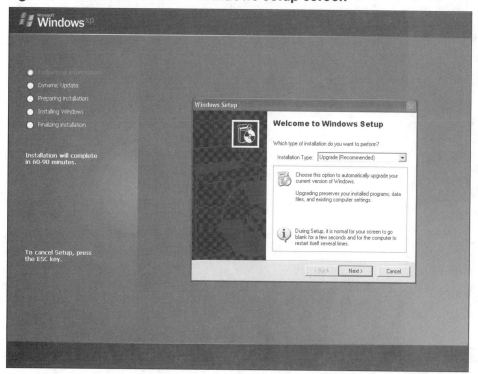

project 2.3

Upgrading a Previous Version of Windows to Windows XP Professional *(cont'd)*

exam objective

Upgrade from a previous version of Windows to Windows XP Professional.

project steps

tip

Windows 95 and Windows NT 3.51 or older cannot be directly upgraded to Windows XP Professional.

4. Click the **I accept this agreement** option button to accept the licensing terms and click **Next**. The **Your Product Key** screen opens **(Figure 2-15)**.

5. Enter the 25-character product key number for Windows XP Professional. The product key is provided with the Windows XP Professional CD.

6. Click **Next**. Setup begins copying installation files and then restarts the computer. Upon restart, Setup continues preparing the installation, a process that can take several minutes.

7. When the preparation phase completes, the computer restarts again and the Installing Windows phase of the installation begins. Again, this phase will take some time (you can see how much time on the left side of the screen). Items such as devices and networking components are installed during this phase. Your screen may flicker occasionally.

8. When the Installing Windows phase completes, the computer restarts. The **Welcome to Microsoft Windows** screen appears with the message **Let's spend a few minutes setting up your computer**. Click the **Next** icon in the lower-right corner of the screen.

9. On the **Ready to activate Windows?** screen, select **No, remind me every few days** and click **Next**. You will learn about activating Windows later in this lesson.

10. On the **Let's get on the Internet** screen, select **Do not set up an Internet connection at this time** and click **Next**.

11. A thank you message appears. Click **Finish** in the lower-right corner of the screen to complete the installation and configuration.

12. The Windows welcome screen opens. Windows applies the default user's personal settings and the default desktop appears with the Start menu open.

Figure 2-15 The Your Product Key dialog box

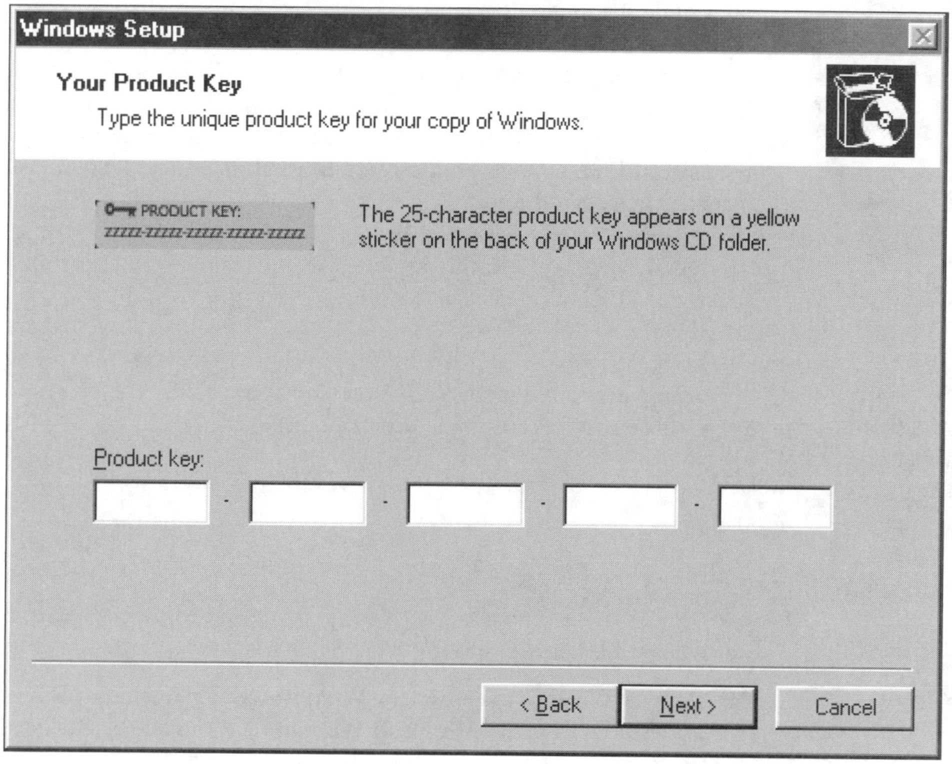

project 2.4

Using the Windows XP Setup Manager

exam objective

Perform and troubleshoot an unattended installation of Windows XP Professional. Create unattended answer files by using Setup Manager to automate the installation of Windows XP Professional.

overview

You next decide to install Windows XP Professional on the 2 computers that have Windows NT 4.0 installed. To automate this process, you will first need to copy Windows XP Setup Manager to your hard disk, and then create answer files using Windows XP Setup Manager. The answer files contain responses to the questions that the setup program asks, making it possible to install Windows XP Professional without any user interaction. You will use the answer files that have been created to perform an unattended installation to the new computers in the next project.

learning objective

After you have completed this project, you will know how to install Windows XP Setup Manager and use it to create answer files.

specific requirements

♦   A computer with Windows XP Professional installed.
♦   A Windows XP Professional installation CD-ROM.

estimated completion time

30 minutes

project steps

Create unattended answer files by using Setup Manager.

1. Log on to Windows and insert the **Windows XP Professional CD** in the **CD-ROM** drive. Close the **Welcome to Microsoft Windows XP** window by clicking **Exit**.
2. Right-click **Start** and click the **Explore** on the shortcut menu to open **Windows Explorer**.
3. Click the **C:** drive.
4. Click **File** on the **Menu** bar, point to **New**, and select the **Folder** command to create a new folder on the C: drive.
5. Type **Deploy** to replace the default name for the folder. You will use this folder to store the files that you will extract from the **Deploy.cab** file on the Windows XP Professional CD. Click the **CD-ROM drive** icon in the left pane of the Windows Explorer window to display the contents of the CD-ROM in the right pane.
6. Double-click the **Support** folder to open the **Support** window.
7. Double-click the **Tools** folder to open the **Tools** window.
8. Double-click the **Deploy** file to open the **Deploy** window (**Figure 2-16**).
9. Open the **Edit** menu and click the **Select All** command to select all of the files in the window.
10. Right-click any file and click the **Extract** command on the shortcut menu. The **Select a Destination** dialog box opens.
11. Click My Computer to display the drives on folders available on your computer. Click the **C:** drive to display the folders stored on that drive.
12. Click the **Deploy** folder and then click **Extract**. Windows XP Professional copies the selected files to the Deploy folder.
13. After Windows XP Professional has finished copying the files to the Deploy folder on your system's **C:** drive, open the Deploy folder to view the copied files.
14. Double-click the **readme** file to read its contents.
15. Close the readme file.
16. Double-click **setupmgr** in the Deploy folder to start the **Setup Manager Wizard**.
17. Click **Next**. The **New or Existing Answer File** dialog box opens.
18. Make sure that the **Create new** option button is selected, as shown in **Figure 2-17**.
19. Click **Next**. The **Type of Setup** dialog box opens.

tip

To select all of the files in the Deploy.cab file, hold down the [Ctrl] key and select each of the files listed. If the file icons are listed within one column, you can also select the files by clicking the first file in the list, holding down the [Shift] key and then clicking the last file in the list.

Figure 2-16 The Deploy File in the Tools Folder

Figure 2-17 New or Existing Answer File dialog box

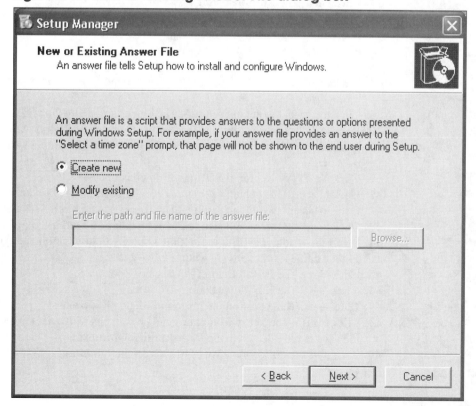

project 2.4

Using the Windows XP Setup Manager (cont'd)

exam objective

Perform and troubleshoot an unattended installation of Windows XP Professional. Create unattended answer files by using Setup Manager to automate the installation of Windows XP Professional.

project steps

caution

Different versions of Setup Manager will differ slightly in the names they give to some dialog boxes, check boxes, and/or option buttons. These steps were completed using Setup Manager version 5.1.2600.1106.

20. Make sure that the **Unattended Setup** option button is selected. Click **Next**. The **Product** dialog box opens.
21. Make sure that the **Windows XP Professional** option button is selected. Click **Next**. The **User Interaction** dialog box opens.
22. Select the **Fully automated** option button, as shown in **Figure 2-18**.
23. Click **Next**. The **Distribution Share** dialog box opens.
24. Leave the **Create a new distribution share** option button selected and then click **Next**. The **Location of Setup** Files dialog box opens.
25. Leave the default option, **On the CD**, selected and click **Next**. The **Distribution Share Location** dialog box opens.
26. Click to accept the default settings. The **License Agreement** opens.
27. Click the **I accept the terms of the License Agreement** check box and click to accept the agreement. The **Name and Organization** dialog box opens.
28. Enter your name in the **Name** text box and your organization name in the **Organization** text box. Click **Next**. The **Display Settings** dialog box opens.
29. The list boxes for Colors, Screen area, and Refresh frequency are set to **Windows default**. Click to accept the default display settings. The **Time Zone** dialog box opens.
30. Select the appropriate time zone setting and click **Next**. The **Product Key** dialog box opens.
31. Enter the appropriate 25-character product key and click **Next**. The **Computer Names** dialog box opens.
32. Type the computer name, **XPPRO2**, in the **Computer name** text box and click **Add**.
33. Repeat this step to add **XPPRO3** and **XPPRO4** to the list of computer names. These names appear in the **Computers to be installed** list box, as shown in **Figure 2-19**.
34. Click **Next**. The **Administrator Password** dialog box opens.
35. Make sure that the **Use the following Administrator password (127 characters maximum; case-sensitive)** option button is selected and type the password, **password 2**, in the **Password** and **Confirm Password** text boxes.
36. Click **Next**. The **Networking Components** dialog box opens.
37. Click to accept the default option, **Typical settings**. The **Workgroup Or Domain** dialog box opens.
38. Click to accept the default settings. The **Telephony** dialog box opens.
39. Provide the appropriate information for the **Country or region**, **Area code or city code**, **Number to dial for access to an outside line**, and **The phone system at this location uses** fields.
40. Click **Next**. The **Regional Settings** dialog box opens.
41. Click to accept the default settings. The **Languages** dialog box opens.
42. Click to accept the default settings. The **Browser And Shell Settings** dialog box opens.
43. Click to accept the default settings. The **Installation Folder** dialog box opens.
44. Select the **A folder with a name that I specify** option button and type **WXPPro** in the **Folder name** text box, as shown in **Figure 2-20**.
45. Click **Next**. The **Install Printers** dialog box opens.
46. Click **Next**. The **Run Once** dialog box opens.
47. Click **Next**. The **Additional Commands** dialog box opens.
48. Click **Finish**. The **Setup Manager** dialog box opens with a default path and file name for the answer file selected in the **Path and file name** text box.
49. Type a new path for the answer file, **C:\Deploy\unattend.txt (Figure 2-21)**, and click **OK**.

Figure 2-18 The Fully automated option in the User Interaction dialog box

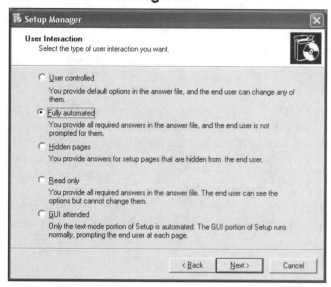

Figure 2-19 Computer Names dialog box

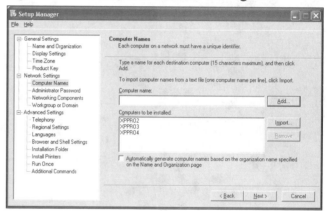

Figure 2-20 Installation Folder dialog box

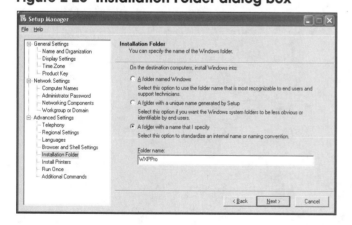

Figure 2-21 Answer file name and path

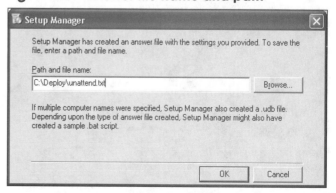

project 2.4

Using the Windows XP Setup Manager *(cont'd)*

exam objective

Perform and troubleshoot an unattended installation of Windows XP Professional. Create unattended answer files by using Setup Manager to automate the installation of Windows XP Professional.

project steps

50. The **Setup Manager** copies distribution files to your computer's hard disk **(Figure 2-22)**.
51. After the files are copied, the **Completing Setup Manager** screen opens, stating that you have created 3 files: **unattend.txt**, **unattend.udb**, and **unattend.bat (Figure 2-23)**.
52. Close the Setup Manager Wizard window. The three files you created now appear in the Deploy window on your hard disk **(Figure 2-24)**. The Setup Manager has also created a folder called **windist** on the hard disk of your computer.
53. Open Unattend.txt and review its contents **(Figure 2-25)**. Open Unattend.udf using either Word or Notepad and review its contents. When you have finished, close all open windows.

Figure 2-22 Copying distribution files

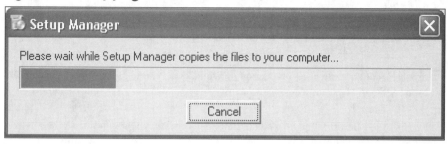

Figure 2-23 The Completing Setup Manager screen

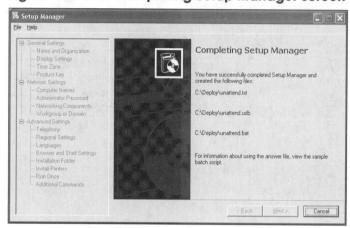

Figure 2-24 New files in the Deploy folder

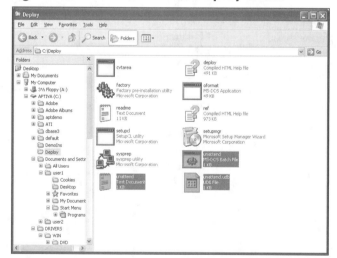

Figure 2-25 unattend.txt

project 2.5

Installing Windows XP Professional Using an Unattended Setup

exam objective

Perform and troubleshoot an unattended installation of Windows XP Professional. Create unattended answer files by using Setup Manager to automate the installation of Windows XP Professional.

overview

Once you have installed Setup Manager and created answer files, you can now use the answer files to help automate the installation of Windows XP Professional on the two computers with Windows NT 4.0 installed.

learning objective

After you have completed this project, you will know how to perform an unattended installation using answer files.

specific requirements

◆ A computer with Windows XP Professional installed. You will install a second copy of Windows XP Professional to this computer using an unattended setup. It will be placed in the \WXPPro directory as was specified in the answer files created in Project 2.4.
◆ Answer files from Project 2.4 stored in the \Deploy folder.
◆ A Windows XP Professional installation CD-ROM.

estimated completion time

45 minutes

project steps

1. Try to write the command line for **winnt32** that would perform an unattended installation using the answer files created in Project 2-4. See **Table 2-2** for command line switches for winnt32.exe.
2. Open **C:\Deploy\Unattend.bat** with notepad to examine the switches that are being used. Compare your command with the contents of Unattend.bat.

tip

In the Unattend.bat file there is a %1 variable. It holds the first argument entered on the command line which in this case is the computer name.

Table 2-2 Comparison of command-line switches for Winnt32 and Winnt

Switch		Description
Winnt32(Use for both new and upgrade installations)	Winnt(Use for new installations only)	
Switch/ checkupgradeonly		Used to verify whether the computer qualifies for an upgrade to Windows XP Professional. This switch also creates a report for upgrade installations.
/copydir: folder_name	/r[:folder]	Creates an additional folder within the folder in which the Windows XP files are installed.
/copysource: folder_name	/rx[:folder]	Creates a temporary additional folder within the folder in which the Windows XP files are installed. Setup deletes the files created using this switch once the installation is complete.
/cmd:command_line	/e[:command]	Used to allow the user to execute a command before the final phase of Setup.
/cmdcons		Used to install the Recovery Console.
/debug[level] [:file_name]		Enables you to create a debug log at the specified level. It creates the C:\Winnt32.log at level 2 (the warning level) by default.
/dudisable		Prevents Dynamic Update from running. Without Dynamic Update, Setup runs only with the original Setup files.
/duprepare:pathname		Carries out preparations on an installation share so that it can be used with Dynamic Update files that you downloaded from the Windows Update Web site. This share can then be used for installing Windows XP for multiple clients.
/dushare:pathname		Specifies a share on which you previously downloaded Dynamic Update files (updated files for use with Setup) from the Windows Update Web site, and on which you previously ran /duprepare:pathname.
/m:folder_name		Forces Setup to copy the replacement files from other locations. If the replacement files are on the computer, this switch asks Setup to use those files and not the files from the default location.
/makelocalsource		Used to copy all of the installation files to the local hard disk. You can use these files later if the CD-ROM drive is not available for installation.
/noreboot		Used to prevent Setup from restarting the computer when the file copy phase of Setup is over. Thus, the user is allowed to enter a command, if required, before completing setup.
/s:source_path	/s[:sourcepath]	Used to determine where the Windows XP Professional installation files source is located. To copy files from multiple paths (up to 8) simultaneously, you use separate /s switches for all source paths.
/syspart: drive_letter		Used to copy the Setup startup files to the hard disk. The drive specified for installation is marked as the active drive. To install Windows XP Professional on another computer, you can install this drive on that computer and the Setup program will start from the next phase on that computer. Note that you cannot use the /syspart switch without the /tempdrive switch.
/tempdrive: drive_letter	/t[:tempdrive]	Used to place temporary files on the specified drive. Windows XP Professional is installed on the same drive.
/unattend[number]: [answerfile]	/u[:answer file]	Used to perform an unattended installation. Used to give custom specifications to the Setup program. If an answer file is not specified, Setup takes the user settings from the previous installation.
/udf:id [,UDB_filename]	/udf:[id],[UDB_ filename]	Used to specify an identifier (ID) used by the Setup program. Setup uses this ID to find out how an answer file is changed by a Uniqueness Database File.
	/a	Provides accessibility options.

project 2.5

Installing Windows XP Professional Using an Unattended Setup (cont'd)

exam objective

Perform and troubleshoot an unattended installation of Windows XP Professional. Create unattended answer files by using Setup Manager to automate the installation of Windows XP Professional.

project steps

3. Insert the **Windows XP Professional CD-ROM** into the CD-ROM drive of your computer. The **Welcome to Microsoft Windows XP** screen asks you what you want to do (**Figure 2-26**). Click **Exit**.

4. Click **Start**, then **Run**, and then enter the command **C:\Deploy\Unattend.bat <computer_name>** in the **Run** window (**Figure 2-27**), where <computer_name> is the name that will be assigned to the computer on which Windows XP Professional will be installed. This computer name is used as an identifier to select which unique settings will be used from the UDB file.

5. Click **OK** to start the unattended installation. The unattended setup will begin collecting information and installing Windows XP Professional (**Figure 2-28**). The initial setup files will be copied to your computer. After they have been copied, the computer will automatically restart with the Windows XP Setup program and Windows XP Professional will automatically install using the information contained in the answer files.

Figure 2-26 Welcome to Microsoft Windows XP screen

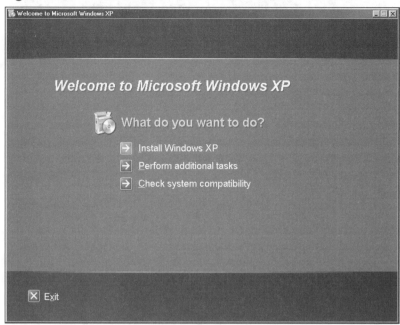

Figure 2-27 Run command dialog box

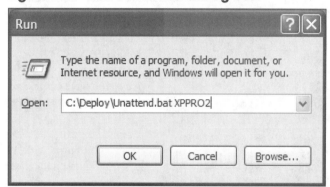

Figure 2-28 Unattended installation

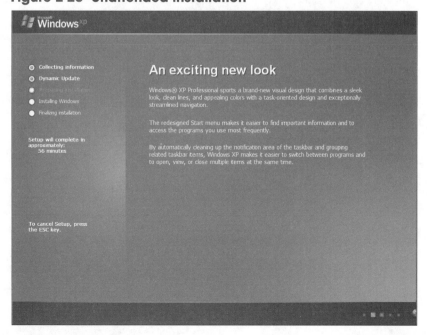

project 2.6

Using the System Preparation Tool

exam objective

Perform and troubleshoot an unattended installation of Windows XP Professional. Install Windows XP Professional by using the System Preparation Tool.

overview

When you have several computers that have identical configurations it is usually most efficient to install Windows XP Professional by creating a disk image and then deploying that image to each computer. In order to be able to use the same disk image for all computers they must use the same mass storage controllers such as a SCSI or IDE. They must also have a Compatible BIOS and use the same hardware abstraction layer (HAL).

caution

Disk duplication will only be successful if the master disk image computer and the clone computers have the same basic hardware (hardware abstraction layer or HAL), hard disk controller, power management, and number of processors.

One of the benefits of deploying Windows XP Professional by using a disk image is that the system can be completely configured and can have user applications installed. Once the system is configured as desired it will be used as the master image. To prepare the image for duplication you must first use the Sysprep program to remove all unique information from the system such as the Computer Name and security identifier (SID). This effectively gives the computer amnesia. After Sysprep has been run a third-party disk imaging application, such as Symantec Ghost or PowerQuest Drive Image, can be used to duplicate the image to other computers.

When the image is deployed to a new computer and the computer is restarted it will require the answer to several questions. To automate this process a Sysprep.inf file can be created using the Setup Manager Program **(Figure 2-29)**.

You will use this method to install Windows XP Professional to the five new identical computers.

learning objective

After you have completed this project, you will know how to use the System Preparation tool to install Windows XP Professional.

specific requirements

◆   A computer with Windows XP Professional installed which has been completely configured with all desired software to be included in the image. It must be a member of a workgroup, not a domain, and the Administrator password must be blank. This computer will act as the distribution model computer. The Windows XP Setup Manager should also be installed.

◆   Third party imaging software such as Symantec Ghost or PowerQuest Drive Image.

estimated completion time

30 minutes

Figure 2-29 Using the Setup Manager to create a Sysprep answer file

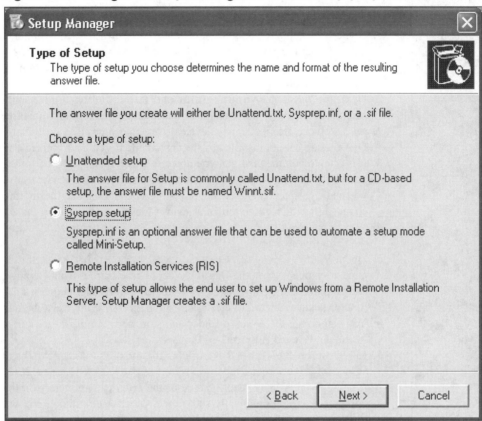

project 2.6

Using the System Preparation Tool
(cont'd)

exam objective

Perform and troubleshoot an unattended installation of Windows XP Professional. Install Windows XP Professional by using the System Preparation Tool.

project steps

Use the **System Preparation** tool.

1. If you were actually going to mass deploy Windows XP Professional, and you wanted to prepare a hard disk so that you could create a disk image, you would first perform a clean installation of the operating system on a computer that was not a member of a domain, leaving the Administrator password blank.

2. Next, log on as an **Administrator** and install and customize applications, such as Microsoft Office or other business-specific programs, that your target computers will need. You can also install any device drivers the clones may need that are not included in **Drivers.cab** (or not installed by the answer file if you have created one).

3. It is often recommended that you now use a third-party auditing tool to audit the system and verify that the image configuration is correct. Do not overwrite any system files when you audit. Sysprep cannot detect or restore system files that the auditing utility may have changed. It is all right to reboot as many times as needed during the auditing process.

4. When your audit is complete, delete any files or folders that the auditing utility added to the hard drive.

5. Open Windows Explorer. Create a new folder on your **%systemdrive%** (usually **C:**) named **Sysprep**. Open the **Deploy** folder (extracted files from Deploy.cab) and move the **Sysprep.exe** and **Setupcl.exe** files to the Sysprep folder **(Figure 2-30)**. If you used the Setup Manager Wizard to create a Sysprep.inf file, it must also be moved to this folder. You can create the Sysprep folder and store Sysprep.inf in it when you run the **Setup Manager Wizard (Figure 2-31)**.

6. Run Sysprep.exe. **Table 2-3** explains the meaning of the switches for Sysprep. The Windows XP System Preparation Tool message box **(Figure 2-32)**, warns you that running Sysprep may modify some of the security parameters on the computer. ACPI computers will automatically shut down. Otherwise, a dialog box will open to let you know that it is safe to shut down the computer.

7. The hard disk of the computer is now programmed to run Plug and Play detection, create new security identifiers (SIDs) (because Setupcl.exe has been copied to %systemroot%\SYSTEM32 and will run at the next boot), and run the Mini-Setup Wizard the next time the system is started.

8. Now you are ready to use an imaging utility to create the master disk image. Copy the image to a shared folder or onto a CD-ROM. The next time you boot up this computer, or any of the clones that were created from the master disk image, the system will detect and re-catalog the Plug and Play devices.

9. When the clone computers are booted up, first Plug and Play detection will take place. Then, the Mini Setup Wizard will run. Users will be prompted to accept the EULA (End-User License Agreement), enter their name and organization, join a workgroup or a domain, enter regional settings, enter TAPI (Telephony Application Program Interface) information, and choose the networking protocols and service to install. If you used a Sysprep.inf file **(Figure 2-33)**, only dialog boxes containing information that was not included in the .inf file will appear.

10. Finally, the local Sysprep folder containing Sysprep.exe, Sysprep.inf, and Setupcl.exe will be deleted, the computer will restart, and the logon dialog box will display.

tip

Test your master image by restarting the computer after running Sysprep. On startup it will go through all of the steps that the clone computers will have to go through. Once you are sure that your Sysprep image works, run Sysprep again and create your disk image.

Table 2-3 Sysprep command line options

/quiet	Runs Sysprep in quiet mode. This switch stops the confirmation dialog boxes from displaying while Sysprep runs on the distribution model computer. It is used when you want to automate Sysprep by adding it to the GuiRunOnce key in the Unattend.txt file.
/pnp	Forces a full device detection on the target computer. This switch is optional. Use it when non-Plug and Play devices that cannot be dynamically detected exist on the target systems.
/reboot	Enables a reboot of the master computer after the image has been created instead of shutting down and then starting the Mini-Setup Wizard. Use this switch for auditing the system and verifying that Mini-Setup is operating correctly.
/nosidgen	Runs Sysprep without generating any security ID. This switch is useful for the Administrator who doesn't intend to clone the computer on which Sysprep is running.

Figure 2-30 System Preparation tool

Figure 2-31 Creating the Sysprep folder and Sysprep.inf with the Setup Manager

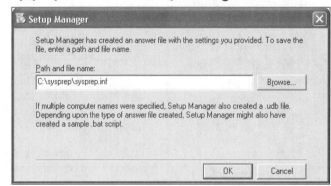

Figure 2-32 Windows XP System Preparation Tool message box

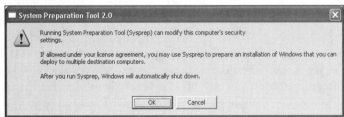

Figure 2-33 Example of a Sysprep.inf answer file

<table>
<tr><td>**project 2.7**</td><td>

Resolving Problems Encountered During Setup

</td></tr>
<tr><td>**exam objective**</td><td>Troubleshoot failed installations.</td></tr>
<tr><td>**overview**</td><td>

Despite following the hardware requirements, checking the HCL, and resolving all compatibility issues, you may still encounter installation problems.

You may encounter media errors and CD-ROM drives that are not supported by Windows XP. These problems can usually be solved by replacing the CD-ROM you are using with a new one or replacing the CD-ROM drive. If you do not want to replace an unsupported CD-ROM drive, you can also simply use the network installation method and later add the driver for the CD-ROM drive, if available.

If you find that you have insufficient disk space, simply create a new partition using the free space available on the hard disk or reformat one of the available partitions to create more space.

If a dependency error occurs (such as that caused by a service that doesn't start or a driver that fails), make sure that you have installed the correct protocol and network adapter in the Network Settings dialog box in the Setup Wizard, that the network adapter has been configured correctly, and that the computer has a unique name on your network.

If you cannot connect to a domain controller, check to see if the DNS server and the domain controller are online and running, and make sure that you have entered the correct domain name. If you cannot locate a domain controller, you must create and join a workgroup and join the domain after installation.

Finally, if the operating system will not install or start, check to see if all hardware has been detected and confirm that it is all on the Hardware Compatibility List.

To assist with troubleshooting installation problems, Windows XP provides several information files, called **log files**, which are generated during the GUI phase of the setup process. These files contain information about the installation process. The files are located in the directory in which Windows XP Professional is installed. The four log files that are created are: **Setupact.log**, **Setuperr.log**, **Setupapi.log**, and **Setuplog.txt**. The action log and the error log are particularly valuable.

♦ **Action log:** The action log, which is stored in the **Setupact.log file (Figure 2-34)**, contains information about the events that transpired during Setup, including the copying of files, the creation of Registry entries, and any errors that may have occurred. Each event is recorded as it happened. Log files are created during the **GUI** phase of setup.
♦ **Error log:** The error log, which is stored in the **Setuperr.log** file, stores a description of the errors that have occurred and an entry indicating the magnitude of each error.

</td></tr>
<tr><td>**learning objective**</td><td>

After you have completed this project you will know how to use the log files to troubleshoot an installation of Windows XP Professional.

</td></tr>
<tr><td>**specific requirements**</td><td>

♦ A computer with Windows XP Professional installed.

</td></tr>
<tr><td>**estimated completion time**</td><td>10 minutes</td></tr>
</table>

Figure 2-34 Action log

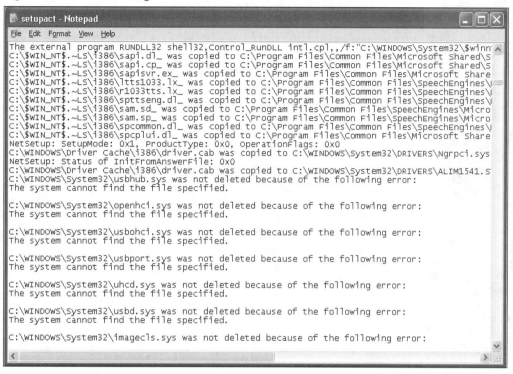

project 2.7

Resolving Problems Encountered During Setup (cont'd)

exam objective

Troubleshoot failed installations.

project steps

1. Log on to the computer.
2. Click **Start**, point to **All Programs**, point to **Accessories** and then click **Windows Explorer**.
3. Double-click the **My Computer** icon, double-click the drive where the installation files are located and then double-click the Windows installation folder, normally C:\Windows.
4. Double-click **setupact.log**. The action log opens in **Notepad**. It provides a list of the events that transpired during Setup, including the copying of files, the creation of Registry entries, and any errors that may have occurred. When you have finished looking at it, close **Notepad**.
5. Double-click **setuperr.log (Figure 2-35)**. The error log opens in **Notepad**. It provides a description of any errors that occurred and what, if any, action the operating system took to rectify the error. If no errors occurred during installation, the file will be empty. Close **Notepad** when you are finished.
6. Close **Windows Explorer**.

Figure 2-35 Error log

project 2.8

Installing Service Packs and Automatic Updates

exam objective

Perform post-installation updates and product activation.

overview

Sometimes Microsoft releases operating system patches to resolve various reliability issues and to provide security related updates. While many of these patches can be applied individually, Microsoft normally distributes complete sets of patches as service packs. In addition to updating your operating system using service packs, Windows XP can also patch your operating system and other applications using **Automatic Updates**.

caution

Service packs can be very large and require a high speed connection for download.

Some previous versions of the Windows operating system required a separate installation for service packs. In fact, if you reconfigured the operating system by adding a particular service, you would have to reinstall the existing service packs. To simplify the use of service packs, Windows XP Professional allows service packs to be applied to a network-based distribution point containing the Windows XP Professional installation files. This process, called service pack slipstreaming, allows installation of Windows XP Professional with the service pack already applied. If changes are later made to the Windows XP Professional installation any required files will be obtained from the slipstreamed distribution point. By using this technique, the need to reapply service packs after making operating system changes is eliminated.

To create a slipstreamed distribution point you must first create an \I386 folder on your disk drive. Then copy the contents of the \I386 folder from a Windows XP Professional installation CD-ROM to that directory. Download the latest Network Installation service pack from the Microsoft support Web site, and then run the executable file for the service pack with the /s:*path_name* option where *path_name* is the full path including the drive letter that points to the parent folder that contains the \I386 folder. If you had created the \I386 folder under a folder called ServicePacks on your C: drive, it would look like: **xpsp1a_en_x86 /s:C:\ServicePacks**

learning objective

In this project you will learn to configure Windows XP Professional to automatically retrieve updates when they are available.

specific requirements

◆ A computer with Windows XP Professional installed.
◆ An internet connection if you want to perform an actual update.

estimated completion time

5–60 minutes (depending on the speed of your Internet connection and the number of updates that your Windows XP Professional installation requires)

project steps

Configure your computer to receive Automatic Updates.

1. Click **Start** and click **Control Panel** to open the Control Panel window.
2. On the left side of the window, click **Switch to Classic View** to display all of the Control Panel icons **(Figure 2-36)**.
3. Double-click the **System** icon to open the **System Properties** dialog box.
4. Click the **Automatic Updates** tab to view its options **(Figure 2-37)**.
5. Make sure that the check box near the top of the tab, labeled **Keep my computer up to date, etc.**, is checked.
6. Make sure the option button labeled **Download the updates automatically and notify me when they are ready to be installed** in the middle of the tab is selected.
7. Click **OK** to close the System Properties dialog box and save the Automatic Update settings. You will be notified of updates that are ready to be installed by pop-up messages appearing from the notification area on the right end of the taskbar.
8. Close the Control Panel window.

Figure 2-36 The Control Panel window in Classic View

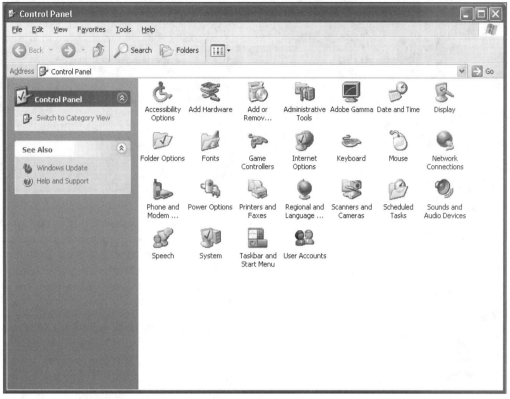

Figure 2-37 Automatic Updates tab

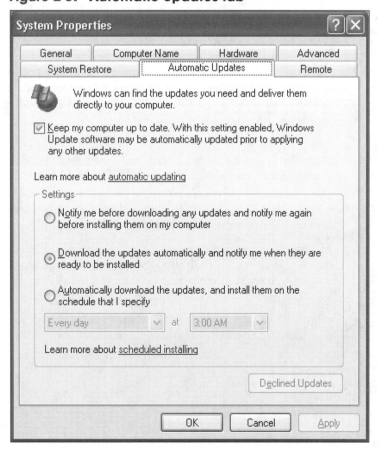

3 Managing Hardware Devices

During the course of your work, you may need to add or change the hardware and peripheral devices connected to your computer. Some of the most common hardware devices that you work with on a daily basis are the mouse, keyboard, CD ROM drive, modem, and printer. These devices can be categorized as either input devices such as the mouse and keyboard, or output devices such as the monitor and printer.

While these hardware devices enable you to work with data, removable media allow you to store data or to backup and archive data on alternatives to the hard drive such as CD-ROMs, DVDs, floppy disks, and tapes. Using removable media to store infrequently used data helps you to save hard disk space.

You may also need to exchange data with computers that are not on your network. Modems are used to exchange data between computers on the Internet using telephone lines. Modems are also used to connect computers to devices such as fax machines. Infrared light is used to connect a digital camera to a computer, whereas external communication lines are used to connect a Web camera to a computer.

These devices must interact with the operating system in order to process data. Windows XP Professional uses programs called device drivers to enable interaction with hardware devices. Device drivers serve as the translators for the operating system, converting commands from Windows into commands that the device can understand and process. A database of device drivers is installed along with the Windows XP Professional operating system. However, you may need to upgrade these drivers periodically when the manufacturers distribute newer versions or if the device is not functioning properly.

Windows XP Professional includes Plug and Play functionality. Any new Plug and Play devices you add to your system will be detected and the settings will be configured automatically after the device driver is located and installed. However, if the system cannot locate the required driver in the driver database because it was not included with the operating system, you will be prompted to install the driver. After the driver is installed, the hardware device will be configured automatically.

As you take on different kinds of tasks, you may also need to install new software on your system. Windows XP Professional uses digitally signed system files and Windows File Protection to ensure that any new software you install does not overwrite the existing system files. This protects your system against data corruption and general system failures.

Scenario

You are the System Administrator at a start-up company. The company has 20 Windows XP Professional computers with a variety of hardware devices installed.

Lesson 3   Managing Hardware Devices

Project	Exam 70-270 Objective
3.1 Configuring I/O Devices	Implement, manage, and troubleshoot input and output (I/O) devices. Monitor, configure, and troubleshoot I/O devices, such as printers, scanners, multimedia devices, mouse, keyboard, and smart card reader.
3.2 Configuring Mass Storage Devices	Implement, manage, and troubleshoot disk devices. Install, configure, and manage DVD and CD-ROM devices. Monitor and configure removable media, such as tape devices.
3.3 Adding a Modem	Install, configure, and manage modems.
3.4 Configuring Fax Devices	Implement, manage, and troubleshoot input and output (I/O) devices.
3.5 Updating Device Drivers	Manage and troubleshoot drivers and driver signing.
3.6 Managing Driver Signing	Manage and troubleshoot drivers and driver signing.
3.7 Managing Universal Serial Bus and Multimedia Devices	Install, configure, and manage USB devices. Monitor, configure, and troubleshoot multimedia hardware, such as cameras. Install, configure, and manage hand held devices.

General Requirements

To complete the projects in this lesson, you will need administrative rights on a Windows XP Professional computer. You will also need a Web camera and a fax modem.

project 3.1

Configuring I/O Devices

exam objective

Implement, manage, and troubleshoot input and output (I/O) devices. Monitor, configure, and troubleshoot I/O devices, such as printers, scanners, multimedia devices, mouse, keyboard, and smart card reader.

overview

A new employee that is left-handed has recently joined the company. Configure the mouse settings on his computer to that he can use the mouse more easily. You will also change some of the other configuration settings.

learning objective

After you have completed this project, you will know how to configure a mouse.

specific requirements

◆ Administrative rights on a Windows XP Professional computer.

estimated completion time

10 minutes

project steps

1. Log on to the computer as an **Administrator**.
2. Click **Start** and click **Control Panel** to open the **Control Panel window**. If necessary, click **Switch to Classic View** to display all of the Control Panel icons.
3. Double-click the **Mouse** icon to open the **Mouse Properties** dialog box. Click each of the tabs and record the information you find on a sheet of paper (**Table 3-1**). The actual tabs that will be displayed may vary depending on the features of the mouse driver that is installed.
4. On the **Buttons** tab, in the **Button Configuration** section, click the **Switch primary and secondary buttons** check box (**Figure 3-1**). In the **Double-click speed** section, slide the slider to the **Fast** setting. Click the **Apply** button to apply the settings.
5. Confirm that the right button on the mouse is now the primary button. Test the **Double-click speed** by double-clicking on the folder icon in the **Double-click speed** section using the right button. Return your mouse to its former configuration, click **Apply** and then test its operation.
6. Click the **Hardware** tab to display the hardware settings. In the **Devices** section, click the mouse name (**Figure 3-2**).
7. Click the **Properties** button to open the **Properties** dialog box for the mouse.
8. Click each of the tabs and record the information you find there on your sheet. On the **Power Management** tab, select the **Allow this device to bring the computer out of standby** check box if it is not already selected (**Figure 3-3**).
9. Click **OK** to close the Device Properties window and save any changes. The Mouse Properties dialog box will become the active window.
10. Click the **Apply** button to apply the change in the settings.
11. Click the **OK** button to close the Mouse Properties dialog box and then close the Control Panel window.

caution

This step will switch the right and left mouse buttons which could make it difficult to use your mouse.

Table 3-1 Tabs in the Mouse Properties dialog box

Buttons	You can configure your mouse for left-handed or right-handed use, set the double-click speed, and turn on ClickLock. In the Double-click speed section, you can test the double-click speed for your mouse.
Pointers	You can specify the look and feel for the mouse pointer. The shape of the pointer acts as a visual cue to indicate the process taking place. For example, the hourglass icon indicates that the computer is processing an event such as opening an application or a file.
Pointer Options	You can set the speed and visibility behaviors with which the mouse pointer moves on your screen. You can also set Snap To to program the mouse pointer to move automatically to the default button in dialog boxes.
Hardware	You can troubleshoot and access the port configuration, advanced settings, driver details, resource settings, and power management settings for the mouse.

Figure 3-1 Modifying mouse settings

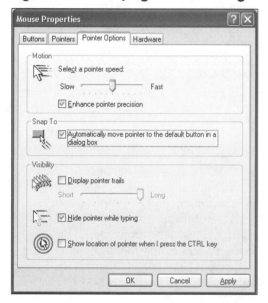

Figure 3-2 The Hardware tab in the Mouse Properties dialog box

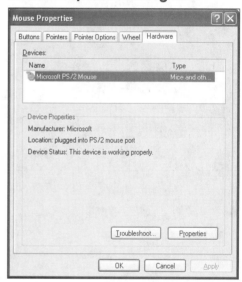

Figure 3-3 The Power Management tab in the Mouse Properties dialog box

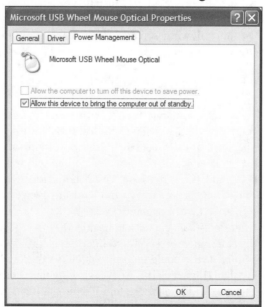

project 3.2 | *Configuring Mass Storage Devices*

exam objective

Implement, manage, and troubleshoot disk devices. Install, configure, and manage DVD and CD-ROM devices. Monitor and configure removable media, such as tape devices.

overview

You need to add additional fault tolerant storage to an existing Windows XP Professional computer. In the spare parts room you have found an older SCSI RAID controller that does not support Plug and Play and four SCSI drives. You decide to install the Mylex 960 controller and 8 Gig SCSI drives into the computer and configure a RAID-5 array.

learning objective

After you have completed this project, you will know how to install and configure mass storage devices.

specific requirements

◆ Administrative rights on a Windows XP Professional.
◆ The actual Mylex controller is **not** required for this project.
◆ The Project Steps assume that the controller is not Plug and Play-compatible. If a Plug and Play-compatible device was used, the Found New Hardware Wizard would automatically launch after you log on to the computer, and the steps used to install the device will differ slightly from those set forth below.

estimated completion time

15 minutes

project steps

The first two steps are only performed if you are installing an actual controller and drives.

1. Shut off the computer. Open the case, install the controller card and drives into the computer and attach and connect all cables as necessary.
2. Turn the computer back on and log on as an **Administrator**.
3. If the **Add Hardware Wizard** does not start automatically, click **Start**, right click on **My Computer** and select **Properties**. On the **System Properties** dialog box click the **Hardware** tab, and then click the **Add Hardware Wizard** button (**Figure 3-4**).
4. The **Welcome to the Add Hardware Wizard** screen appears (**Figure 3-5**). Click **Next**.
5. The Wizard will begin searching for hardware that has been attached to the computer but has not yet been configured. If it does not find any new hardware the **Is the hardware connected**? dialog box will open. Select **Yes, I have already connected the hardware** and click **Next**.
6. A list of hardware already installed on your computer will open (**Figure 3-6**). Scroll to the bottom of the list, highlight **Add a new hardware device** and click **Next**.
7. On the following screen select **Search for and Install Hardware Automatically (Recommended)** then click **Next**. The **Add Hardware Wizard** will search for hardware (**Figure 3-7**).
8. If no new hardware is found, you will receive a message that says **The wizard did not find any new hardware on your computer**. Click **Next** to open a screen which will allow you to manually select the device from a list. Select the **SCSI and RAID controllers** option in the **Common Hardware Type** list box (**Figure 3-8**) and click **Next**.
9. The **Select the device driver you want to install for this hardware** screen opens with a list of manufacturers and models for the selected device. Click **Mylex** then select **Mylex DAC960 Disk Array Controller (non-pnp)** (**Figure 3-9**), and click **Next**.
10. **The wizard is ready to install your hardware** dialog box will list the hardware that will be installed when you click **Next**.
11. After the system copies and installs the drivers for the Mylex controller the **Completing the Add Hardware Wizard** dialog box will open. There will be a message indicating that the device could not start which is expected because the physical card has not been installed (**Figure 3-10**). After reviewing this screen click **Finish**.
12. Click **OK** to close the **System Properties** dialog box.

tip

Remember to set the SCSI IDs to a unique value for each drive and to terminate the last device on the cable.

Figure 3-4 The System Properties Hardware tab

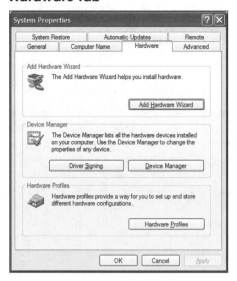

Figure 3-5 The Add Hardware Wizard

Figure 3-6 Hardware already installed on your computer

Figure 3-7 Searching for new hardware devices

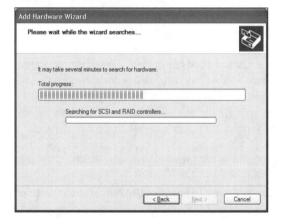

Figure 3-8 Selecting the type of hardware to install

Figure 3-9 Choosing the specific hardware driver

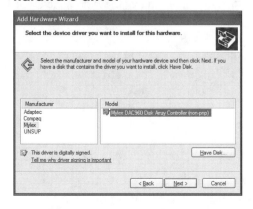

Figure 3-10 Completing the installation

project 3.3 — *Adding a Modem*

exam objective

Install, configure, and manage modems.

overview

You recently added a fax modem to a computer used by one of the firm's employees, Ken Stewart. However, now that you have done this, he finds that each time he attempts to connect to the Internet, he is unable. You want to verify that the modem is working and, additionally, your ISP suggests that you to set the maximum port speed to 57600 to sustain connectivity.

learning objective

After you have completed this project, you will know how to configure a modem.

specific requirements

◆   A Windows XP Professional computer with a fax modem installed.

estimated completion time

15 minutes

project steps

Verify that a modem is installed and operating, configure it to wait for the dial tone before it starts dialing, and set the port speed to 57600.

1. Open the **Control Panel** window and switch to **Classic View** if necessary.
2. Double-click the **Phone and Modem Options** icon to open the **Phone and Modem Options** dialog box.
3. Click the **Modems** tab to display the list of modems installed on your computer (**Figure 3-11**).
4. Select a modem and click to open the **Properties** dialog box for the modem. The **General** tab opens by default.
5. Click the **Diagnostics** tab and click the **Query Modem** button. The diagnostics will attempt to communicate with the modem and will return values for a number of AT commands (**Figure 3-12**). If the diagnostics returns values for the queries, it can be assumed that the drivers are communicating with the modem correctly. This does not test the ability of the modem to transmit and receive data over a phone line.
6. Next click the **Modem** tab.
7. In the **Maximum Port Speed** section, click the list arrow and select **57600** as the port speed for transmitting data (**Figure 3-13**).
8. In the **Dial Control** section, the **Wait for dial tone before dialing** check box is selected by default. This will program the modem to detect the dial tone before it begins dialing out.
9. Click **OK** to apply the changes and to close the Properties dialog box, then click **OK** again to close the Phone and Modem Options dialog box. Close the Control Panel.

Figure 3-11 List of installed modems

Figure 3-12 Modem Diagnostics tab

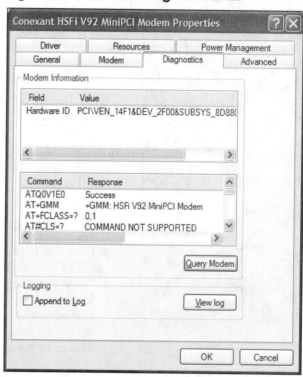

Figure 3-13 Modem Properties dialog box

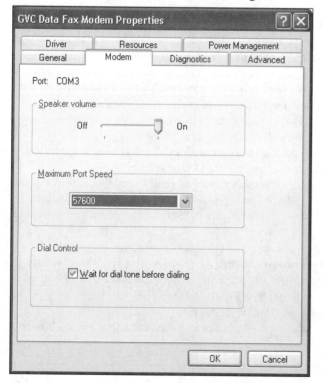

project 3.4

Configuring Fax Devices

exam objective

Implement, manage, and troubleshoot input and output (I/O) devices.

overview

The old fax device in your organization has been malfunctioning and you have installed a new fax modem. The CEO's Administrative Assistant needs to access the fax machine on a daily basis. As the Administrator, you must assign the necessary permissions and configure the fax settings so that they match the old settings for the number of retries, minutes between retries, and number of days an unsent fax is kept.

learning objective

After you have completed this project, you will know how to configure fax support.

specific requirements

◆ Administrative rights on a Windows XP Professional computer with a fax modem installed.
◆ A user account.

estimated completion time

20 minutes

project steps

Start and configure the Fax Service on the local computer and configure a fax device.

1. Click **Start** and click **Printers and Faxes**. Click **Set up faxing** on the left side of the window.
2. The **Insert Disk** dialog box asks you to insert your Windows XP Professional CD. After you insert the CD, Windows configures your fax modem and adds a Fax icon to the Printers and Faxes window.
3. Click **Start** and click **Control Panel**. Double-click **Administrative Tools** and double-click **Computer Management** to open the Computer Management window.
4. Double-click **Services and Applications** to expand the node. Click **Services**.
5. Locate and right-click **Fax** in the list of services in the Details pane. Click **Start** on the context menu to start the fax service. You may receive a message saying that the service started and then stopped because it has no work to do. Click **OK** to close the Computer Management window and then close the **Administrative Tools** window.
6. Double-click the Fax icon in the Printers and Faxes window to open the **Fax Configuration Wizard**. Complete the steps of the Wizard as instructed on its screens. When you complete the final step, the **Fax Console** opens. Close the Fax Console.
7. Right-click the **Fax** icon in the Printers and Faxes window and click **Properties** to open the **Fax Properties** dialog box. By default, the **General** tab opens.
8. Click the **Devices** tab. Select the device whose properties you want to configure and click **Properties (Figure 3-14)** to open the Properties dialog box for that device.
9. On the **Send** tab, make sure that the **Enable device to send** check box is selected and enter your fax number in the TSID text box. This will identify any faxes you transmit.
10. Type **4** in the **Number of retries** text box **(Figure 3-15)** to add an additional attempt to transmit.
11. In the **Retry after** text box, type **5** to wait five minutes between each attempt.
12. Click the **Receive** tab. Make sure that the **Enable device to receive** check box is selected.
13. In the **Answer mode** section of the tab, click the **Automatic after** option button, if necessary, and type **1** in the **rings** text box **(Figure 3-16)**.
14. Click **OK** to apply the changes and close the dialog box.
15. Close the **Fax Properties** dialog box, the **Printers and Faxes** window, and the **Control Panel**.

caution

Once this has been configured your computer fax will answer all incoming calls on the first ring.

Figure 3-14 Fax Properties Devices tab

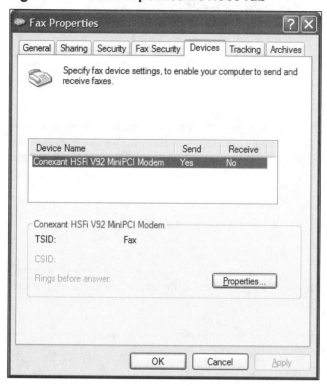

Figure 3-15 Setting Send properties

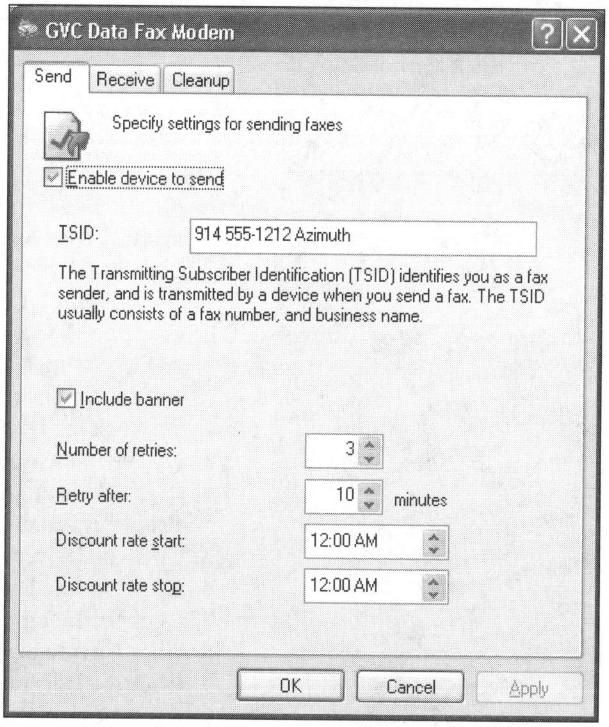

Figure 3-16 Setting Receive properties

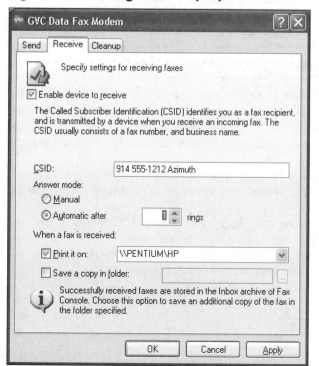

project 3.5 — *Updating Device Drivers*

exam objective

Manage and troubleshoot drivers and driver signing.

overview

The CEO's Administrative Assistant notifies you that, for some reason, she is unable to send faxes. You determine that this is due to a corrupt driver. You also discover that the manufacturer for the modem has recently released a new version of the driver for the fax modem, which you have downloaded to the local computer. You now need to update the driver for the modem.

learning objective

After you have completed this project, you will know how to update device drivers.

specific requirements

◆ Administrative rights on a Windows XP Professional computer with a fax modem added to it and an updated device driver for the modem.

estimated completion time

15 minutes

project steps

Update the drivers for the modem attached to your system.

1. Click **Start** and click **Control Panel**. Double-click **Administrative Tools** and double-click **Computer Management** to open the Computer Management window.
2. Click the **Device Manager** node to display all of the devices that are currently installed on the system. Alternatively, you can click **Start**, point to **Settings**, click **Control Panel**, and double-click **System** to open the **System Properties** dialog box. On the **Hardware** tab, click the **Device Manager** button to open the Device Manager.
3. Double-click **Modems** to display the modems installed on the computer.
4. Right-click the modem name, for example, **GVC Data Fax Modem**, and click the **Properties** command to open the **Properties** dialog box for the modem.
5. Click the **Driver** tab (**Figure 3-17**).
6. Click **Update Driver** to open the **Hardware Update Wizard**.
7. Click the **Install from a list or specific location (Advanced)** option button.
8. Click **Next** to open the **Please choose your installation options** screen.
9. Click the **Don't search. I will choose the driver to install** option button.
10. Click **Next** to open the **Install New Modem** screen.
11. Select the driver that you would like to use for the modem that you are updating from the **Models** list (**Figure 3-18**). If you need to upgrade the drivers from a disk, you can click **Have Disk**. This will allow you to select the path to the manufacturer's files so that they can be copied to the hard drive.
12. Click **Next**. The Hardware Update Wizard installs the software for the device.
13. The Completing the Update Hardware Wizard screen opens. Click **Finish** to complete the update procedure.
14. Close the modem **Properties** dialog box. The **System Settings Change** dialog box may prompt you to restart the system so that the changes can take effect.
15. If needed, click **Yes** to restart the system and apply the settings; otherwise, close the **Computer Management** and the **Administrative Tools** windows.

Figure 3-17 Fax Modem Properties Driver tab

Figure 3-18 The Install New Modem screen

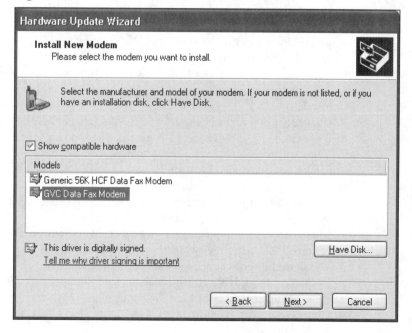

project 3.6 *Managing Driver Signing*

exam objective

Manage and troubleshoot drivers and driver signing.

overview

As the System Administrator, you must occasionally install new hardware for specific projects. While you are installing a device on a file server, a message box warns you that the device drivers are not digitally signed, and you are not allowed to install the hardware. You decide to modify the driver signing options so that you will be warned before installing an unsigned driver and given the option to either continue or cancel the installation. You also want to verify whether any other unsigned drivers have been installed on the server.

tip

Critical systems should be set to require digitally signed drivers to ensure their stability.

learning objective

After you have completed this project, you will know how to manage driver signing.

specific requirements

◆ Administrative rights on a Windows XP Professional computer.

estimated completion time

15 minutes

project steps

Set driver signing options to block the installation of unsigned files.

1. Open the **Control Panel** window in Classic View.
2. Double-click the **System** icon to open the **System Properties** dialog box.
3. Click the **Hardware** tab to display the hardware setting options.
4. Click **Driver Signing** to open the **Driver Signing Options** dialog box.
5. Click the **Warn—Prompt me each time to choose an action** option button in the **What action do you want Windows to take**? section to allow the installation of unsigned drivers after a warning prompt is displayed (**Figure 3-19**).
6. Make sure that the **Apply setting as the system default** check box is selected in the **Administrator option** section to apply the default setting for all users who log on to the computer.
7. Click **OK** to apply the changes and close the **Driver Signing Options** dialog box.
8. Click **OK** to close the **System Properties** dialog box. Close the Control Panel.
9. You want to be sure that no other unsigned drivers have been installed on the system. Click **Start** and then click **Run**.
10. On the **Open** line in the **Run dialog box** type **sigverif** and click **OK**.
11. The **File Signature Verification** screen will open (**Figure 3-20**). Click **Start** to scan all system files for digital signatures.
12. When the scan completes, the **Signature Verification Results** window will open (**Figure 3-21**). After reviewing it's contents click **Close**.
13. The signature verification report is also stored as a text file that can be opened and printed by clicking the **Advanced** button on the **File Signature Verification** screen. Then click the **Logging** tab and click **View Log** to open the report file.
14. Close the report window, click **OK**, and click **Close** to exit the **File Signature Verification** screen.

Figure 3-19 Setting driver signing options

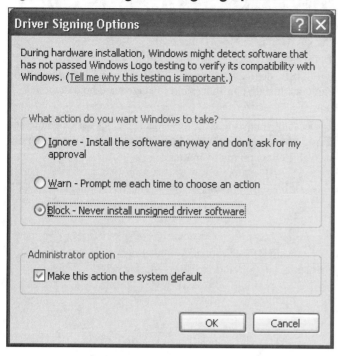

Figure 3-20 File Signature Verification screen

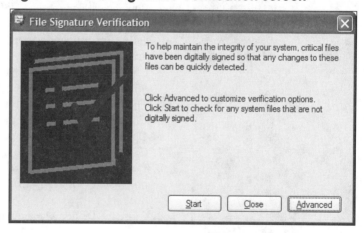

Figure 3-21 Signature Verification Results window

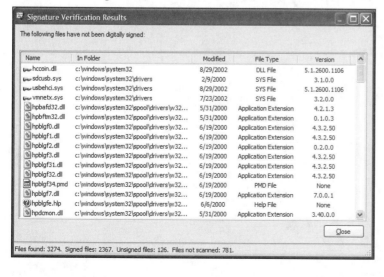

project 3.7

Managing Universal Serial Bus and Multimedia Devices

exam objective

Install, configure, and manage USB devices. Monitor, configure, and troubleshoot multimedia hardware, such as cameras. Install, configure, and manage hand held devices.

overview

Your company's CEO is in the process of finalizing a business deal. He has asked you to set up video conferencing capabilities on his computer so that he can discuss last minute details with the client. You will install a Web camera on his computer.

learning objective

After you have completed this project, you will know how to install a Web camera.

specific requirements

◆ Administrative rights on a Windows XP Professional computer.
◆ A USB connected Web camera with supported drivers for Windows XP.

estimated completion time

10 minutes

project steps

Install and configure a digital camera.

1. Plug the camera into the USB port and turn on the camera.
2. The **Found New Hardware Wizard** opens. Leave the **Install the software automatically (Recommended)** option button selected. If you have a disk containing the device drivers, insert the disk.
3. Click **Next**. The Wizard searches for the proper device driver. When the driver is located, the Wizard installs the necessary software.
4. The **Completing the Found New Hardware Wizard** screen opens (**Figure 3-22**).
5. Click **Finish** to complete the installation of the camera.
6. Open the **Control Panel**, double-click the **System** icon, and click the **Hardware** tab.
7. Click **Device Manager** to open the Device Manager window.
8. Double-click the **Universal Serial Bus controllers** node. The camera you just installed is now listed (**Figure 3-23**). You can configure the properties of the camera by double-clicking it.
9. Close the Device Manager, the System Properties dialog box, and the Control Panel.

tip

USB supports hot connection and removal of devices

Figure 3-22 Installing hardware device drivers

Figure 3-23 Installed camera in the Device Manager window

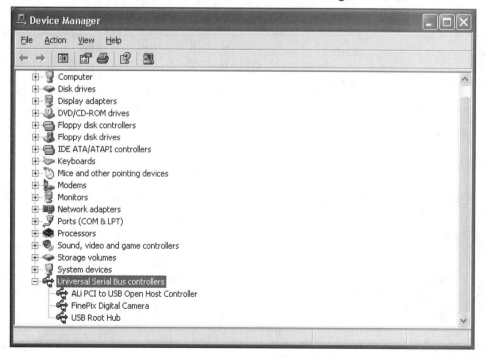

Working with the Control Panel

In Windows XP Professional, the Control Panel is used to customize many different system settings to suit users' tastes and needs. For example, you may want to change the screen resolution, screen colors, language support, or keyboard and mouse functionalities. In the Control Panel, you can configure many different options to control the basic functionality and administration of your system.

The Control Panel includes the following utilities: (The System and Display utilities are most commonly used.)

◆ System: You can use the System properties to manage hardware profiles, configure system devices, optimize system performance, configure automatic updates, activate remote assistance, and configure the system for restoration.

◆ Regional and Language Options: You can configure multiple-language support on your computer and designate location-specific settings, such as the currency that will be used in monetary calculations, and the date and time format.

◆ Accessibility Options: This applet is used to configure a system for users with visual, auditory, or physical impairments. For example, you can configure the system to display visual effects or captions when the computer makes a sound, or you can use the MouseKeys setting to allow users to control the pointer using the number pad instead of the mouse.

◆ Display: You can use the Display properties to define and modify the screen resolution, color scheme, color quality, and other properties that affect the appearance of the desktop and application interfaces. You can also set up multiple displays to expand the size of your desktop across more than one monitor.

In the Control Panel, you will also find the Power Options utility, which is used to configure the power management functions in the Windows XP environment. The contents of this dialog box will vary depending on the particular power-saving features of the computer. Typically, however, it allows you to implement or create power schemes that will dictate when to turn off the monitor and hard disk, when to put the computer into Standby mode, and when to put it into Hibernate mode (if you so choose). Power-saving capabilities are particularly important when you are using a laptop or notebook computer because they help you to extend the life of the computer's battery. The PCMCIA (Personal Computer Memory Card International Association) or PC card is another important mobile computer hardware device. These card devices are used to change laptop configurations by adding memory, a NIC, modem, or portable hard drive. Card services do not have a utility in the Control Panel. The operating system automatically carries out most of the functions that are needed to administer PC card support. The main thing you will need to know about configuring card services is that you should make sure that the system stops using the PC card before you remove it.

Scenario

You have just been hired as the System Administrator for a small graphics design company with responsibility for maintaining a variety of Windows XP Professional computers. Some of the computers are quite old and barely meet the requirements for running Windows XP.

Lesson 4   Working with the Control Panel

Project	Exam 70-270 Objective
4.1 Tuning System Performance	Monitor, optimize, and troubleshoot performance of the Windows XP Professional desktop. Optimize and troubleshoot application performance. Optimize and troubleshoot memory performance.
4.2 Configuring Internet Settings	Configure, manage, and troubleshoot Internet Explorer security settings.
4.3 Configuring Scheduled Tasks	Configure, manage, and troubleshoot Scheduled Tasks.
4.4 Setting Display Properties	Implement, manage, and troubleshoot display devices. Configure and manage user profiles and desktop settings.
4.5 Configuring Multiple Displays	Implement, manage, and troubleshoot display devices. Configure multiple-display support.
4.6 Configuring Power Options	Manage, monitor, and optimize system performance for mobile users. Configure Advanced Configuration Power Interface (ACPI).

General Requirements

Administrative rights on a computer with Windows XP Professional installed. You will also need administrative rights on a laptop with Windows XP Professional installed for Project 4.6. For Project 4.5, you will need two monitors and administrative rights on a Windows XP Professional computer equipped with a PCI or AGP video adapter for each monitor.

project 4.1 | *Tuning System Performance*

exam objective

Monitor, optimize, and troubleshoot performance of the Windows XP Professional desktop. Optimize and troubleshoot application performance. Optimize and troubleshoot memory performance.

overview

Several of the computers in your company are quite old and barely meet the minimum requirements to run Windows XP Professional. You do not have a sufficient budget to replace the systems and so you want to configure them to operate with the best performance possible. You plan to configure the systems so that processor intensive tasks like visual effects will be used minimally, and you will also configure the paging file to provide the best performance.

learning objective

After you complete this project, you will know how to tune Windows XP Professional to obtain the best possible performance.

specific requirements

Administrative rights on a Windows XP Professional computer.

estimated completion time

10 minutes

project steps

First, set both the initial size and the maximum size of the paging file to equal values to reduce fragmentation in the swap file and improve memory performance. Then, disable visual effects to provide the best system performance.

1. Click **Start** and click **Control Panel** to open the **Control Panel** window. If necessary, click **Switch to Classic View**.
2. Double-click the **System** icon to open the **System Properties** dialog box, and click the **Advanced** tab.
3. In the **Performance** section, click **Settings** to open the **Performance Options** dialog box (**Figure 4-1**).
4. Click the **Advanced** tab, and then click **Change** in the **Virtual memory** section to open the **Virtual Memory** dialog box.
5. Select the **Custom size** option button, if necessary, and change the **Initial size (MB)** value so that it matches the **Maximum size (MB)** value (**Figure 4-2**).
6. Click **Set** to set the initial and maximum sizes of the paging file.
7. Click **OK** to close the **Virtual Memory** dialog box then click the **Visual Effects** tab (**Figure 4-3**).
8. Select **Adjust for best performance** and then click **OK** to close the **Performance Options** dialog box. Observe the changes that are made to the appearance of the windows and menus on the computer.
9. Click **OK** to close the **System Properties** dialog box and then close the **Control Panel**.

Figure 4-1 Performance Options dialog box

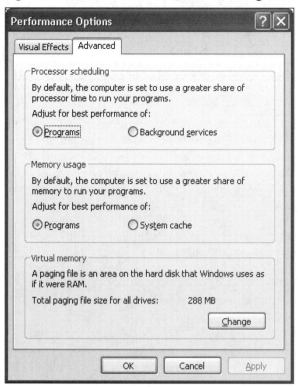

Figure 4-2 Virtual Memory dialog box

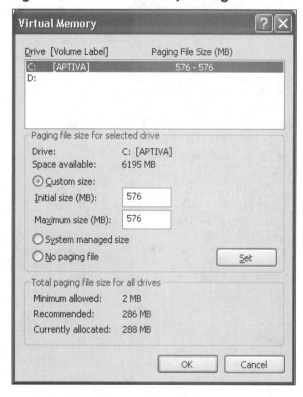

Figure 4-3 Visual Effects dialog box

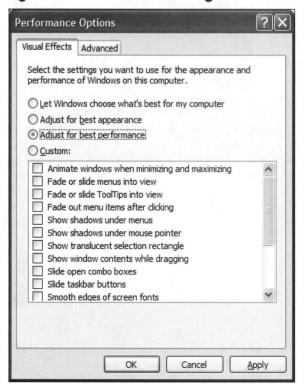

project 4.2

Configuring Internet Settings

exam objective

Configure, manage, and troubleshoot Internet Explorer security settings.

overview

The management of your organization is concerned with the security of the Windows XP Professional computers that are used to browse the Internet. You need to configure these systems so that users can transparently access the corporate intranet and also securely access the Internet. You want to define different security zones for each type of access and also pre-load a certificate onto the client machines to allow encrypted communications with your internal Web server.

learning objective

After completing this project you will have learned how to configure security zones for Internet explorer and also how to import and export certificates.

specific requirements

Administrative rights on a Windows XP Professional computer.

estimated completion time

25 minutes

project steps

First, you will configure the Security Settings for your intranet security zone to provide access to only your internal corporate Web site. You will also configure the intranet security zone to automatically connect to the Web server using the current user's username and password.

1. Click **Start** then click **Control Panel**.
2. If necessary, click **Switch to Classic View**, then Double-click **Internet Options**.
3. The **Internet Properties** dialog box will open. Click the **Security** tab (**Figure 4-4**).
4. Click the **Local intranet** icon and then click the **Sites** button. The **Local intranet** dialog box will open which allows you to define which Web sites will be included in the Local intranet zone. Click the **Advanced** button.
5. In the **Add this Web site to the zone** text box, enter the URL for your internal Web site: **www.yourcompany.com**.
6. Click **Add** to place the URL in the list of Web sites that will be part of the intranet zone, and then click **OK** to close the window (**Figure 4-5**).
7. Click **OK** to close the **Local intranet** dialog box.
8. In the **Security level for this zone** section, click **Custom Level**. Scroll to the bottom of the **Settings** list in the **Security Settings** dialog box (**Figure 4-6**) and click **Automatic logon with current user name and password**.
9. Click **OK** to close the **Security Settings** dialog box. A warning dialog box will appear. Click **Yes** to confirm the changes that you have made to the Security Settings for this zone.

tip

Using the Internet Explorer Administration Kit (IEAK) downloaded from Microsoft's Web site enables automated customization, deployment, and management of your Internet Explorer installations.

Figure 4-4 Setting Security levels for security zones

Figure 4-5 Configuring a Web site to belong to a security zone

Figure 4-6 Configuring Security Settings

project 4.2

Configuring Internet Settings (cont'd)

exam objective

Configure, manage, and troubleshoot Internet Explorer security settings.

project steps

So that you will have a certificate available to import later in this lab, you will first export a certificate. In the present scenario with the corporate Web server, an Administrator would have already configured a Certificate Authority and issued a certificate for the Web server.

10. Click the **Content** tab. In the **Certificates** section click the **Certificates** button.
11. The **Certificates** dialog box will open. Click the **Trusted Root Certification Authorities** tab and then scroll to the bottom of the list box (**Figure 4-7**). Select **Xcert EZ by DST** and click **Export**.
12. The **Certificate Export Wizard** will open. Click **Next**.
13. In the **Export File Format** dialog box, click **Next** to accept the default export format (**Figure 4-8**). The **File to Export** dialog will open.
14. In the **File Name** input box, type **C:\MyCertificate** and click **Next**. The Wizard will add a **.cer** extension to the filename.
15. The **Completing the Certificate Export Wizard** screen will open. Click **Finish** to save the certificate. A message box indicating that the export was successful will appear. Click **OK**.

Next, you want to pre-load a certificate that will be used to enable encrypted SSL Connections with your Web server.

16. The **Certificates** dialog box should still be open. Click **Import**.
17. The **Certificate Import Wizard** will open. Click **Next**. The **File to Import** dialog box will open (**Figure 4-9**). In the **File Name** input box type **C:\MyCertificate.cer** and click **Next**.
18. When the **Certificate Store** dialog box opens, select **Place all certificates in the following store** and click **Browse**. The **Select Certificate Store** list box will open.
19. Select **Trusted Publishers** from the list and click **OK** to close the window. Click **Next** to accept the settings and open the **Completing the Certificate Import Wizard** window.
20. Click **Finish** to complete the certificate import. Click **OK** to close the message box indicating that the import was successful.
21. The imported certificate will appear in the **Trusted Publishers** list (**Figure 4-10**).
22. Click **Close** to close the **Certificates** window and click **OK** to close **Internet Properties**, and then close the **Control Panel**.

Figure 4-7 Managing Certificates

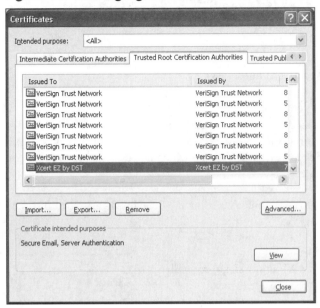

Figure 4-8 Exporting a Certificate

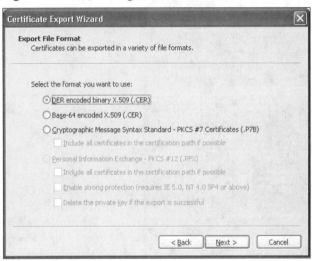

Figure 4-9 Importing a Certificate

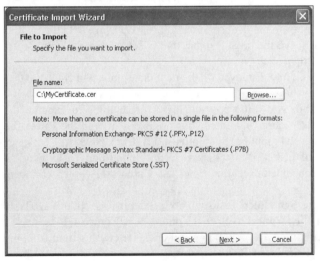

Figure 4-10 Viewing an Imported Certificate

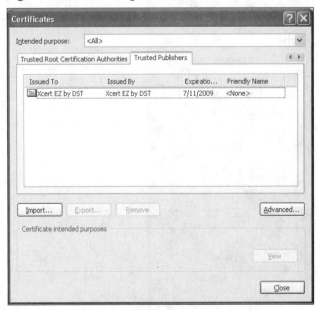

project 4.3 · *Configuring Scheduled Tasks*

exam objective

Configure, manage, and troubleshoot Scheduled Tasks.

overview

There are several repetitious tasks that must be executed at the same time every day. To save your users unnecessary effort, you plan to set up those tasks so that they will run automatically. You will use the **Scheduled Task Wizard** which makes it simple to run a task according to any required schedule.

learning objective

In this project you will learn how to configure tasks using the Scheduled Task Wizard.

specific requirements

Administrative rights on a Windows XP Professional computer.

estimated completion time

15 minutes

project steps

1. Click **Start** then click **Control Panel**. When the **Control Panel** opens, click **Switch to Classic View** if necessary, and double-click **Scheduled Tasks**.
2. The **Scheduled Tasks** window will open. Double-click **Add Scheduled Task** to run the **Scheduled Task Wizard** and then click **Next**.
3. Select the **Calculator** program from the list box and click **Next (Figure 4-11)**.
4. In the following dialog box, leave the default name that is set for this task and select **Perform this task Daily** and then click **Next**.
5. Add three minutes to the **Start Time** displayed on the next dialog box and click **Next**.
6. Scheduled tasks can run when a user is not logged on or may need to run using a specific user account. For this reason, you must provide logon credentials to execute the scheduled task. Accept the user name and enter your password in both the **Enter the password** and **Confirm password** input boxes **(Figure 4-12)**. Click **Next**.
7. Click **Finish**. The **Calculator** task will now appear in the **Scheduled Tasks** window **(Figure 4-13)**. Wait for the scheduled execution time. The **Calculator** applet will open. Close the **Calculator** applet.
8. Double-click **Calculator** in the **Scheduled Tasks** window. Examine the options available on each of the tabs and then click **Cancel** to close the dialog box **(Figure 4-14)**.
9. Select **Calculator** in the **Scheduled Tasks** window and click **Delete this item** from the **Folder Tasks** box. Close the **Scheduled Tasks** window.

tip

A scheduled task is often used to run system backups and antivirus scans but it could be used to run any program or script.

tip

Very complex schedules can be configured by enabling Show Multiple Schedules.

Figure 4-11 Selecting a program to schedule

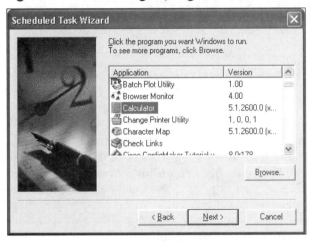

Figure 4-12 Entering credentials for scheduled task

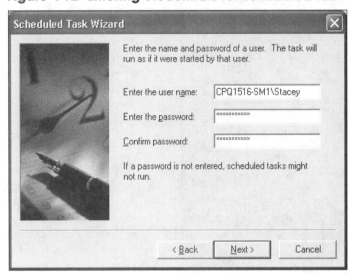

Figure 4-13 Viewing status of scheduled tasks

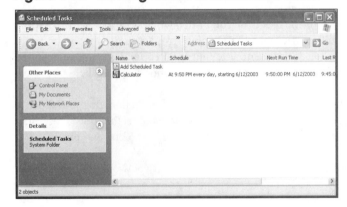

Figure 4-14 Scheduled task properties dialog

project 4.4

Setting Display Properties

exam objective

Implement, manage, and troubleshoot display devices. Configure and manage user profiles and desktop settings.

overview

Your company has recently undertaken a new graphics project. One aspect of the project involves creating and working with a large number of graphical images. Many of the graphics are large and with your present monitor resolution setting you will be unable to view the complete image without scrolling up and down. Your new hardware budget has allowed for the purchase of several large monitors for this project. You want to increase the video resolution on the systems that will receive the new displays.

learning objective

In this project you will learn how to configure video display settings.

specific requirements

◆ Administrative rights on a Windows XP Professional computer.
◆ A monitor that supports 1152 x 864 pixel resolution. However, if you do not have access to such a monitor, you can still do the project. Just change the resolution to the highest resolution that your monitor supports.

estimated completion time

5 minutes

project steps

1. Log on to the computer as an **Administrator**.
2. Double-click the **Display** icon in the **Control Panel** window to open the **Display Properties** dialog box. You can also open the **Display Properties** dialog box by right-clicking an open area on your desktop and clicking the **Properties** command on the context menu. Click each of the tabs and record the information you find there on a sheet of paper.
3. Click the **Settings** tab (**Figure 4-15**). In the **Screen resolution** section, drag the slider to the right toward **More**. The numbers indicating the resolution at the bottom of the slider will increase. Release the mouse button when the resolution is 1152 by 864 pixels.
4. Click the **Apply** button.
5. The **Monitor Settings** message box prompts you to indicate if you would like to keep the setting.
6. Click the **Yes** button to apply the new desktop setting.
7. Click the **Settings** tab on the **Display Properties** dialog box.
8. Click the **Advanced** button to open the hardware specific **Properties** dialog box. Click each of the tabs and record the information you find there on your sheet.
9. Click the **Troubleshoot** tab. In the **Hardware acceleration** section, drag the slider all the way to the right next to **Full**. This controls the level of acceleration and performance supplied by your graphics hardware (**Figure 4-16**).
10. Click the **OK** button.
11. Close the **Display Properties** dialog box and the **Control Panel** window.

caution

Setting video resolution to a value higher than that supported by your monitor could damage your monitor.

tip

If you have previously used the selected settings the system will not prompt for confirmation.

Figure 4-15 Changing video settings

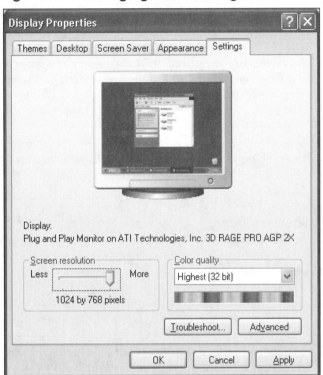

Figure 4-16 Controlling hardware acceleration

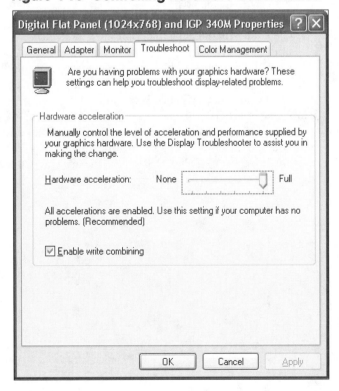

project 4.5
Configuring Multiple Displays

exam objective

Implement, manage, and troubleshoot display devices. Configure multiple-display support.

overview

The accounting department in your company is working with an Excel spreadsheet that has many columns. They find that they must constantly scroll left and right to view and edit it. They would like to test the use of two monitors to display more of the spreadsheet at one time. One of their systems already has an AGP video adapter built on the motherboard and you found a PCI video adapter in the spare parts box.

learning objective

Once this project is completed you will know how to configure multiple monitors.

specific requirements

◆ Two monitors.
◆ A Windows XP Professional computer equipped with a Peripheral Component Interconnect (PCI) or Accelerated Graphics Port (AGP) video adapter for each monitor.

estimated completion time

30 minutes

project steps

1. Shut down the computer, insert an additional **Peripheral Component Interconnect (PCI)** or **Accelerated Graphics Port (AGP)** video adapter into an available slot, plug your additional monitor cable into the display adapter, restart the computer and log on as an **Administrator**.
2. Windows XP detects the new video adapter and installs the appropriate drivers.
3. Open the **Control Panel** window and double-click the **Display** icon to open the **Display Properties** dialog box.
4. Click the **Settings** tab.
5. Click the **Monitor** icon that represents the monitor you want to use in addition to your primary monitor.
6. Click the **Extend my Windows desktop onto this monitor** check box (**Figure 4-17**).
7. Select the color depth and resolution for the secondary display. Record the settings you choose on a sheet of paper.
8. Click **Identify** to display a large number on each of your monitors, showing which monitor corresponds with each monitor icon (**Figure 4-18**).
9. Drag the **Monitor** icons to positions that represent the physical arrangement of the monitors, and then click **OK** to view the changes. Close the **Control Panel**.

tip

Windows XP supports up to 10 separate monitors.

Figure 4-17 Configuring multiple monitors

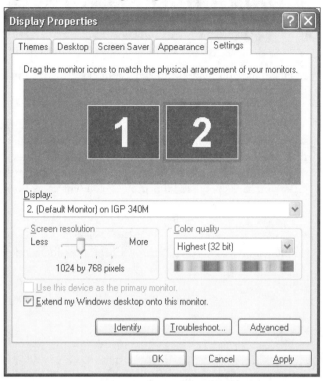

Figure 4-18 Identifying multiple monitors

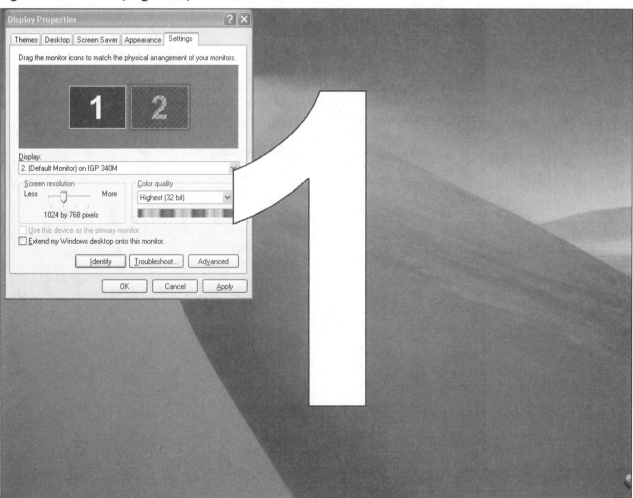

project 4.6	# *Configuring Power Options*
exam objective	Manage, monitor, and optimize system performance for mobile users. Configure Advanced Configuration Power Interface (ACPI).
overview	John uses a laptop when he is working from home. He wants to reduce power consumption when he is not working and the computer is idle. You will configure his laptop so that the hard disk and the monitor automatically switch off after a specified time period.
learning objective	After you have completed this project, you will know how to configure power options.
specific requirements	Administrative rights on a Windows XP Professional laptop that supports APM or ACPI.
estimated completion time	10 minutes
project steps	Configure the Power options on a laptop.

project steps

Configure the Power options on a laptop.

1. Click **Start** and click **Control Panel** to open the **Control Panel** window.
2. Double-click the **Power Options** icon to open the **Power Options Properties** dialog box.
3. Select the **Portable/Laptop** option in the **Power schemes** list box, as shown in **Figure 4-19**.
4. In the **Settings for Portable/Laptop power scheme** section, click the **After 10 mins** option in the **Turn off monitor** list box. This programs the monitor to automatically switch off after 10 minutes when it is not in use.
5. Click the **After 20 mins** option in the **Turn off hard disks** list box. This programs the hard disk to automatically switch off after 20 minutes when it is not in use.
6. Select **After 30 mins** in the **System standby** list box. Then click **Save As** to save the scheme. This opens the **Save Scheme** dialog box.
7. Type **Laptop Settings** as the name of the power scheme in the **Save this power scheme as** text box.
8. Click **OK** to close the **Save Scheme** dialog box.
9. Click **Apply** to apply the saved scheme to the system.
10. Open the list box in the **Power schemes** section to make sure that your newly created power scheme is on the list **(Figure 4-20)**.
11. Close the list and click the **Hibernate** tab.
12. Make sure that the **Enable hibernation** check box is selected and click **Apply**.
13. Click **OK** to close the **Power Options Properties** dialog box. You have now successfully configured Power options.
14. Close the **Control Panel**.

Figure 4-19 Setting power schemes

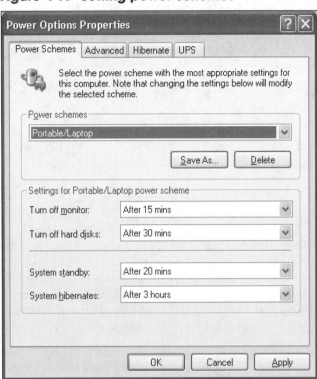

Figure 4-20 Saved power scheme

5 Managing Data Storage

In order to store your programs and data, you must learn how to properly configure and manage the physical drives in your system. In Windows XP Professional, a fixed disk drive can be configured using one of two data storage types: basic or dynamic. In basic storage the hard disk is divided into primary partitions, extended partitions, and logical drives. In dynamic storage the entire physical hard disk is viewed as a single entity, which can be divided into volumes. These volumes consist of portions of one or more physical disks. Dynamic disks are not supported on portable computers, removable disks, or disks connected using USB or IEEE 1394. Each storage type, either a basic partition or a dynamic volume, must be formatted with a file system, either NTFS or FAT/FAT32, before you can use it for storage.

Effective data storage involves more than storing data in volumes. You may need to compress data, assign disk quotas, and perform disk maintenance, such as deleting files that are no longer needed, and organizing your hard disk for effective data storage. The NTFS file system can store large amounts of data on a hard disk by compressing entire volumes, folders, subfolders, and files. Using NTFS, you can also limit the disk space assigned to specific users or groups by assigning disk quotas so that users will not be able to consume excess disk space. NTFS is the preferred file system because it provides many features that FAT/FAT32 does not.

You can also improve file access speed by using the Disk Defragmenter utility to organize the files on the hard disk into consecutive clusters, rather than having them scattered over the hard disk. Although NTFS provides a file system that resists fragmentation, you will still need to run the Disk Defragmenter occasionally to optimize the speed with which the system locates and retrieves files.

Scenario

You are the System Administrator of a small architectural firm. You have been asked to address the data storage issues currently being experienced by various members of the firm.

Lesson 5 Managing Data Storage

Project	Exam 70-270 Objective
5.1 Upgrading a Basic Disk to a Dynamic Disk	Monitor and configure disks.
5.2 Creating Volumes	Monitor, configure, and troubleshoot volumes.
5.3 Converting File Systems	Convert from one file system to another file system.
5.4 Introducing Disk Quotas	Monitor and configure disks.
5.5 Copying and Moving Compressed Files and Folders	Configure, manage, and troubleshoot file compression.
5.6 Using Disk Defragmenter	Optimize and troubleshoot disk performance.

General Requirements

To complete the projects in this lesson, you will need administrative rights on Windows XP Professional computer that has two hard disks and a CD-ROM drive. Both of the hard disks should use basic storage and the FAT32 file system. There should be at least 500 MB of unallocated disk space on both disks. **Unallocated space** is free space that does not belong to any partition or volume.

project 5.1

Upgrading a Basic Disk to a Dynamic Disk

exam objective

Monitor and configure disks.

overview

Windows XP Professional uses basic storage to initialize a hard disk by default. However, you may want to convert a basic disk to a dynamic disk in order to take advantage of the additional features offered by dynamic disks. Under Windows XP Professional, dynamic disks allow the creation of three volume types (**Table 5-1**).

You can upgrade a basic disk to a dynamic disk using the **Disk Management** snap-in. Before upgrading, you need to make sure that:
◆   All programs running on the hard disk are closed.
◆   There is at least 1 MB of unallocated space on the hard disk.
◆   The disk to be upgraded has been backed up. *While the upgrade process is non-destructive, you could lose your data if there is an error or power loss during the upgrade.*

When you convert a basic disk to a dynamic disk, the existing partitions on the basic disk are converted to simple volumes. You can change a dynamic disk to a basic disk, but if you do so, you will lose all of the data stored on that disk.

Caroline Jones currently has a system that has two hard drives, both of which use the basic storage type. You decide to convert one of her hard disks to dynamic so that she can take advantage of the benefits offered by this storage type.

caution

Fault-tolerant volumes such as RAID 5 and mirrored volumes cannot be created on computers running Windows XP Professional.

learning objective

After you have completed this project, you will know how to upgrade a basic disk to a dynamic disk.

specific requirements

A Windows XP Professional computer with two hard disk drives, one of which uses the basic storage type.

estimated completion time

15 minutes

project steps

Convert a basic disk to a dynamic disk.
1. Click **Start**, right-click **My Computer**, and click **Manage** to open the **Computer Management** console.
2. Click the **Disk Management** node under **Storage**.
3. In the lower-right pane of the **Computer Management** window, right-click the disk that you want to upgrade, for example, **Disk 1** (**Figure 5-1**).
4. Click the **Convert to Dynamic Disk** command to open the **Convert to Dynamic Disk** dialog box.
5. Click **OK** to open the **Disks to Convert** dialog box.
6. Click **Convert**. The **Disk Management** message box opens, warning you that, once you upgrade to a dynamic disk, you will not be able to boot other installed operating systems from any volume on this disk (**Figure 5-2**).
7. Click **Yes** to confirm the conversion of the disk. The **Convert Disk to Dynamic** message box informs you that file systems on any of the disks to be converted will be dismounted.
8. Click **Yes**. Windows converts the disk from basic to dynamic.
9. Close the Computer Management console.

caution

Dynamic disks are unique to Windows 2000/2003 and XP Professional and are not recognized by other operating systems.

tip

DiskPart is a command line tool that is an alternate means for configuring and managing disks.

Table 5-1   Dynamic Volumes

Volume Type	Properties
Simple	• Contains space from a single disk • Equivalent to a basic partition
Spanned	• Up to 32 volume segments from two or more drives that are combined sequentially to provide one large volume • No performance increase • Additional volume segments can be added at any time to increase size
Striped	• Up to 32 segments from two or more separate drives combined by striping to provide one large volume • Increases read/write performance • Size cannot be changed once created • RAID 0
Mirrored	• **Cannot be created under Windows XP Professional** • Can be created under Windows 2000/2003 Server • Provides fault tolerance • RAID 1
RAID 5	• **Cannot be created under Windows XP Professional** • Can be created under Windows 2000/2003 Server • Provides fault tolerance • Striped volume with parity

Figure 5-1 Converting a disk

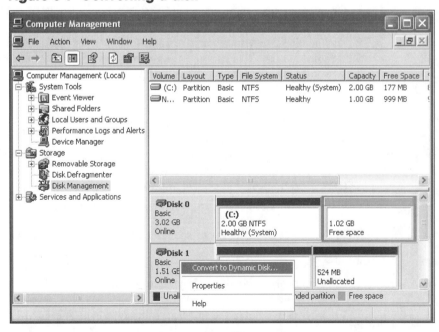

Figure 5-2 Disk Management message box

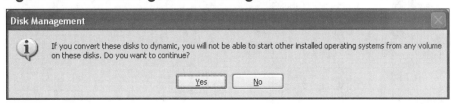

project 5.2   *Creating Volumes*

exam objective

Monitor, configure, and troubleshoot volumes.

overview

A simple volume consists of disk space from a single disk. However, it can be extended to include any available free space on the disk. Simple volumes can be formatted with the FAT, FAT32, or NTFS file systems; however, you can extend a volume only if it is formatted with NTFS.

Now that you have created a dynamic disk on Caroline's system, you can create a volume on it.

learning objective

After you have completed this project, you will know how to create a simple volume and view its properties.

specific requirements

To complete this project, you must have a Windows XP Professional computer with a dynamic disk with unallocated space.

estimated completion time

15 minutes

project steps

Create a simple volume.

1. Click **Start**, and then click **Control Panel** to open the Control Panel window. If necessary, click **Switch to Classic View** to display all of the Control Panel icons.
2. Double-click the **Administrative Tools** icon to open the Administrative Tools window.
3. Double-click the **Computer Management** icon to open the Computer Management console.
4. Click **Disk Management** under **Storage** on the left side of the **Computer Management** console.
5. In the lower-right pane of the **Computer Management** console, right-click the unallocated space on the dynamic disk where you would like to create the volume, and select the **New Volume** command (**Figure 5-3**). The **New Volume Wizard** is initialized and the first screen **Welcome to the New Volume Wizard** opens.
6. Click **Next** to display the **Select Volume Type** screen.
7. The **Simple** option button is selected by default (**Figure 5-4**). Click **Next** to display the **Select Disks** screen.
8. In the **Select the amount of space in MB** spin box, type **200** to specify the disk size (**Figure 5-5**).
9. Click **Next** to display the **Assign Drive Letter or Path** screen.
10. The **Assign the following drive letter** option button is selected by default. If necessary, select **F** in the list box.
11. Click **Next** to display the **Format Volume** screen. The **Format this volume with the following settings** option button is selected by default.

Figure 5-3 Selecting unallocated space on the dynamic disk to create a volume

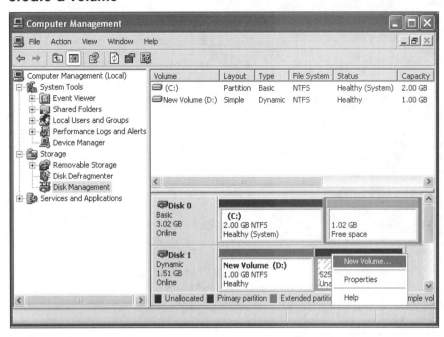

Figure 5-4 Selecting the volume type

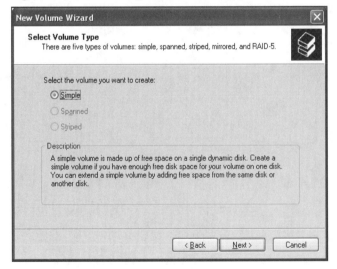

Figure 5-5 Selecting the disk where the volume will be created

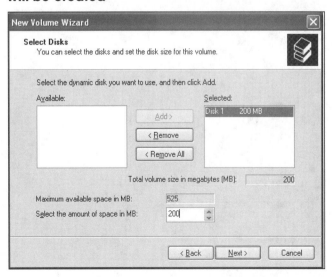

project 5.2

Creating Volumes (cont'd)

exam objective

Monitor, configure, and troubleshoot volumes.

project steps

12. Select the **FAT32** file system in the **File system** list box.
13. Make sure that **Default** is selected in the **Allocation unit size** list box.
14. Type **SimpleVol** in the **Volume label** text box to enter a label for the volume **(Figure 5-6)**.
15. Select the **Perform a Quick Format** check box.
16. Click **Next** to display the final screen, **Completing the New Volume Wizard**. This screen displays the settings that you have selected.
17. Click **Finish** to complete the process of creating a simple volume.
18. In the **Computer Management** console, under Disk Management, right-click the volume that was just created and then click the **Properties** command on the context menu.
19. The **Properties** dialog box for the volume will open. Click each of the tabs and record the information you find there on your sheet. After you have recorded the information, close the **Computer Management** console.

Figure 5-6 Formatting the volume

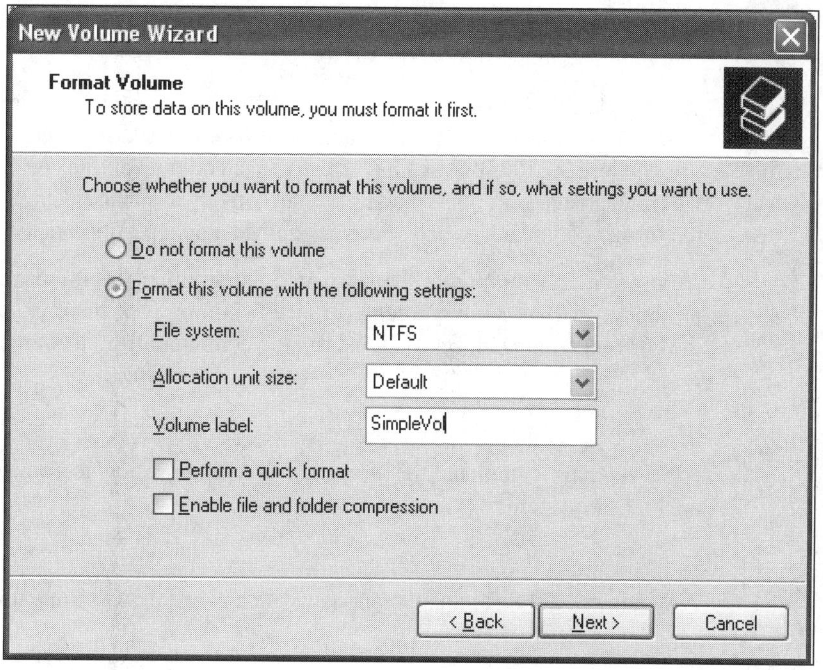

project 5.3

Converting File Systems

exam objective

Convert from one file system to another file system.

overview

NTFS is a much more robust file system than FAT/FAT32 and provides many features such as encryption, compression, and security.

You decide that it would be best to convert the simple volume on Caroline's dynamic disk from FAT32 to NTFS to take advantage of its enhanced features. Caroline is concerned that she will lose the files that she has already saved on the volume. You assure her that the process will not damage her data. You will use the convert command, which is non-destructive, unlike the format command, which will erase any data on a partition or volume.

A partition or volume may be formatted using either the **format** command at a command prompt or in **Disk Management (Figure 5-7)**; however, there is no graphical equivalent for the **convert** command, so you must run the command from a command prompt.

caution

To convert from NTFS to FAT, you must back-up the data on the volume, delete the volume, recreate it, format it, and then restore the data from the backup.

learning objective

After you have completed this project, you will know how to convert from one file system to another file system.

specific requirements

A Windows XP Professional computer with a partition or volume formatted with FAT/FAT32.

estimated completion time

15 minutes

project steps

Convert a **FAT** partition to **NTFS**.
1. Click **Start**, point to **All Programs**, point to **Accessories**, and click **Command Prompt** to open the Command Prompt window.
2. Type **convert** *x:* **/fs:ntfs /v** and press **[Enter]**. *Note that there is a space between each option switch in the command.* The x represents the drive letter of the volume you are converting, and the **/v** indicates that the command should be run in verbose mode. In **verbose mode**, all of the messages generated during the conversion are displayed **(Figure 5-8)**.
3. Enter **SimpleVol** as the current volume label, and press **[Enter]** to perform the conversion.
4. Type **Exit**, and press **[Enter]** to exit the command prompt window and to return to the Windows XP desktop.

tip

Only Windows XP, 2000/2003 and NT 4.0 Service Pack 4 can use NTFS 5.0 file systems.

Figure 5-7 Formatting a drive in the Disk Management snap-in

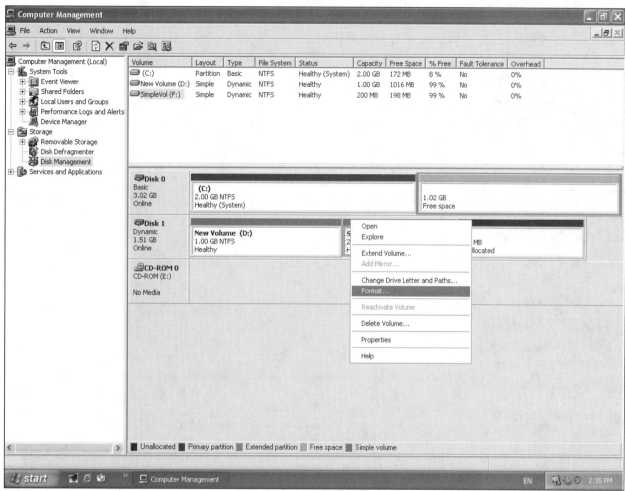

Figure 5-8 Convert command in the Command Prompt window

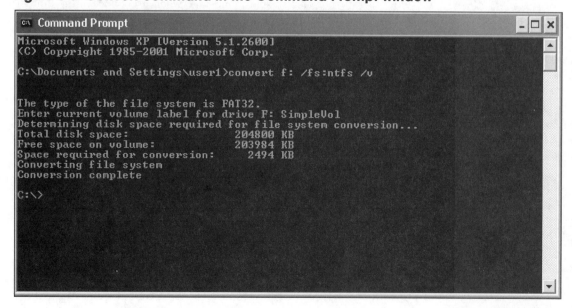

project 5.4   *Introducing Disk Quotas*

exam objective

Monitor and configure disks.

overview

Last week the computer acting as a workgroup server ran out of storage space on the volume that holds your user's home directories. Upon examination you found that three users had copied their entire laptop's data to their home directories, using all available space on the volume. After reminding the users of the acceptable use policy for the network and deleting the offending files, you decide to prevent the problem from ever occurring again by implementing disk quotas to limit the maximum amount of space each user can use.

learning objective

In this project, you will learn how to enable and configure disk quotas to control disk usage on a per-user basis.

specific requirements

A Windows XP Professional computer with a partition or volume formatted with NTFS.

estimated completion time

15 minutes

project steps

Enable quotas on a drive, setting the default limit to **20 MB** and the warning level to **16 MB**. Add a quota entry for the **Guest** account.

1. Click **Start**, point to **All Programs**, point to **Accessories**, and click **Windows Explorer** to open the Explorer window.
2. Click the **My Computer** icon, right-click the **F:** drive in the left panel, and click the **Properties** command to open the Properties dialog box on the **General** tab.
3. Click the **Quota** tab to display the options for setting disk quotas. By default, disk quotas are disabled.
4. Select the **Enable quota management** check box.
5. Select the **Deny disk space to users exceeding quota limit** check box. This selection will send an "out of disk space" message when users exceed the limit. To track and generate hard disk usage information without preventing users from saving data, you can clear the **Deny disk space to users exceeding quota limit** check box.
6. Select the **Limit disk space to** option button, and type **20** in the **Limit disk space to** text box.
7. Type **16** in the **Set warning level to** text box.
8. Specify the unit size by opening the list boxes next to the **Limit disk space to** and **Set warning level to** text boxes and by selecting the MB option for both values (**Figure 5-9**).
9. Click **Apply**. The **Disk Quota** message box opens to warn you that, if you enable disk quotas, the volume will be rescanned to update disk usage statistics.
10. Click **OK** to enable disk quotas.
11. Click **Quota Entries** on the **Quota** tab to open the **Quota Entries for SimpleVol (F:)** window.
12. Click **Quota** on the Menu bar, and click the **New Quota Entry** command (**Figure 5-10**) to open the **Select Users** dialog box.

tip

Only the Administrator can modify quota settings.

Figure 5-9 Setting disk quotas

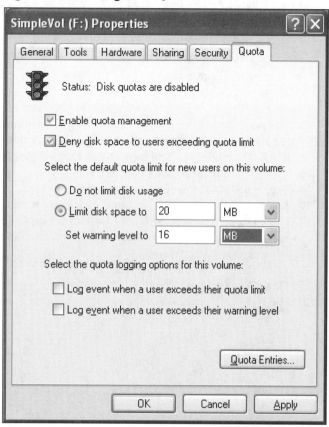

Figure 5-10 Quota entries for the SimpleVol (F:) window

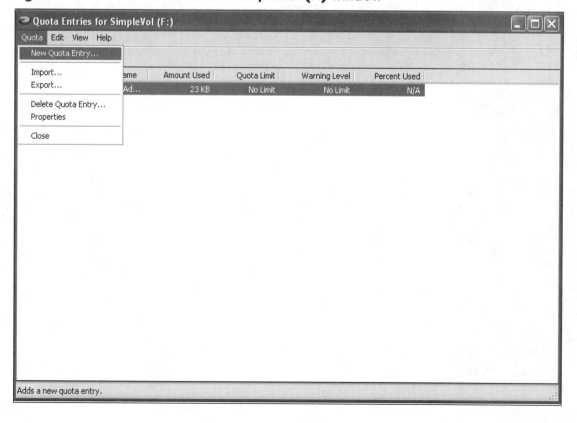

project 5.4   *Introducing Disk Quotas (cont'd)*

exam objective

Monitor and configure disks.

project steps

13. Make sure the object type is set to **Users** and the **location** is set to the local computer name. Type **Guest** in the **Enter the object names to select** text box.

14. Click **OK** to open the **Add New Quota Entry** dialog box (**Figure 5-11**).

15. Type **10** in the **Limit disk space to** text box.

16. Type **8** in the **Set warning level to** text box.

17. Select the MB unit size in the **Limit disk space to** and **Set warning level to** list boxes.

18. Click **OK** to return to the **Quota Entries** window (**Figure 5-12**). The quota entry you created for the Guest account now appears in the window.

19. Close the **Quota Entries** window.

20. Click **OK** to close the **Properties** dialog box.

21. Close Windows Explorer.

Figure 5-11 Setting a quota entry for a user

Figure 5-12 Quota entry for the Guest account

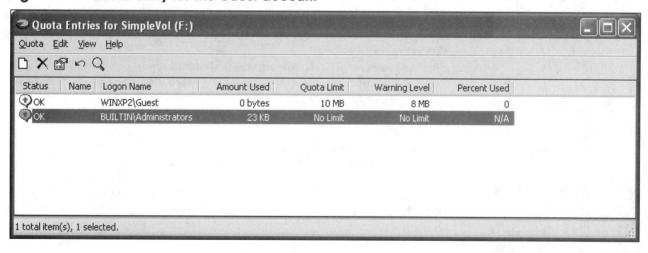

Copying and Moving Compressed Files and Folders

exam objective

Configure, manage, and troubleshoot file compression.

overview

Your company uses MS Excel spreadsheets to forecast production schedules. Each week a new spreadsheet is created from the previous week's spreadsheet and the old spreadsheet is kept to allow historical analysis of your projections. To conserve storage space on your workstations, you want to have your users place all old file versions in a folder that has compression enabled.

learning objective

In this project, you will learn what effect copying and moving compressed files has on the compression attribute of the file.

specific requirements

A Windows XP Professional computer with a partition or volume formatted with NTFS.

estimated completion time

15 minutes

project steps

Compress a folder in an **NTFS** volume and change the display color of the compressed folder.

1. Create a folder called **SourceFolder** and a folder called **CompFolder** on the C: drive.
2. Right-click the **CompFolder** folder, and click **Properties** to open the **CompFolder Properties** dialog box.
3. Click **Advanced** to open the **Advanced Attributes** dialog box.
4. Select the **Compress contents to save disk space** check box in the **Compress or Encrypt attributes** section (**Figure 5-13**).
5. Click **OK** to close **Advanced Attributes** dialog box and to display the **Properties** dialog box for the folder.
6. Click **OK** to close the **Properties** dialog box for the folder.
7. By default, **Windows XP Professional** displays compressed files in blue. You want to confirm that the system is configured to use the default settings for displaying compressed files and folders. Right-click **Start**, and click the **Explore** command.
8. Open the **Tools** menu, and click the **Folder Options** command to open the **Folder Options** dialog box.
9. Click the **View** tab.
10. In the **Advanced Settings** list box, make sure that the **Show encrypted or compressed NTFS files in color** check box is selected (**Figure 5-14**).
11. Click **OK** to apply any changes. The names of the compressed files and folders are displayed in blue in the **Windows Explorer** window.
12. Double-click the **SourceFolder** folder to open it. In the **Windows Explorer** window, click the **File** menu, click **New**, and then click **Text Document**.
13. Type **file1.txt**, for the new file name and press [**Enter**].
14. Repeat this process to create another file called **file2.txt**.
15. Select **file1.txt** and click **Copy this file** under the **File and Folder Tasks** section (**Figure 5-15**). The **Copy Items** dialog box will open (**Figure 5-16**). Browse the directory list, and select the **CompFolder** folder then click **Copy**.

tip

If the folder you are compressing contains files or subfolders you will be prompted to select if you want the change to apply only to this folder or this folder, subfolders, and files.

Figure 5-13 Setting the Compress attribute

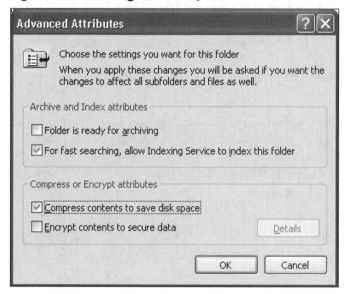

Figure 5-14 Displaying compressed NTFS files and folders in color

Figure 5-15 Copying file1.txt

Figure 5-16 Selecting destination for file1.txt

project 5.5

Copying and Moving Compressed Files and Folders (cont'd)

exam objective

Configure, manage, and troubleshoot file compression.

project steps

16. Next, select **file2.txt**, and click **Move this file** under the **File and Folder Tasks** section. The **Move Items** dialog box will open (**Figure 5-17**). Browse the directory list, and select the **CompFolder** folder then click **Move**.
17. Change directories to **CompFolder**. Notice that **file1.txt** is displayed in blue because it is compressed and that **file2.txt** is not displayed in blue because it is not compressed (**Figure 5-18**).
18. Close **Windows Explorer**.

tip

Any time that you copy or move a file between two volumes, it will always inherit the compressed attribute of its new location. The only time a file will keep its compressed attribute is if you move it within a single volume.

Figure 5-17 Selecting the destination for file2.txt

Figure 5-18 Viewing files in CompFolder

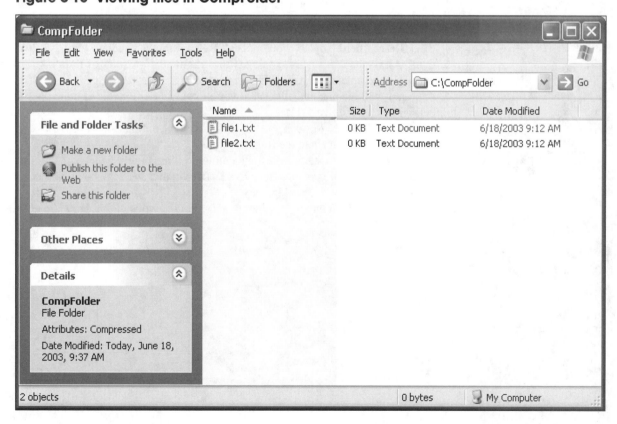

project 5.6

Using Disk Defragmenter

exam objective

Optimize and troubleshoot disk performance.

overview

Several users have complained that their computers that run Windows XP Professional have become slower lately and that, when they access files, the hard drive light stays on for a long time. You realize that their volumes must have become fragmented over time as files were created and deleted. You plan to teach the users how to defragment their own volumes, but first you want to write down each step of the procedure.

learning objective

In this project you will learn how to defragment a volume using Disk Defragmenter.

specific requirements

A computer running Windows XP Professional.

estimated completion time

15-30 minutes

project steps

Analyze a volume to determine its fragmentation level and defragment the volume using the **Disk Defragmenter**.

1. Right-click **Start** and click **Explore** to open the **Windows Explorer** window.
2. Right-click the **C:** drive, and click **Properties** to open the **Properties** dialog box for the **C:** drive.
3. Click the **Tools** tab **(Figure 5-19)**.
4. Click **Defragment Now** to open the **Disk Defragmenter** window **(Figure 5-20)**.
5. Click **Analyze**. The system analyzes the fragmentation state of the disk. When the analysis is complete, the **Analysis Complete** dialog box opens.
6. A prompt will recommend either that you defragment or that the volume does not need defragmenting **(Figure 5-21)**.
7. Click **View Report** to open the **Analysis Report** dialog box **(Figure 5-22)**, which displays information about the fragmented files.
8. Click **Defragment** to start the defragmenting process **(Figure 5-23)**.
9. After the disk is defragmented, the **Disk Defragmenter** message box will display.
10. Click **Close** to close the message box.
11. Close the Disk Defragmenter window and the Properties dialog box. Close Windows Explorer.

Figure 5-19 The Tools tab in the Properties dialog box

Figure 5-20 The Disk Defragmenter

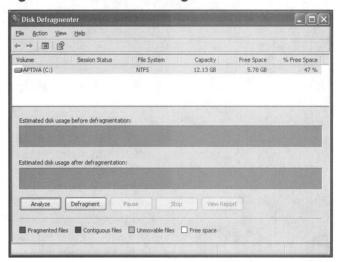

Figure 5-21 Analyzing the fragmentation of the disk

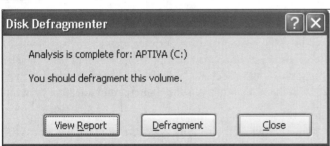

Figure 5-22 The Analysis Report dialog box

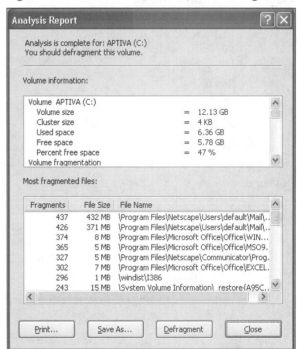

Figure 5-23 Defragmenting the disk

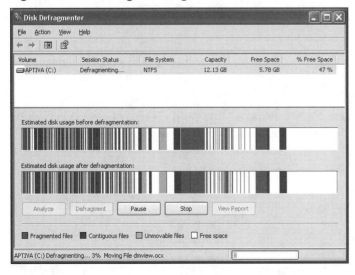

6 Installing and Configuring Network Protocols

A protocol is a set of rules and conventions for sending information over a network. These rules manage the content, format, timing, sequencing, and error control for messages exchanged among network devices. The protocol explains how the clients and servers on a network must arrange data in order to deliver it to other computers on the network and how they can interpret data that is delivered to them. In addition, computers on a network must "speak the same language" in order for data transfers to be possible. Windows XP Professional supports several protocols that networks follow when transferring data. The main protocol is TCP/IP (Transmission Control Protocol/Internet Protocol), which is the core protocol for the Internet. TCP/IP is a scalable and routable protocol. It is scalable because it can be used for both large and small networks, and data can be transferred across networks and between computers using different operating systems with widely varying structural designs. TCP/IP is a routable protocol because it ensures that data can cross a router, which is a special computer used to transfer data between networks. Networking protocols today are put into practice as a suite of protocols. A protocol suite is a combination of several different networking applications and services that function jointly to make network communications possible. The protocol suite outlines the stages involved in packaging data so that it can be sent and received on the network. Each packet of data must be correctly formatted, ordered, compressed, and checked for errors. Therefore, each computer on a network must be configured with the same protocol suite if intercommunication between them is required.

If your network uses computers running Microsoft operating systems and you must access the resources on servers running a version of Netware that predates 4.0, you must use the NWLink protocol. Netware 4.0 servers and above support TCP/IP. NWLink can also be used in an exclusively Microsoft environment; however, you will not be able to use Active Directory because it is only compatible with TCP/IP. If a Microsoft client needs to access file and print resources on a NetWare server, Client Service for NetWare (CSNW), the redirector that is compatible with NetWare, must also be installed. Alternatively, you can install Novell's redirector, Novell Client for Windows NT/2000/XP.

Network bindings are used to set the order in which the protocols that are configured on a system will be used. When a network connection is initiated, the bindings set the order in which the system will attempt to use protocols to establish links.

On computers running Windows XP Professional, you can use Network Bridge to connect segments of a LAN without implementing routers. Network Bridge greatly simplifies the process of combining multiple media types that use multiple protocols in one network.

Scenario

You are a Network Administrator for a small company that produces artwork for greeting cards. The organization has recently expanded. It currently has a TCP/IP-based Windows XP network. To deal with increased demand for print services, you have decided to create a dedicated print server for a group of artists. You must configure this Windows XP Professional computer with a static IP address and test the connection. Your artists also need to access resources on a Netware server that does not support the TCP/IP protocol, so you must install the NWLink Protocol and Client Services for NetWare (CSNW) on their client computers. Finally, you must set the binding order for the protocols to ensure optimal network performance.

Lesson 6   Installing and Configuring Network Protocols

Project	Exam 70-270 Objective
6.1 Configuring TCP/IP to Use a Static IP Address	Configure and troubleshoot the TCP/IP protocol.
6.2 Troubleshooting TCP/IP Problems	Configure and troubleshoot the TCP/IP protocol.
6.3 Installing NWLink on a System	Basic knowledge
6.4 Configuring Network Bindings	Optimize and troubleshoot network performance.
6.5 Configuring Network Bridge	Optimize and troubleshoot network performance.

General Requirements

A network connected computer running Windows XP Professional.

project 6.1

Configuring TCP/IP to Use a Static IP Address

exam objective

Configure and troubleshoot the TCP/IP protocol.

overview

You recently decided to make one of the Windows XP Professional client computers on your Microsoft-based TCP/IP network a dedicated print server for ten of your artists. First, you will check the network components installed on the computer, and then reconfigure the TCP/IP settings to give the print server a static IP address. When you manually assign an IP address, Windows XP Professional automatically assigns a subnet mask to divide the network ID from the host ID.

learning objective

After completing this project, you will know how to:
◆   Assign a static IP address.
◆   Configure TCP/IP to use a static IP Address.

specific requirements

Administrative rights on a Windows XP Professional computer that has the TCP/IP protocol installed.

estimated completion time

15 minutes

project steps

Configure TCP/IP to use a static IP address.

1. Click **Start**, click **Control Panel** on the Start menu, and double-click the Network Connections icon to open the **Network Connections** window.
2. Right-click the **Local Area Connection** icon, and select **Properties** to open the **Local Area Connection Properties** dialog box.
3. Select **Internet Protocol (TCP/IP) (Figure 6-1)**.
4. Click **Properties** to open the **Internet Protocol (TCP/IP) Properties** dialog box. Record the settings for all options on the **General** tab so that you can return your TCP/IP configuration to its original settings after you complete this project.
5. Click the **Use the following IP address** option button.
6. Click in the **IP address** text box, and type **198.164.1.204 (Figure 6-2)**.
7. Click in the **Subnet mask** text box. Windows XP Professional automatically assigns the default subnet mask based on the class of the given IP address. In this case, the address is a Class C address that has a default mask of 255.255.255.0.
8. Click **OK** to confirm the settings.
9. Click **OK** to close the Local Area Connection Properties dialog box.
10. Close the Network Connections window.
11. Repeat the steps above to return the TCP/IP settings to their original configuration.

tip

Computers operating as servers often have a static IP address.

Figure 6-1 Local Area Connection Properties dialog box

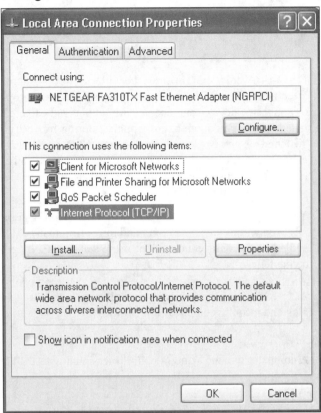

Figure 6-2 Configuring a static IP address

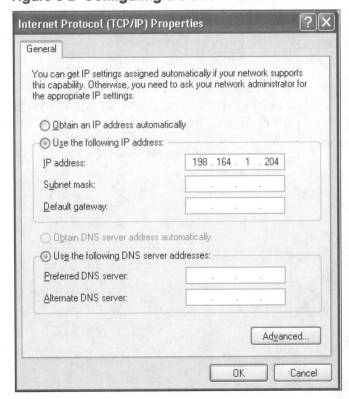

project 6.2   *Troubleshooting TCP/IP Problems*

exam objective

Configure and troubleshoot the TCP/IP protocol.

overview

Network Administrators must be able to troubleshoot network connectivity problems effectively. Frequently, network problems are traced to simple physical problems such as disconnected devices and accidentally unplugged cables. Before you use any of the utilities listed below, you should start troubleshooting by verifying that everything is plugged in, switched on, and connected. Next, check the Device Manager to ensure that the driver for the network adapter is set up and functioning properly.Finally, you can use several troubleshooting utilities included in Windows XP Professional to inspect your network protocols. All are run from the Command Prompt window.

You will execute the **ping** command and the **ipconfig** command to test the TCP/IP connectivity. You will use the ping command to confirm that TCP/IP is bound to the network adapter, and use the ipconfig command to ensure that the TCP/IP protocol has initialized itself on your computer.

learning objective

After completing this project, you will know how to troubleshoot TCP/IP problems using the ping and ipconfig command-line utilities.

specific requirements

A computer running Windows XP Professional with TCP/IP installed and configured.

estimated completion time

5 minutes

project steps

1. Open the **Start** menu and click the **Run** command. Type **cmd** in the **Open** text box, and click **OK** to open the **Command Prompt** window.
2. At the command prompt, type **ipconfig /all** and press **[Enter]**. The details of the **Ethernet adapter Local Area Connection** will display (**Figure 6-3**). Record the IP address for your system on a sheet of paper for use in the next step.
3. At the command prompt, type **ping <ip_address_of_client_computer>** and press **[Enter]**. This command verifies that the TCP/IP protocol is correctly installed and configured on the computer (**Figure 6-4**). Record the results on your sheet.
4. Close the **Command Prompt** window.

Figure 6-3 Using the ipconfig /all command

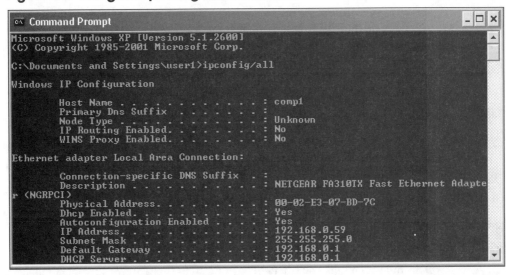

Figure 6-4 Using the ping command

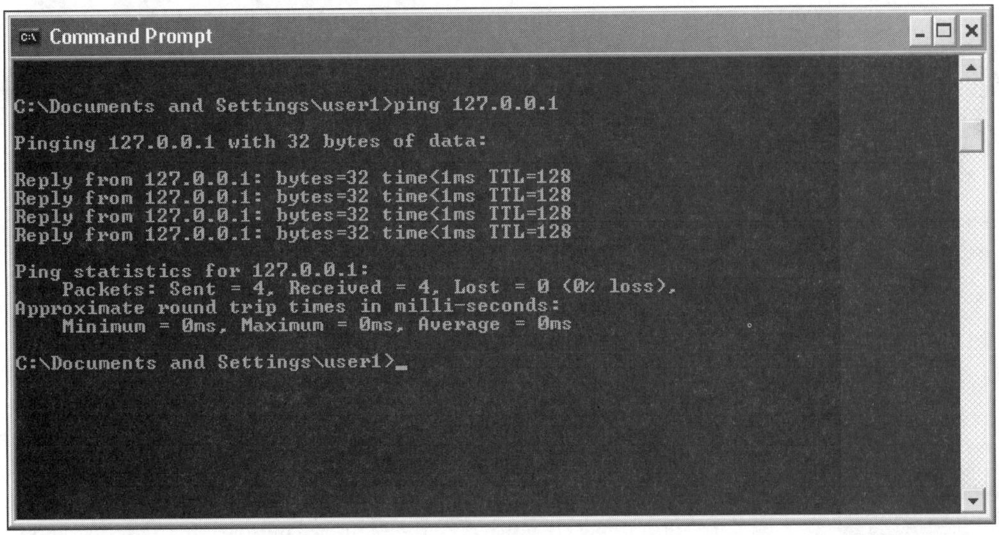

project 6.3

Installing NWLink on a System

exam objective

Basic Knowledge

overview

The Art department needs to access resources on an older NetWare server that does not support TCP/IP. You must install the NWLink protocol and Client Services for NetWare (CSNW) on their computers so that they can access the required files.

learning objective

After you have completed this project, you will know how to install NWLink and Client Services for NetWare (CSNW) on a Windows XP Professional computer.

specific requirements

◆ A computer running Windows XP Professional that is connected to the network.
◆ A NetWare server (optional).

estimated completion time

15 minutes

project steps

Install NWLink and Client Service for Netware (CSNW) on your computer.

1. Click **Start**, click **Control Panel**, and double-click the **Network Connections** icon in the Control Panel window to open the **Network Connections** window.
2. Right-click the **Local Area Connection** icon, and click **Properties** on the shortcut menu to open the **Local Area Connection Properties** dialog box.
3. Click **Install** to open the **Select Network Component Type** dialog box.
4. Select the **Protocol** option in the **Click the type of network component you want to install** box.
5. Click **Add**. The **Select Network Protocol** dialog box opens.
6. Select the **NWLink IPX/SPX/NetBIOS Compatible Transport Protocol** option in the **Network Protocol** section (**Figure 6-5**).
7. Click **OK** to apply the changes. In addition to the NWLink IPX/SPX/NetBIOS Compatible Transport Protocol, the NWLink NetBIOS protocol has been added (**Figure 6-6**). This addition ensures backward compatibility with earlier Microsoft networks. The additional protocol is needed to make IPX/SPX/NetBIOS compatible.
8. Select **NWLink IPX/SPX/NetBIOS Compatible Transport Protocol**, and click **Properties (Figure 6-7)**.
9. The **Internal network number** should be set to a unique hexadecimal value. Type **A90001FC**.
10. In the **Adapter** section set the **Frame type** to **Ethernet 802.2**. The **Network number** must match the Network number on all other systems that will communicate on the local network segment. Normally, Windows XP Professional will automatically detect the Network number. If you know the Network number that is in use, you can manually set the **Network number** value.
11. Click **OK** to close the **NWLink IPX/SPX/NetBIOS Compatible Transport Protocol** dialog box.
12. Click **Install** to open the **Select Network Component Type** dialog box again.

tip

When using NWLink IPX/SPX/NetBIOS, all computers that will communicate must use the same frame type. Netware 3.11 and older versions used 802.3 for the default frame type. Netware 3.12 and newer versions use 802.2 for the default frame type.

Figure 6-5 Select Network Protocol dialog box

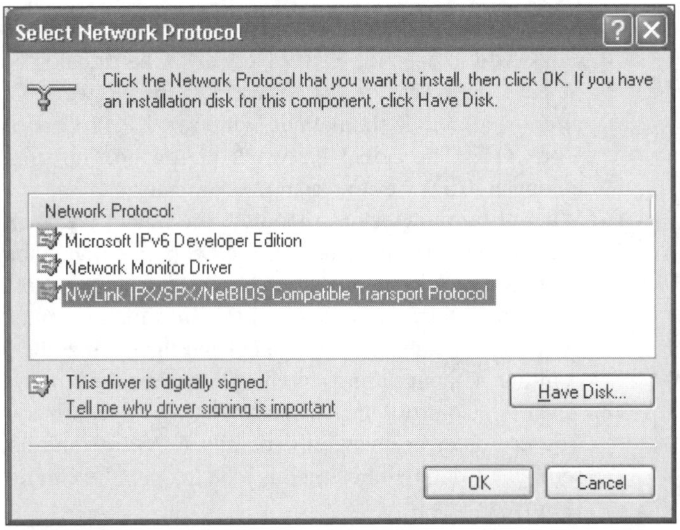

Figure 6-6 Protocols configured for this Network Connection

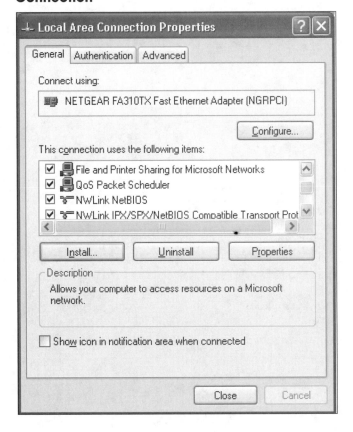

Figure 6-7 NWLink/SPX/NetBIOS Compatible Transport Protocol Properties dialog box

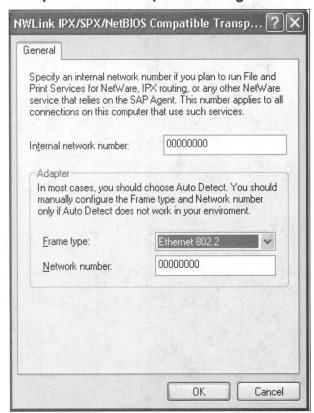

project 6.3

Installing NWLink on a System (cont'd)

exam objective

Basic knowledge

project steps

13. Select **Client** in the **Click the type of network component you want to install** box.
14. Click **Add** to open the **Select Network Client** dialog box.
15. Select **Client Service for Netware** in the **Network Client** box. (This will be the only client available if the default Windows XP Professional installation was performed.) Click **OK**. The **Local Network** dialog box informs you that you must restart the computer. Click **Yes** to restart the computer.
16. When the computer has rebooted, the **Select NetWare Logon** dialog box opens. You must have ready the name of the NDS (Novell Directory Services) **tree** and the location of the server object **(context)** to which the client computer will connect. If you have access to a Netware Server and this information, enter it in the **Tree** and **Context** text boxes. If not, simply click **Cancel** and then **Yes** in the **NetWare Network** dialog box to continue without setting a preferred server.
17. Open the Control Panel window. A **CSNW** icon has been added to the Control Panel. You can enter or change the default **NDS** tree and context settings and other **CSNW** settings by double-clicking this icon to open the **Client Service for Netware** dialog box **(Figure 6-8)**.
18. Click **OK** to Close the Client Service for Netware dialog box, and then close the Control Panel window.

Figure 6-8 Client Service for Netware dialog box

project 6.4

Configuring Network Bindings

exam objective

Optimize and troubleshoot network performance.

overview

On a client computer on which multiple protocols are configured, you may adjust the **binding order** for the protocols. The binding order establishes which protocol will be used first when a network connection is attempted. It is the *client* computer that determines which protocol will be used to establish the connection. Since your artists will be accessing the Netware server only occasionally, you do not want the NWLink IPX/SPX/NetBIOS Compatible Transport Protocol to be the first protocol used when a session is established. Furthermore, for the most part your Art department will be accessing a LAN server that uses TCP/IP, so you want it to be the top protocol.

learning objective

After you have completed this project, you will know how to configure the network bindings on a computer.

specific requirements

A Windows XP Professional computer on which the TCP/IP and NWLink protocols have been installed.

estimated completion time

10 minutes

project steps

Configure the network bindings on your computer.

1. Open the Control Panel, and double-click the Network Connections icon to open the **Network Connections** window.
2. Open the **Advanced** menu, and select the **Advanced Settings** command to open the Advanced Settings dialog box (**Figure 6-9**).
3. Select **Local Area Connection** in the **Connections** section of the **Adapters and Bindings** tab.
4. In the **Bindings for Local Area Connection** scrolling list box, under **File and Printer Sharing for Microsoft Networks**, select **Internet Protocol (TCP/IP)**.
5. Click the **Up Arrow** once to move the selected protocol above **NWLink IPX/SPX/ NetBIOS Compatible Transport Protocol**.
6. Under **Client for Microsoft Networks**, select **Internet Protocol (TCP/IP)**. Click the **Up Arrow** again to position Internet Protocol (TCP/IP) above NWLink (**Figure 6-10**).
7. Click **OK** to apply the changes.
8. Close the Network Connections window.

tip

Disabling unused network bindings will improve network performance.

Figure 6-9 Advanced Settings dialog box

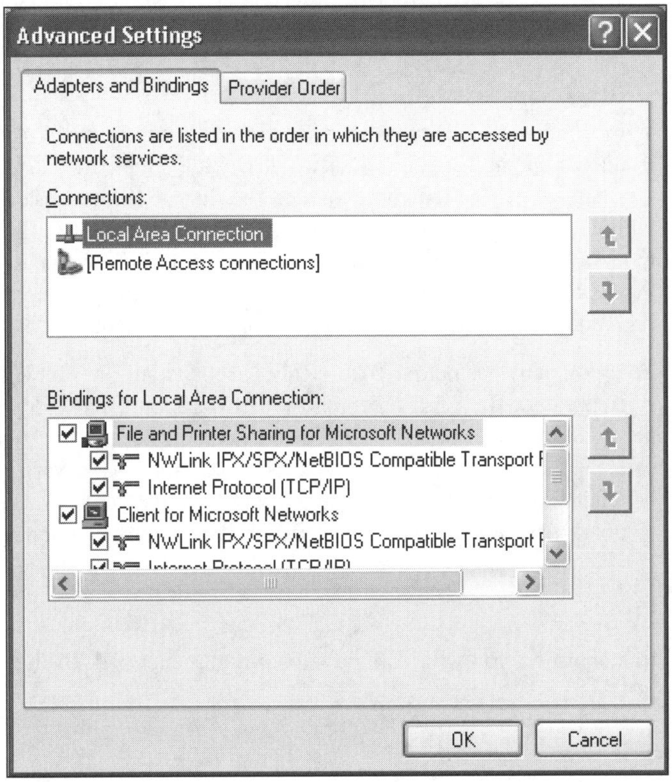

Figure 6-10 Protocol binding order changed

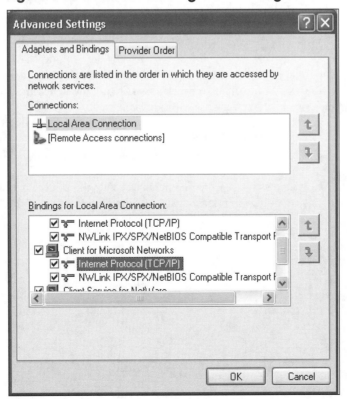

project 6.5

Configuring Network Bridge

exam objective

Optimize and troubleshoot network performance.

overview

With Windows XP Professional, Microsoft has introduced a new networking feature to the Windows operating system. **Network Bridge** simplifies the process of connecting different segments of networked computers on the same LAN because it allows them to communicate without requiring the use of separate subnets. **Network Bridge** operates at layer 2 of the OSI model, and it allows the connection of different media types, if required. Before Windows XP Professional, systems engineers had to configure routing to connect separate network segments that require unique subnets for each segment.

Your company has both a Token Ring LAN and an Ethernet LAN that use addresses with the same network ID. Until recently, the networks operated independently; but now there is the need for some resource sharing. You must connect the two networks without requiring any changes to their existing network address schemes. After verifying that there are no duplicate host addresses on the two networks, you have decided that you will be able to use the new Network Bridge feature of Windows XP Professional to connect the two LANs.

tip

Bridges join segments belonging to the same network. Routers join segments from separate networks.

tip

No two computers on a bridged network can share an IP address.

learning objective

In this project you will learn how to configure Network Bridge.

specific requirements

A Windows XP Professional computer with two configured network connections.

estimated completion time

15 minutes

project steps

Configure Network Bridge on a Windows XP Professional computer.

1. Click **Start**, click **Control Panel**, and double-click the **Network Connections** icon to open the **Network Connections** window.
2. Select the network connections you wish to bridge in the Network Connections window under **LAN or High-Speed Internet (Figure 6-11)**.
3. Right-click any of the selected network connections, and click **Bridge Connections** on the shortcut menu.
4. Windows takes a few moments to create the bridge. A bridge icon then appears in the Network Connections window (**Figure 6-12**).
5. Close the Network Connections window.

Figure 6-11 Network connections selected for Network Bridge

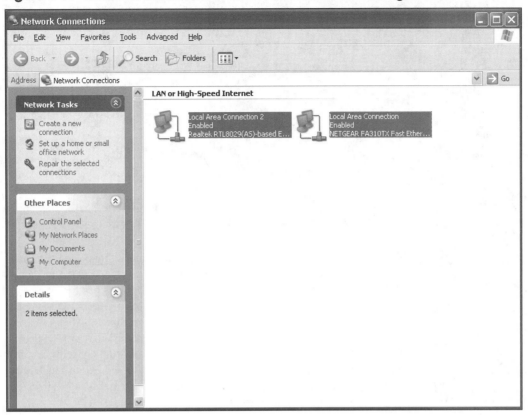

Figure 6-12 Network Bridge created

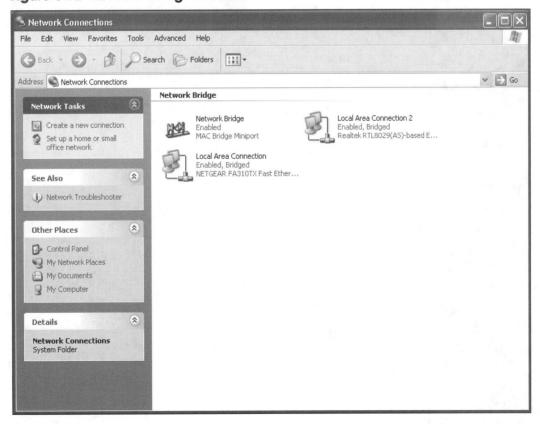

7 Performing Administrative Tasks

Windows XP Professional includes various administrative tools that you can use in order to centralize administrative tasks and perform them efficiently. The Microsoft Management Console (MMC) is used to create a set of tools for performing administrative tasks. MMC acts as a container for other administrative tools and displays them as consoles. Consoles consist of one or more applications called snap-ins that aredesigned to perform specific administrative functions. Windows XP Professional provides certain predefined consoles, and you can also create custom consoles by combining multiple preconfigured snap-ins into one console. You can also add extensions to custom snap-ins in order to provide additional administrative functionality. Taskpad views can be created to provide a simplified interface for specific administrative tasks.

Scripting languages can provide powerful administrative control and Windows XP Professional provides excellent support for scripting. Logon and Logoff scripts can be executed each time a user logs on or off a system. Startup and shutdown scripts can be run each time a computer starts or is shutdown. Scripts can also be automated to run at specified intervals by using the Task Scheduler as can many other system tools. In addition, scripting can be used to save time when repetitious tasks must be executed.

Scenario

You have just joined a firm as an Assistant Systems Administrator in charge of the administration and maintenance of a Windows XP network. One of the tasks you will be responsible for will be the creation of customized management consoles for other administrators use. Initially you will review the existing management consoles that Windows XP Professional provides so that you can determine what customizations will be required for your environment. You will also be required to configure Logon scripts for users.

Lesson 7   Performing Administrative Tasks

Project	Exam 70-270 Objective
7.1 Viewing Preconfigured Microsoft Management Consoles	Basic knowledge
7.2 Creating Custom Consoles	Basic knowledge
7.3 Creating Taskpad Views	Basic knowledge
7.4 Adding Extensions to Snap-ins	Basic knowledge
7.5 Configuring Logon/Logoff Scripts	Basic knowledge

General Requirements

To complete the projects in this lesson, you must have administrative rights on a Windows XP Professional computer.

project 7.1

Viewing Preconfigured Microsoft Management Consoles

exam objective

Basic knowledge

overview

Your first task is to become familiar with the preexisting consoles available on the system and the functionality that each provides.

learning objective

After you have completed this project, you will know how to access preconfigured consoles, and enable the display of the administrative tools on the Start menu.

specific requirements

Administrative rights on a Windows XP Professional computer.

estimated completion time

25 minutes

project steps

1. Log on to the computer as an **Administrator**.
2. Open the **Control Panel** window and then double-click the **Taskbar and Start Menu**. The **Taskbar and Start Menu Properties** dialog box will open (**Figure 7-1**).
3. Click the **Start Menu** tab and then click the **Customize** button (**Figure 7-2**).
4. The **Customize Start Menu** dialog box will open. Click the **Advanced** tab. Scroll to the bottom of the **Start menu items** list box and under the **System Administrative Tools** node, select **Display on the All Programs menu (Figure 7-3)**.
5. Click **OK** to close the **Customize Start Menu** dialog box, and then click **OK** to close the **Taskbar and Start Menu Properties** dialog box.
6. Close the **Control Panel**.
7. Click on **Start**, **All Programs**, and **Administrative Tools**, and on a piece of paper, record the preexisting tools that are provided with **Windows XP Professional**.
8. Click **Computer Management** to open the **Computer Management** console window. Expand the **System Tools** node and the **Storage** node, if necessary, and then examine each of the tools available in the console (**Figure 7-4**). On a piece of paper, list and describe the functionality of each tool. If you need help, open the **Action** menu and click **Help** to open the **Microsoft Management Console Help** window, where you can obtain further information about the **Computer Management** console (**Figure 7-5**). When you have finished, close the **Computer Management** console window.
9. Click **Performance** in the **Administrative Tools** menu to open the **Performance** console (**Figure 7-6**). On a piece of paper, list and describe the functionality of each tool you find. If you need help, open the **Action** menu and click **Help** to open the **Microsoft Management Console Help** window, where you can obtain further information about **Performance Logs and Alerts**. When you have finished, close the **Performance** console window.
10. Follow the same procedure set forth above for each of the other preconfigured consoles that you find in the **Administrative Tools** menu.

tip

Administrative Tools may also be accessed by double-clicking the Administrative Tools icon under the Control Panel.

Figure 7-1 The Taskbar and Start Menu Properties dialog box

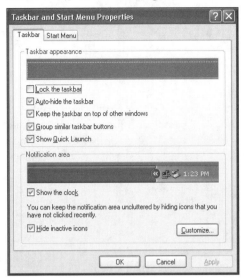

Figure 7-2 Accessing the Customize button for the Start Menu

Figure 7-3 Enabling the display of Administrative Tools on the Start menu

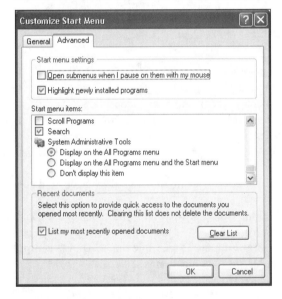

Figure 7-4 Examining tools available in the Computer Management console

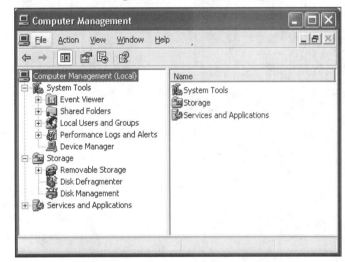

Figure 7-5 Getting help for a Management console

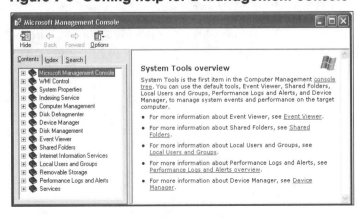

Figure 7-6 Examining the Performance console

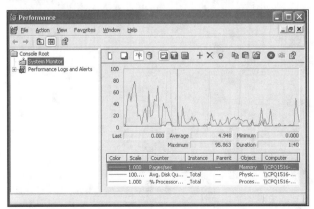

project 7.2 | *Creating Custom Consoles*

exam objective

Basic knowledge

overview

As a part of his duties as a Junior System Administrator, a new employee needs to be able to reset passwords for users and run the Disk Defragmenter utility on a regular basis. He has asked you to create a custom console that enables both of these tasks to be performed from the same interface. You will save this console as an icon to the Desktop of your computer so that it can be easily accessed.

learning objective

After you have completed this project, you will know how to:
◆ Create a custom console.
◆ Add a snap-in to a customized console.
◆ Save a console in Author mode.

specific requirements

◆ Administrative rights on a computer running Windows XP Professional.

estimated completion time

10 minutes

project steps

1. Click **Start**, and then click the **Run** command to open the **Run** dialog box.
2. Type **MMC** in the **Open** list box (**Figure 7-7**).
3. Click **OK**. MMC is initialized and displays the default empty console.
4. Open the **File** menu and click the **Add/Remove Snap-in** command to open the **Add/Remove Snap-in** dialog box with the **Standalone** tab active by default.
5. Click **Add** to open the **Add Standalone Snap-in** dialog box. This dialog box lists all available snap-ins.
6. Click the **Local Users and Groups** snap-in to select it to be added to the custom console (**Figure 7-8**).
7. Click **Add**. The **Choose Target Machine** dialog box prompts you to select the computer you want the snap-in to manage (**Figure 7-9**).
8. Most of the time you will select the local computer. Make sure that the **Local computer: (the computer this console is running on)** option button is selected.
9. Click **Finish** to close the **Choose Target Machine** dialog box.
10. In the **Add Standalone Snap-in** dialog box, select **Disk Defragmenter** and click **Add** then click **Close**.
11. Click **OK** to close the **Add/Remove Snap-in** dialog box.
12. In order to use the console again, you must save it. You may first set the mode it will be saved in: your choice of Author mode or 3 types of User modes. Open the **File** menu and click the **Options** command to open the **Options** dialog box (**Figure 7-10**). Note that the default **Console mode** is set to **Author mode**. Read the descriptions for **Author Mode** and all **User modes**.

tip

Selecting the computer that the console will manage is called setting the focus of the console.

Figure 7-7 Opening an empty MMC

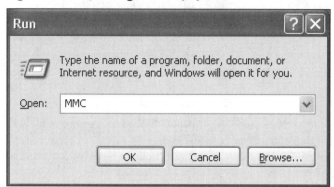

Figure 7-8 Selecting a snap-in

Figure 7-9 Focusing the snap-in on a computer

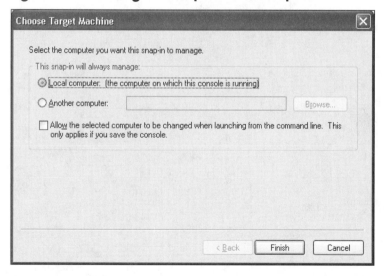

Figure 7-10 Setting the Console mode

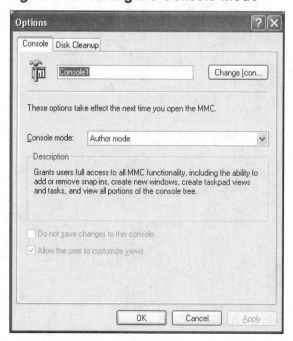

project 7.2

Creating Custom Consoles (cont'd)

exam objective

Basic knowledge

project steps

13. Select **Author Mode** and click **OK** to close the **Options** dialog box. Author mode will allow changes to be made to the Management console later.
14. Now the console may be saved. Open the **File** menu and click the **Save As** command to open the **Save As** dialog box.
15. To save the console on the desktop, select **Desktop** in the **Save in** list box.
16. Type **Password Reset and Defrag** in the **File name** text box **(Figure 7-11)**.
17. Click **Save**. The console name appears in the MMC title bar **(Figure 7-12)**.
18. **Close** the **Password Reset and Defrag** console. The Password Reset and Defrag icon is added to the desktop.

Figure 7-11 Saving a console to the desktop

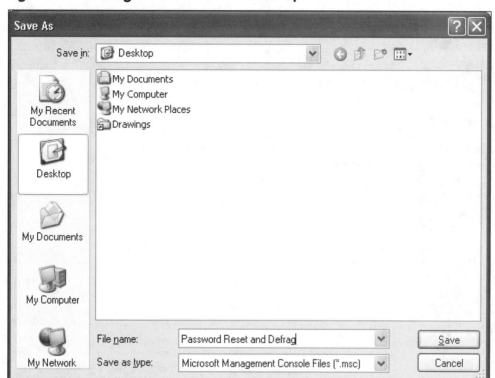

Figure 7-12 New Password Reset and Defrag console

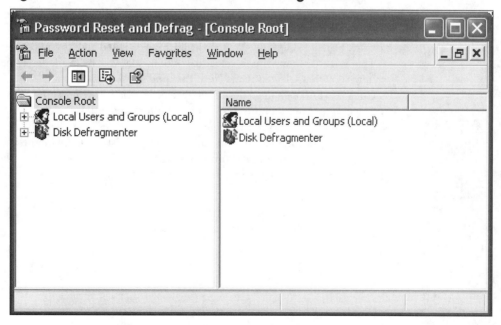

project 7.3

Creating Taskpad Views

exam objective

Basic knowledge

overview

You have decided to make some tasks easier for the new Junior System Administrator. You will modify the Management console that you created earlier by configuring a taskpad view that will make it simpler to reset user passwords, and then save the console so that it cannot be modified.

learning objective

After you have completed this project, you will know how to:
- Create a taskpad view for a Management console.
- Save a console in User mode.

specific requirements

- Administrative rights on a computer running Windows XP Professional.

estimated completion time

25 minutes

project steps

1. Double-click the **Password Reset and Defrag** icon on your desktop to open the custom console you created in Project 7.2.
2. Expand the **Local Users and Groups (Local)** node and select the **Users** container under it.
3. Open the **Action** menu and click the **New Taskpad View** command.
4. The **New Taskpad View Wizard** will appear. Click **Next** to open the **Taskpad Display** dialog box **(Figure 7-13)**. This dialog box allows you to control the display format for the Taskpad.
5. Click **Next** to accept the default settings and to open the **Taskpad Target** dialog box which controls the items that the taskpad will affect.
6. Ensure that **All tree items that are the same type as the selected tree item** is selected and click **Next**.
7. On the **Name and Description** dialog box, enter **Simple Password Reset** in the **Name** text box **(Figure 7-14)**, and click **Next**.
8. Click **Finish** to close the **New Taskpad View Wizard** and to start the **New Task Wizard**. This Wizard allows you to select the actions that will be available in the taskpad for the items that you selected in the **New Taskpad View Wizard**.
9. Click **Next** to open the **Command Type** selection box **(Figure 7-15)**.
10. Select the **Menu command** option button and click **Next**. The **Shortcut Menu command** dialog box will appear.
11. Make sure that the **Command source** is set to **List in details pane** and then select **Set Password** in the **Available commands:** list box **(Figure 7-16)**. Click **Next**.
12. Click **Next** to accept the default name and description for this task.

Figure 7-13 Selecting Taskpad display layout

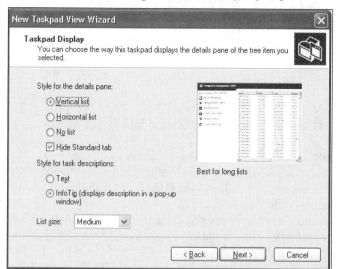

Figure 7-14 Naming a taskpad

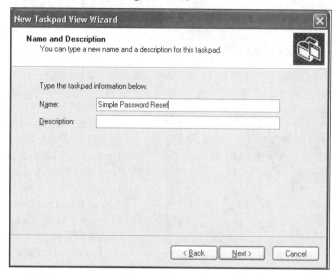

Figure 7-15 Choosing a command type for a taskpad

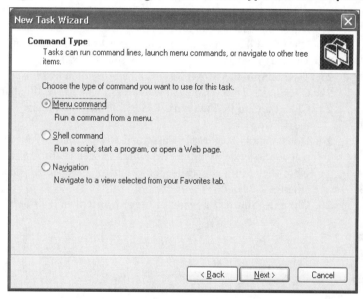

Figure 7-16 Selecting the command for the taskpad

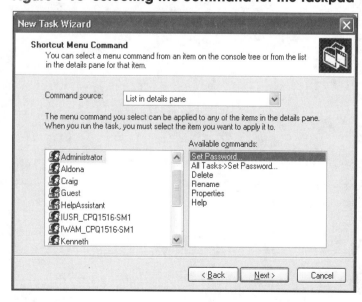

project 7.3

Creating Taskpad Views *(cont'd)*

exam objective

Basic knowledge

project steps

13. Select an icon from the **Icons provided by MMC** list on the **Task Icon** dialog box, and then click **Next (Figure 7-17)**.
14. On the **Completing the Task** screen, click **Finish** to save the task.
15. Now that you have created the taskpad view, you want to simplify the appearance of the console and save it so that it cannot be modified. Open the **View** menu and click the **Large Icons** command **(Figure 7-18)**.
16. Open the **View** menu again and click the **Customize** command. The **Customize View** dialog will open. Clear the check marks for the top three options and click **OK** to accept the changes **(Figure 7-19)**.
17. Open the **File** menu option and then click the **Options** command. The **Options** dialog will open.
18. Change the description in the first text box to **Simple Password Reset**. Set the **Console mode** to User mode — limited access, single window and clear the check mark beside **Allow the user to customize views**. Click **OK** to save these options.
19. Open the **File** menu and click the **Save As** command to open the **Save As** dialog box.
20. To save the console on the desktop, select **Desktop** in the **Save in** list box.
21. Type **Simple Password Reset** in the **File name** text box.
22. Click **Save**. The console name appears in the MMC title bar.
23. Close the **Simple Password Reset** console. The Simple Password Reset icon is added to the desktop.
24. Double-click the **Simple Password Reset** icon on your desktop. Note that the console can no longer be modified. Select a user icon to display the tasks available for that item. Note that this taskpad is dedicated to the specific task of setting user passwords **(Figure 7-20)**.
25. Close the **Simple Password Reset** Management console.

Figure 7-17 Assigning an icon to the task

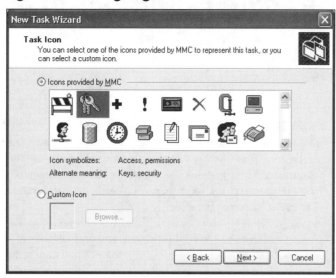

Figure 7-18 Taskpad view before simplification

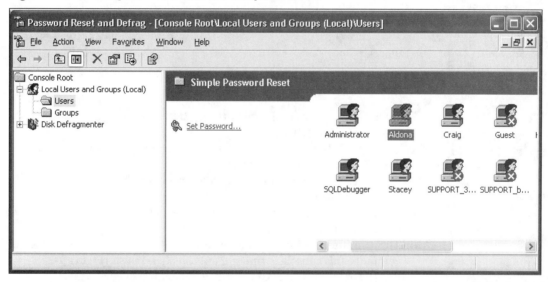

Figure 7-19 Customizing console view options

Figure 7-20 The completed Simple Password Reset Management console

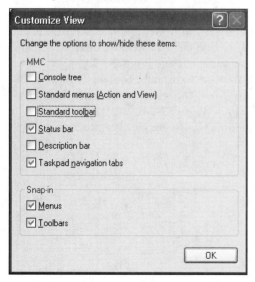

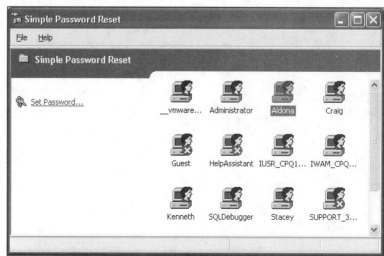

project 7.4 *Adding Extensions to Snap-ins*

exam objective

Basic knowledge

overview

You want to create a console that is similar to the Computer Management console but does not include certain features. You have learned that certain snap-ins have sub components called extensions that can be added or removed from a custom console. You plan to add the **Computer Management** snap-in to the **Reset Passwords and Defrag** custom console, and remove the extensions for managing users and defragmenting hard drives from under the Computer Management node.

learning objective

After you have completed this project, you will know how to:
◆ Add and remove extensions for a snap-in in a management console.

specific requirements

◆ Administrative rights on a computer running Windows XP Professional.

estimated completion time

10 minutes

project steps

1. Double-click the **Reset Passwords and Defrag** icon on the desktop to open the **Reset Passwords and Defrag** console.
2. Open the **File** menu and click the **Add/Remove Snap-in** command to open the **Add/Remove Snap-in** dialog box.
3. Click the **Add** button on the **Standalone** tab to open the **Add Standalone Snap-in** dialog box.
4. Select **Computer Management** from the list of available snap-ins and click **Add** (**Figure 7-21**).
5. The **Computer Management** window will open. Select **Local Computer: (the computer this console is running on)** and click **Finish** (**Figure 7-22**).
6. Click **Close** to close the **Add Standalone Snap-in** dialog box.
7. On the **Add/Remove Snap-in** window, click the **Extensions** tab to display the extension snap-ins available in the Reset Passwords and Defrag console.
8. In the **Snap-ins that can be extended** list box, select **Computer Management**.
9. Clear the **Add all extensions** check box.
10. Clear the **Disk Defragmenter** and **Local Users and Groups** check boxes in the **Available extensions** list box, and click **OK** to close the **Add/Remove Snap-in** window, and add the **Computer Management** snap-in to the console (**Figure 7-23**).
11. Expand the **Computer Management (Local)** node. Expand the **System Tools** node and the **Storage** node. The Disk Defragmenter and Local Users and Groups extensions do not appear under the Computer Management snap-in (**Figure 7-24**).
12. Close the **Reset Password and Defrag** window, and save the changes you have made.

Figure 7-21 Adding the Computer Management snap-in

Figure 7-22 Focusing the Computer Management snap-in

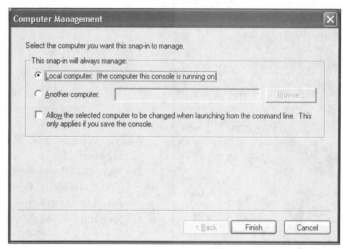

Figure 7-23 Selecting extensions for a snap-in

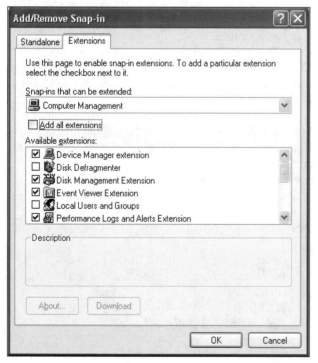

Figure 7-24 The completed console

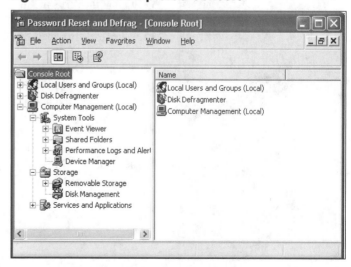

project 7.5 — *Configuring Logon/Logoff Scripts*

exam objective

Basic knowledge

overview

You need to ensure that certain tasks execute each time a user logs on or logs off of their computer. Because the same scripts will apply to all users, you have decided to use the Logon/Logoff scripts feature of the Local computer policy. Scripts can be very powerful.

learning objective

In this project you will learn:
◆ To create a Management console for configuring local computer policy settings.
◆ To configure Logon and Logoff scripts

specific requirements

◆ Administrative rights on a computer running Windows XP Professional.

estimated completion time

15 minutes

project steps

1. First you need to create the scripts that will run at logon and logoff, and then you will setup the system to run them. Open **Notepad** by clicking **Start**, then **All Programs**, and then **Accessories**.
2. Type **echo Logon: %username% %date% %time% >> c:\log.txt** on a single line (**Figure 7-25**).
3. Open the **File** menu and click the **Save** command. The **Save As** dialog box will open. Type **C:\WINDOWS\System32\GroupPolicy\User\Scripts\LogON\logonscript1.bat** and click **Save** (**Figure 7-26**).
4. Open the **File** menu and click the **New** command.
5. Type **echo Logoff: %username% %date% %time% >> c:\log.txt** on a single line.
6. Open the **File** menu and click the **Save** command. The **Save As** dialog box will open. Type **C:\WINDOWS\System32\GroupPolicy\User\Scripts\LogOFF\logoffscript1.bat** and click **Save**.
7. Close **Notepad**.
8. Next, you will configure a MMC that will allow you to set the Logon and Logoff scripts. Click **Start**, and then click the **Run** command to open the **Run** dialog box.
9. Type **MMC** in the **Open** list box.
10. Click **OK**. MMC is initialized and displays the default empty console.
11. Open the **File** menu and click the **Add/Remove Snap-in** command to open the **Add/Remove Snap-in** dialog box with the **Standalone** tab active by default.
12. Click **Add** to open the **Add Standalone Snap-in** dialog box. This dialog box lists all available snap-ins.
13. Click the **Group Policy** snap-in to select it to be added to the Custom console.
14. Click **Add**. The **Select Group Policy Object** dialog box prompts you to select the group policy object you want the snap-in to manage.
15. Select the **Local Computer** and click **Finish**.
16. Click **Close** to close the **Add Standalone Snap-in** dialog box.
17. Click **OK** to close the **Add/Remove Snap-in** window.
18. Expand the **Local Computer Policy** node, the **User Configuration** node and the **Windows Settings** node. Select **Scripts (Logon/Logoff)** (**Figure 7-27**).

Figure 7-25 Creating a Logon script

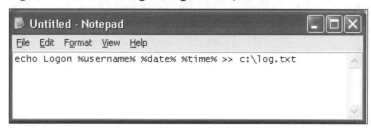

Figure 7-26 Saving a Logon script

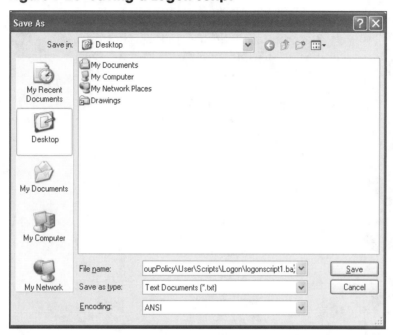

Figure 7-27 Managing scripts through Local Computer Policy

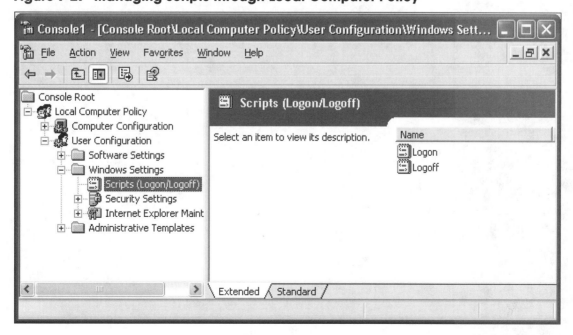

project 7.5

Configuring Logon/Logoff Scripts
(cont'd)

exam objective

Basic knowledge

project steps

caution

The scripts that are created in this lab should be disabled after the lab on any computer used for production work. Otherwise, the log.txt file will continue to grow with each logon and logoff.

19. On the right hand pane, double-click **Logon** to open the **Logon Properties** dialog box (**Figure 7-28**).
20. Click the **Add** button to open the **Add a Script** dialog box.
21. Click **Browse** to select the logon script from a directory list. Highlight **logonscript1.bat** and click **Open (Figure 7-29)**.
22. Click **OK** to close the **Add a Script** dialog box.
23. Click **OK** to close the **Logon Properties** dialog box and save the changes.
24. Repeat steps 18 through 22 for the **Logoff** script. Make sure that you select **logoffscript1.bat** for the script.
25. Close the console and save it as **Local Computer Policy**.
26. Log off of the computer and then log on again.
27. Using **Notepad** open **C:\LOG.TXT**. The file should have recorded your logons and logoffs (**Figure 7-30**).
28. Close **Notepad**.

Figure 7-28 The Logon Properties dialog box

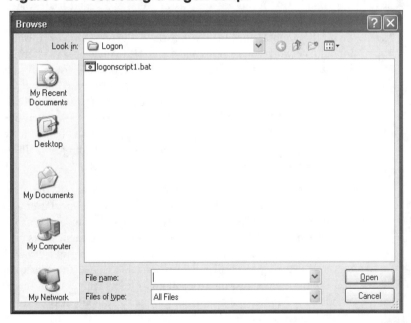

Figure 7-29 Selecting a Logon script

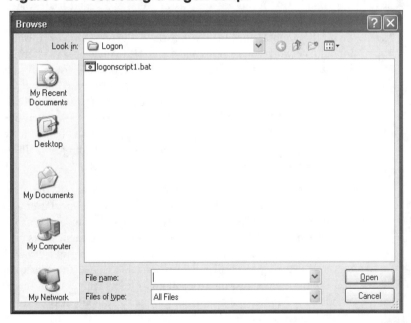

Figure 7-30 Confirming proper function of the Logon/Logoff scripts

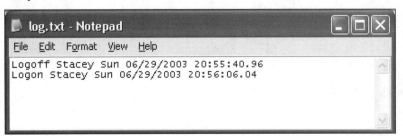

Administering User Accounts and Groups

In Windows XP Professional, user accounts are used to store relevant details about network users and to distinguish one user from another. There are three types of user accounts: local user accounts, domain user accounts, and built-in user accounts. With a local user account, the account can only be assigned permissions to resources on the computer on which the account was created. Conversely, with a domain user account, you can assign permissions for the user to access resources on any computer on the domain or trusting domains. Built-in user accounts are created when you install Windows XP Professional. The Administrator and Guest accounts are the two built-in user accounts.

In a peer-to-peer or workgroup network, where there is no dedicated server and no central logon authority, resources such as printers, disks, and folders are accessed using local user accounts and group names. Microsoft recommends that workgroup networks contain no more than 10 computers because Windows XP Professional will only allow a maximum of 10 inbound network connections and the effort to manage a workgroup increases significantly as its size increases. Windows XP Professional is all you will need to create a workgroup network. However, if you want to create a domain-based network, you will have to create at least one central server (domain controller) that stores Active Directory. Active Directory is the database that stores all of the information about users and groups, and manages logging on to the network. In order to create a domain controller you must have Windows 2000 Server or Windows Server 2003 installed. You primarily use only domain user accounts in a domain-based network.

Setting up user accounts in either type of network is the first line of defense against unauthorized access to network resources. You create local user accounts and groups to allow multiple users to access resources on a particular standalone or workgroup computer. Then, you assign permissions to the groups and to individual users so that they can access only certain resources and folders on the machine. A group is, therefore, a collection of user accounts that require similar permissions and rights. In order to create local user accounts, you use the Computer Management console, which is one of the Administrative Tools in the Windows XP Professional operating system. You can also modify existing user accounts by changing their properties.

Scenario

You are the Network Administrator for a small business, Blossoms Inc., which uses a workgroup network. Some new sales representatives have been hired and you must create local user accounts for the new employees, and assign them to local groups.

Lesson 8   Administering User Accounts and Groups

Project	Exam 70-270 Objective
8.1 Creating a Local User Account	Configure, manage, and troubleshoot local user and group accounts.
8.2 The User Accounts utility	Configure, manage, and troubleshoot local user and group accounts.
8.3 Managing User Accounts	Configure, manage, and troubleshoot local user and group accounts.
8.4 Creating and Using a Password Reset Disk	Configure, manage, and troubleshoot local user and group accounts.
8.5 Creating Local Groups	Configure, manage, and troubleshoot local user and group accounts.
8.6 Adding Members to a Group	Configure, manage, and troubleshoot local user and group accounts.

General Requirements

To complete the projects in this lesson, you will need administrative rights on a Windows XP Professional computer.

project 8.1

Creating a Local User Account

exam objective

Configure, manage, and troubleshoot local user and group accounts.

overview

You must create local user accounts for the new employees in your company so that they can logon to their respective machines and start working. You have already decided to use a standard naming convention for your user names consisting of the user's first name, followed by enough letters from the user's last name to create a unique user name. As part of your corporate security policy, all new user accounts must also be assigned a unique password that the user must change during their first logon.

Local user accounts are stored in the local security accounts manager (SAM) database of the computer. When you create a local user account you create a new Security Identifier (SID), which is a unique number stored in the local security database. The SID is used to identify the user account in the operating system.

When you are setting up a workgroup network, you will want to create local user accounts for the primary user of each computer, as well as for anyone else who shares the computer or connects to its resources. One way to create local user accounts on a workgroup workstation is by using the **Local Users and Groups** snap-in in the **Computer Management** console. Another method is to use the **User Accounts** applet in the **Control Panel**.

learning objective

After completing this project, you will know how to create user accounts and set their properties.

specific requirements

Administrative rights on a Windows XP Professional computer.

estimated completion time

15 minutes

project steps

Create local user accounts using the **Local Users and Groups** snap-in.
1. Log on as the default local user or as an **Administrator**.
2. Click **Start** and click the **Control Panel** command to open the **Control Panel** window.
3. If necessary, click **Switch to Classic View** to display all of the Control Panel icons (**Figure 8-1**).
4. Double-click the **Administrative Tools** icon to open the **Administrative Tools** window (**Figure 8-2**).
5. Double-click the **Computer Management** icon to open the **Computer Management** console.
6. Double-click the **Local Users and Groups** node to open it. There are two folders in the node: **Users** and **Groups**.
7. Right-click **Users** and click the **New User** command on the shortcut menu (**Figure 8-3**) to open the **New User** dialog box.
8. Type **ChristineL** in the **User name** text box.
9. Type **Christine Landon** in the **Full name** text box.
10. Type **Temp Worker** in the **Description** text box. (The description is not required and may be omitted.)
11. Type **123!abc** in the **Password** text box. Notice that the password appears as a series of large dots.
12. Re-type the password in the **Confirm password** text box.

tip

Always have new users change their passwords the first time they log on in order to ensure that their password is known only to them.

Figure 8-1 Control Panel window

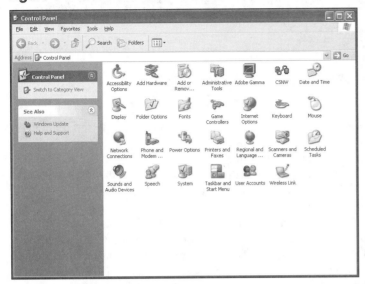

Figure 8-2 Administrative Tools window

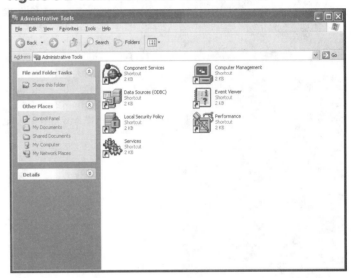

Figure 8-3 Computer Management snap-in

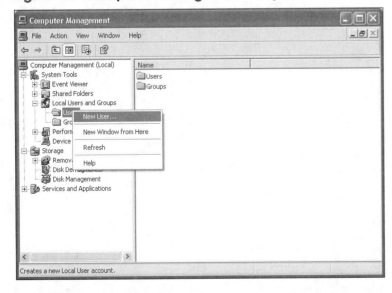

project 8.1

Creating a Local User Account (cont'd)

exam objective

Configure, manage, and troubleshoot local user and group accounts.

project steps

13. The **User must change password at next logon** check box is selected by default. **Figure 8-4** illustrates steps 8 to 13.

14. Click **Create**. A local user account is now created.

15. The New User dialog box remains open so that you can create another user account, if necessary. Using **Table 8-1** create the remaining four user accounts using steps 8 to 14.

16. Close the New User dialog box.

17. Close the Computer Management snap-in and the Administrative Tools window.

18. To test the local user account, click **Start** and click **Log Off**. Next, click **Switch User**. (*Note:* The Fast User Switching feature is not available on computers that are members of a domain. If your computer is a member of a domain, you will have to log off the current user account and log on to the ChristineL account using the **Log On to Windows** dialog box.)

19. When the list of user accounts appears, click **Christine Landon**. Type **123!abc** in the password text box that opens and press **[Enter] (Figure 8-5)**.

20. The Logon Message, **You are required to change your password at first logon** appears. Click **OK**. The **Change Password** window opens.

21. Type a new password, such as **c@b#777**, in both the **New Password** and **Confirm New Password** text boxes.

22. Click **OK**. The Change Password window displays the message, **"Your password has been changed"**.

23. Click **OK**. You are now successfully logged on as Christine Landon.

tip

Teach your users to always choose secure passwords.

Table 8-1 New users

User name	Full name	Description	Password
ChristineL	Christine Landon	Temp Worker	123!abc
TomR	Tom Randolph	Accounting Dept.	234!abc
RonJ	Ron James	Plant Manager	345!abc
DavidN	David Naws	Order Entry	456!abc
JanetJ	Janet Jones	Graphic Design	789!abc

Figure 8-4 New User dialog box

Figure 8-5 Windows XP logon screen

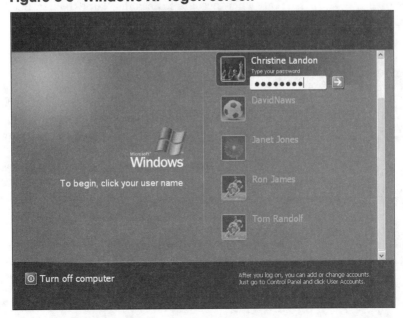

project 8.2 *The User Accounts Utility*

exam objective

Configure, manage, and troubleshoot local user and group accounts.

overview

The other tool you can use to create and manage user accounts is the **User Accounts** utility in the Control Panel. You will only be able to open this utility if you log on with the Administrator account or another user account that is a member of the Administrators group. If you are not currently logged on as an Administrator when you attempt to open the applet, the **User Accounts** utility will offer limited options only; those geared toward modifying the account that is currently logged on. On the Administrator account, the User Accounts tool lists all local user accounts, the groups to which they belong, and if the accounts are password protected. You can add new accounts to the computer, change existing accounts, or change the way users log on or off. If you choose to modify an existing account, your options include changing the name of the account, changing the password, removing the password, changing the picture associated with the account, changing the account type, and deleting the account. However, if you want to change the group to which an account belongs, you will need to use the Local Users and Groups snap-in. Furthermore, you can only create groups in the Local Users and Groups snap-in. You can also use the Local Users and Groups snap-in to make a user a member of several groups.

learning objective

After completing this project, you will know how to use the User Accounts utility to create user accounts.

specific requirements

Administrative rights on a Windows XP Professional computer.

estimated completion time

15 minutes

project steps

Create a local user account using the User Accounts utility.
1. Log on as an **Administrator**.
2. Click **Start** and click the **Control Panel** command to open the **Control Panel** window.
3. Double-click the **User Accounts** icon to open the User Accounts dialog box (**Figure 8-6**).
4. Click **Create a new account** to open the **Name the new account** screen.
5. Type **John Simmons** in the text box provided.
6. Click **Next** to open the **Pick an account type screen**.
7. Select the **Limited** option button (**Figure 8-7**). (*Note:* If this is the first time you have created an account with this Wizard, you will be required to make the first user a Computer Administrator; the Limited account type will be unavailable.)
8. Click **Create Account**. The John Simmons account now appears on the main screen of the User Accounts window with the other existing user accounts.
9. Click the John Simmons account in the **or pick an account to change** section of the window.
10. On the **What do you want to change about John Simmons's account**? screen, click **Create a password**.
11. The **Create a password for John Simmons's account** screen explains the ramifications of creating a password for the account. Since the account was just created, the likelihood of losing important data is minimal.
12. Type **P@ssw0rd** in the **Type a new password** text box and confirm the password in the next text box. Leave the password hint text box blank.
13. Click **Create Password**. The John Simmons account is now password protected.
14. Close the User Accounts window and the Control Panel.

tip

The steps in this exercise describe the process of creating a local user account on a computer that is a member of a workgroup. The process and the screens that you will see will be different if your computer is a domain member.

Figure 8-6 User Accounts window

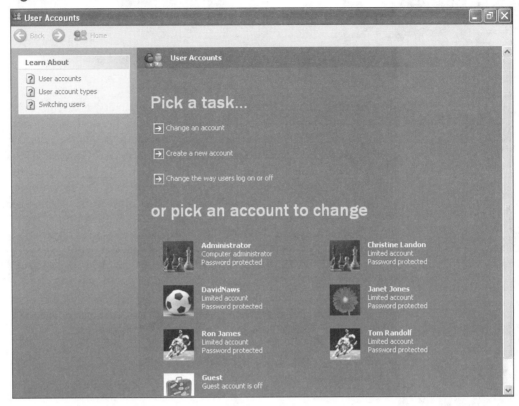

Figure 8-7 Pick an account type screen

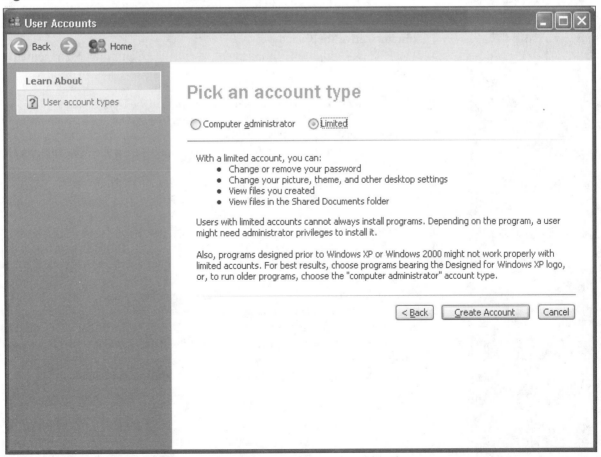

project 8.3   *Managing User Accounts*

exam objective

Configure, manage, and troubleshoot local user and group accounts.

overview

Christine Landon has been recruited as a temporary replacement and will only be working for your company for a short while. You have been advised that she will only need her password for a limited time, so you are going to assign the User cannot change password property to her account. **Tom Randolph** needs to take a leave of absence, so you are going to disable his account. **Ron James** has resigned, so you will delete his user account. **David Naws** has forgotten his password, so you will set a new password for this account. Finally, **Janet Jones** was just married and has changed her name to **Janet Smith**. You will need to rename her user account.

learning objective

After completing this project, you will know how to modify user account properties.

specific requirements

◆ Administrative rights on a Windows XP Professional computer.
◆ Completion of Project 8.1.

estimated completion time

15 minutes

project steps

1. Log on to the computer as an **Administrator**.
2. Open the **Control Panel** window. If necessary, click **Switch to Classic View** to display all of the Control Panel icons. Double-click **Administrative Tools** to open the **Administrative Tools** window.
3. Double-click **Computer Management** to open the **Computer Management** console window.
4. Double-click **Local Users and Groups** to expand it.
5. Click the **Users** folder to display a list of the users in the Details pane.
6. Right-click **ChristineL** and then click **Properties** on the shortcut menu to open the **Properties** dialog box for this user.
7. On the General tab, verify that the **User must change password at next logon** check box is not checked.
8. Select the **User cannot change password** check box (**Figure 8-8**). The **User must change password at next logon** check box is now grayed out indicating that it is unavailable.
9. Click **OK** to close the dialog box.
10. Right-click **TomR** and then click **Properties** to open the **TomR Properties** dialog box.
11. On the **General** tab, select the **Account is disabled** check box (**Figure 8-9**), and then click **OK** to close the dialog box.
12. Right-click **RonJ** and then click **Delete** on the shortcut menu.
13. A **Local Users and Group** message box appears (**Figure 8-10**), asking you to confirm that you wish to delete the user account. Click **Yes**. Notice that when the Computer Management console window reappears, that the **RonJ** account is no longer listed in the Details pane.
14. Right-click **DavidN** and then click **Set Password** on the shortcut menu.

caution

Changing a password using this method will make any encrypted email, saved internet passwords, and files encrypted by this user, inaccessible from their user account.

Figure 8-8 User cannot change password check box

Figure 8-9 Account is disabled check box

Figure 8-10 Confirming deletion of a user account

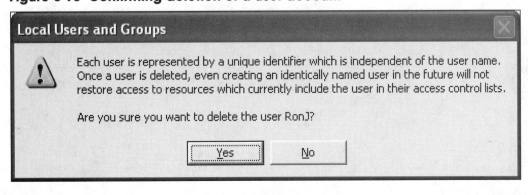

project 8.3

Managing User Accounts (cont'd)

exam objective

Configure, manage, and troubleshoot local user and group accounts.

project steps

tip

Show users how to create a password reset disk for themselves so that forgotten passwords don't result in data loss, and have them store it in a secure place.

15. The **Set Password for DavidN** warning dialog box appears (**Figure 8-11**). Users should normally manage their passwords and change them either when prompted or by using the **Change my password** command in the **User Accounts** utility. David did not create a password reset disk and has told you that he has not used any encryption for email or files so you decide to proceed. Click the **Proceed** button.

16. The **Set Password** dialog box appears. Type a new password in the **New password** and **Confirm password** text boxes (**Figure 8-12**), and then click **OK**. A message box appears informing you that the password has been set. Click **OK**.

17. Right-click **JanetJ** and then click **Rename** on the shortcut menu. Type a new user name (**JanetS**) for the user and then press [**Enter**].

18. Right-click **JanetS** and then click the **Properties** command. Replace the contents of the **Full Name** text box with **Janet Smith** and click **OK**.

19. Close the **Computer Management** console window and the **Administrative Tools** window.

Figure 8-11 The Set Password warning dialog box

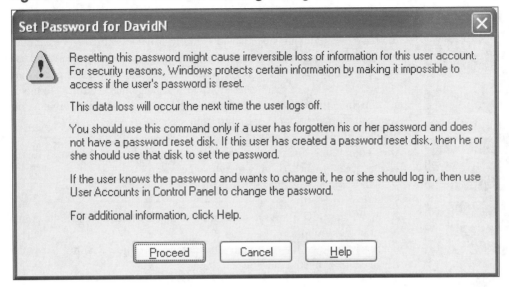

Set Password for DavidN

Resetting this password might cause irreversible loss of information for this user account. For security reasons, Windows protects certain information by making it impossible to access if the user's password is reset.

This data loss will occur the next time the user logs off.

You should use this command only if a user has forgotten his or her password and does not have a password reset disk. If this user has created a password reset disk, then he or she should use that disk to set the password.

If the user knows the password and wants to change it, he or she should log in, then use User Accounts in Control Panel to change the password.

For additional information, click Help.

[Proceed]   [Cancel]   [Help]

Figure 8-12 The Set Password dialog box

Set Password for DavidN

New password: ●●●●●●●●

Confirm password: ●●●●●●●●

If you click OK, the following will occur:

- This user account will immediately lose access to all of its encrypted files, stored passwords, and personal security certificates.

- Any password reset disks the user has created will no longer work.

If you click Cancel, the password will not be changed and no data loss will occur.

[OK]   [Cancel]

project 8.4

Creating and Using a Password Reset Disk

exam objective

Configure, manage, and troubleshoot local user and group accounts.

overview

You have been thinking since David Naws lost his password, you have now decided that you should document the procedure that all users should follow to create and use a password reset disk. You are concerned that if the disks fell into the possession of an unauthorized person, they would be able to gain access to the user's accounts. To mitigate this risk, after creating and labeling the Password Reset disk, all users are to deliver it to one of the System Administrators for storage in a fireproof safe.

learning objective

After completing this project, you know how to create a Password Reset disk and how to recover access to an account with a lost password.

specific requirements

◆ A Windows XP Professional computer that is either a standalone computer or a member of a workgroup.
◆ A user account for John Simmons (created in project 8.2).
◆ A blank formatted diskette.

estimated completion time

20 minutes

project steps

Log on as a normal user and record the steps required to create a Password Reset disk.

1. Log on as **John Simmons** using **P@ssw0rd** for the password.
2. Click **Start** and click the **Control Panel** command to open the **Control Panel** window.
3. Click the **User Accounts** icon to open the User Accounts window dialog box. If Control Panel is set to Classic View, double-click the **User Accounts** icon.
4. The **Pick a Task** user accounts screen will open for John Simmons (**Figure 8-13**). Click **Prevent a forgotten password** in the **Related Tasks** section.
5. The **Forgotten Password Wizard** will start. Click **Next**.
6. The **Create a Password Reset Disk** screen will open (**Figure 8-14**). Insert a blank formatted floppy disk into the indicated drive and click **Next**.
7. On the **Current User Account Password** screen in the **Current user account password** text box, type **P@ssw0rd** and then click **Next** (**Figure 8-15**).
8. The computer will begin writing to the diskette. When the progress indicator displays 100% complete, click **Next**.
9. Click **Finish** to close the **Completing the Forgotten Password Wizard** screen.
10. Remove the diskette from the floppy drive and label it with the user's name. Because anyone can use the diskette to gain access to the current user's account, it should be stored in a secure location.
11. Close the **User Accounts** window and the **Control Panel**.

Figure 8-13 Pick a Task for the current user account

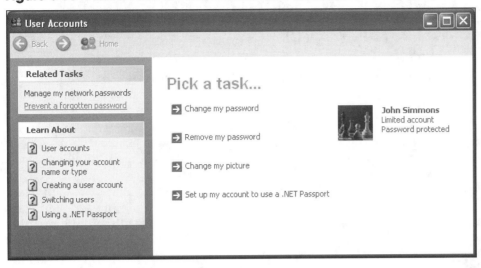

Figure 8-14 The Create a Password Reset Disk screen

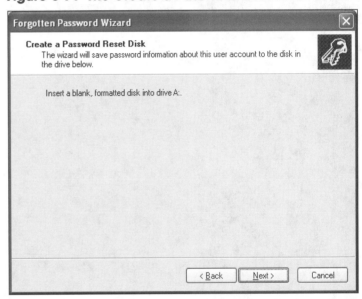

Figure 8-15 Entering the current user account password

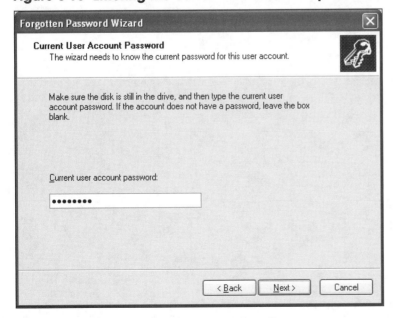

project 8.4

Creating and Using a Password Reset Disk (cont'd)

exam objective

Configure, manage, and troubleshoot local user and group accounts.

project steps

You want to test the Password Reset disk and record the procedure for its use.

12. Log off from the computer.

13. Click **John Simmons** on the Windows Welcome screen and then press **[Enter]**. The log on screen with a help bubble will appear (**Figure 8-16**).

14. Click the **use your password reset disk** link in the help bubble. The **Password Reset Wizard** will start. Click **Next**.

15. Insert the Password Reset disk and click **Next** on the **Insert the Password Reset Disk** screen.

16. On the **Reset the User Account Password** screen, type a new password in the **Type a new password** text box and type it again in the next text box (**Figure 8-17**). Click **Next** to save the new password.

17. Click **Finish** to close the **Completing the Password Reset Wizard** screen.

18. Log on as **John Simmons** using the new password to confirm the password change.

Figure 8-16 Starting the Password Reset Wizard

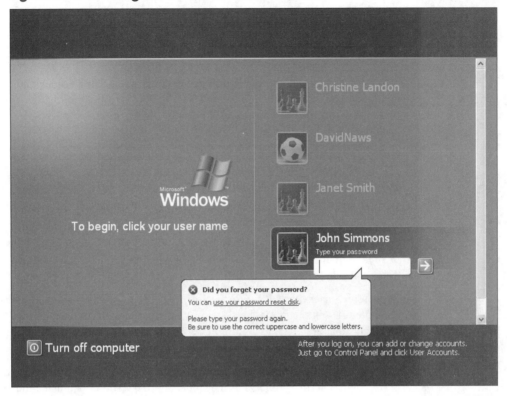

Figure 8-17 Entering a new password

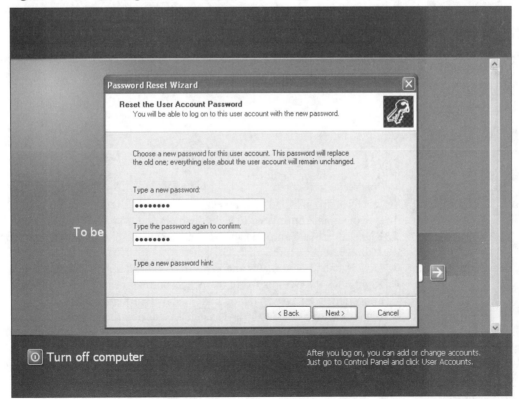

project 8.5

Creating Local Groups

exam objective

Configure, manage, and troubleshoot local user and group accounts.

overview

You need to give all of your employees access to a shared folder and a printer on your computer. You have decided to create a local group for all of your users so that you can grant them access to the shared resources without having to assign permissions individually for each user.

Groups are used to make it easy to assign permissions and rights to users with similar needs. It is much easier to assign permissions and rights to a group of users rather than having to assign permissions and rights on an individual basis.

Permissions are used to assign the capabilities a user has when he or she gains access to a resource. For example, students in a class would likely be assigned permission to read the files in a professor's folder, but would not be able to modify them. First, to assign permissions to such a group, you create a Students group and give that group the Read-only permission. Then, you add the user accounts for these students to the Students group.

Rights give users the ability to perform system tasks such as changing the time on the computer or shutting down the system. A member of a group receives all of the permissions and rights that are given to a group. Users can belong to multiple groups, and one group can belong to another group in a domain.

Local groups reside in the local security database on a single computer and are used to assign permissions and rights to local user accounts for the resources on that computer. Local groups are used in peer-to-peer or workgroup networks. For the most part, they should not be used on domain-based networks. Windows XP Professional can only create and manage local groups. A local group cannot be a member of any other group.

learning objective

After completing this project, you will know how to create local groups on Windows XP Professional.

specific requirements

Administrative rights on a Windows XP Professional computer.

estimated completion time

5 minutes

project steps

Create a local group called **Employees**.
1. Log on as an **Administrator**.
2. Right-click **My Computer** on the Start menu and click **Manage** to open the **Computer Management** window.
3. Double-click **Local Users and Groups** to expand it.
4. Right-click the **Groups** folder to open a shortcut menu. Click the **New Group** command to open the **New Group** dialog box, as shown in **Figure 8-18**.
5. Enter the group name **Employees** in the **Group name** text box.
6. Enter the group description **Employees of Blossoms Creations** in the **Description** text box (**Figure 8-19**).
7. Click **Create**. Close the New Group dialog box and the Computer Management window.

Figure 8-18 New Group dialog box

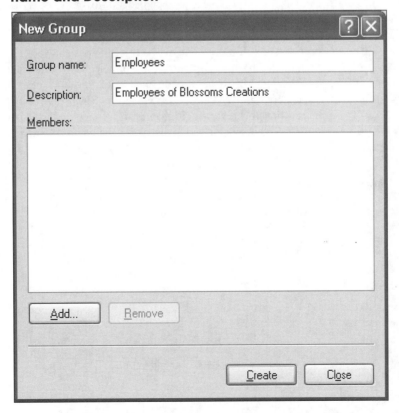

Figure 8-19 New Group dialog box showing the Group name and Description

Adding Members to a Group

exam objective

Configure, manage, and troubleshoot local user and group accounts.

overview

You have to add all of the user accounts to the employees group so that they can access the resources for which the group has permission. Also, as new employees join your organization, you will have to add their user accounts to various groups that are relevant to the projects they will be working on. This will help you to effectively manage the rights and permissions of employees working on different projects or in different departments. To add members to a group, you use the Select Users and Groups dialog box, which is accessed in the Computer Management console.

learning objective

After completing this project, you will know how to add users to local groups.

specific requirements

◆   Administrative rights on a Windows XP Professional computer.
◆   An **Employees** local group (created in project 8.5).

estimated completion time

10 minutes

project steps

Add all users to the **Employees** group.
1. Open the **Computer Management** window and expand the **Local Users and Groups** node.
2. In the left pane of the Computer Management window, click **Groups** to display a list of all of the available groups in the details pane.
3. Double-click **Employees** to open the **Employees Properties** dialog box (**Figure 8-20**).
4. Click **Add. The Select Users or Groups** dialog box opens.
5. Make sure that **Users or Built-in security principals** appears in the **Select this object type** text box. If it does not, click **Object Types** and select **Users**.
6. Make sure that the computer on which you are working appears in the **From this location** text box. If it does not, click **Locations** and select the computer.
7. Type **ChristineL;DavidN;JanetS;John Simmons;TomR** in the **Enter the object names to select** text box (**Figure 8-21**). Notice that multiple names can be separated by semi-colons. You can verify that you have entered the names correctly by clicking the **Check Names** button.
8. Click **OK**. The Employees Properties dialog box displays the selected user's name in the **Members** section, as shown in **Figure 8-22**.
9. Click **OK** to close the Employees Properties dialog box. Close the **Computer Management** window.

tip

You can browse for user names by clicking the **Advanced** button.

Figure 8-20 Employees Properties dialog box

Figure 8-21 Adding users to a group

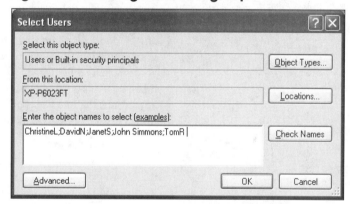

Figure 8-22 Viewing members of a group

Working with Shared Folders

S ince the main function of any network of computers is to share resources, providing accessibility to files and folders, as well as making sure that the correct levels of access are enforced, is crucial to a functional and secure system. If you do not grant sufficient access, users may be unable to perform their duties. On the other hand, if the access you grant is too liberal, you risk the inadvertent, or even intentional, loss or destruction of vital enterprise data.

Shares are like doorways through which users on a network may gain access to a computer's resources. When a network user attempts to connect to a share, their credentials are examined at the 'door', or share, that they are using to access that computer's resource. They can be granted or denied access to the resource based on a security check that utilizes the user's access token, which is generated when they log on to a computer on the network. The access token contains a list of Security Identifiers (**SIDs**) that represent the user's logon account and any groups that the user belongs to. For example, if John Simmons belongs to three groups, his access token might contain SIDs that match the following four entries:

<u>**Access Token**</u>
John Simmons
Group1
Group2
Group3

If the **Share Permissions** for the shared resource that is being accessed contain any entries that match any entries in the user's access token, the permissions for each entry will be added together to obtain the user's effective permission for that resource. Let's assume that the following Share Permissions have been set:

<u>**Share Permissions**</u>

John Simmons	Read
Group2	Change
Group3	Read
Group100	Full Control

This list would be compared with the access token to determine the access permission for the user. Using the examples given above, the effective permission for the user would be the Change permission because the Share Permissions for the resource have matching entries for John Simmons, Group2 and Group3. These permissions add up to Change. Because the user does not belong to Group100, he does not obtain the Full Control permission.

If the **Deny** permission is set for any user or group that exists in the user's access token, the effective permission for that access level will be **Deny**. The **Deny** permission should only be used when absolutely necessary to keep permission management as simple as possible. It is normally used to block access for a specific user or group to a resource where they would otherwise obtain access to the resource through some other group membership.

If you are using NTFS volumes, you can also use NTFS permissions to control access to both files and folders on the local computer. You can use Share Permissions in conjunction with NTFS permissions to control network access if a folder resides on an NTFS partition. When shared folder permissions and NTFS permissions are both used, they are compared and the most restrictive permission of the two will become the effective permission.

Using Share Permissions, you can permit particular users to access only certain folders and, to some degree, you can control the level of access or the tasks they will be able to perform after they have opened the folder. In this lesson, we will concentrate on how to create Share Permissions.

Network sharing is controlled by the File and Printer Sharing for Microsoft Networks service (also known more simply as the Server service), which is automatically configured on all Windows XP Professional computers, and starts as soon as the operating system is initiated. The Server service uses the Server Message Block (SMB) protocol to communicate with other Windows computers so that file and print resources can be shared between network users.

After you assign permissions, you will also need to monitor user access to shared folders in order to maintain and secure the data. To do this, you can view a list of open files that are located in the shared folders, as well as the users who are currently using the files. Additionally, you can make the shared folders available offline by storing copies of the files in a reserved portion of disk space on the client machine called the cache. This enables you to work on the latest version of files even when you are not connected to the network.

Scenario

You are a Network Administrator at Pinnacle Corp. The Project Manager at Pinnacle has created a shared folder named General that contains, among other things, a list of tasks and the planned time to finish those tasks. He wants to make the General folder available to his team over the network and he needs you to assign appropriate permissions to different users. He also wants you to configure offline files so that he can work on the files in the Plan folder when the system is down.

Lesson 9 Working with Shared Folders

Project	Exam 70-270 Objective
9.1 Sharing a Folder	Create and remove shared folders.
9.2 Introducing Types of Permissions for Shared Folders	Control access to files and folders by using permissions. Control access to shared folders by using permissions.
9.3 Monitoring Access to Shared Folders	Manage and troubleshoot access to shared folders. Monitor, manage, and troubleshoot access to files and folders.
9.4 Configuring and Managing Offline Files and Folders	Manage and troubleshoot access to and synchronization of offline files. Optimize access to files and folders.

General Requirements

To complete this lesson, you will need administrative rights on a Windows XP Professional computer, a folder named General, a Word document named Schedule and a user account named John Simmons.

project 9.1

Sharing a Folder

exam objective

Create and remove shared folders.

overview

To create a shared folder, you use the **Sharing tab** in the Properties dialog box for that folder. By default, the name that is given to the shared folder will be the original folder name, but you can change this if you want. This way you can use one name for opening the folder locally and another name for accessing it over the network. On the Sharing tab, you can set various options for sharing the folder, as well as set the properties for the shared folder. Some of the options are listed below:

◆ **Share this folder:** Makes the contents of the folder available to network users.
◆ **Share name:** This is the name assigned to the folder that you want to share. Network users will use this name to access the shared folder.
◆ **Comment:** This is a description of the shared folder.
◆ **User limit:** This option is used to set the number of users who can simultaneously access a shared folder over a network. If you click the **Maximum allowed** option button, Windows XP Professional will allow ten users to connect to the shared folder, or you can specify a lower number. A maximum of ten simultaneous users is allowed because Windows XP Professional is designed for workgroup or peer-to-peer networks. Windows 2000 Server and Server 2003, on the other hand, allow a maximum number of users to simultaneously access a shared folder based on licensing terms.
◆ **Permissions:** This button is used to assign access permissions to ensure that only authorized users can connect to the shared folder.
◆ **Caching:** This button is used to designate how the contents of a shared folder can be accessed offline.

caution

The options available on the Sharing tab will be different depending on whether the computer is a member of a workgroup or a domain.

You can also stop sharing a folder to make its contents unavailable over the network. To do this, click the **Do not share this folder** option button on the **Sharing** tab. You can also create a shared folder using the **Create Shared Folder Wizard**. This Wizard guides you through the process of selecting the folder you want to share, making it available to network users, and assigning permissions to the various users who will be accessing it. You access the Create Shared Folder Wizard in the **Computer Management** window.

The Project Manager for your company has created a folder named General on his system. He wants his team to plan their work according to the information in the folder, so he wants you to share this folder so that his team can view the contents of the folder.

learning objective

After completing this project, you will know how to share a folder.

specific requirements

◆ Administrative rights on a Windows XP Professional computer.
◆ A folder named C:\General.

estimated completion time

15 minutes

project steps

Share a folder named **General** and verify that network users will be able to connect to it.

1. Right-click **Start**, and click the **Explore** command on the shortcut menu to open the **Windows Explorer** window.
2. Right-click the folder that you want to share, for example **General**. Then click the **Properties** command on the shortcut menu to open the **General Properties** dialog box.
3. Click the **Sharing** tab. If Sharing has not previously been enabled on this computer, the **Sharing** tab will appear as shown in **Figure 9-1**.

Figure 9-1 Sharing tab before enabling file sharing

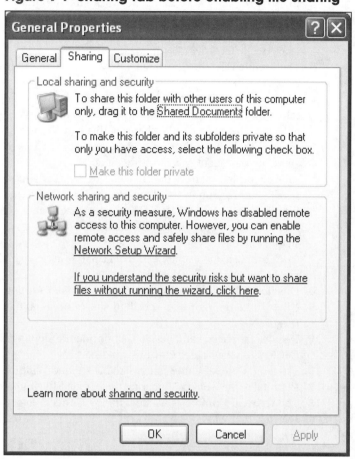

Sharing a Folder (cont'd)

exam objective

Create and remove shared folders.

project steps

tip

Folder options can also be accessed from any Windows Explorer window by clicking the Tools menu.

4. Click **If you understand the security risks but want to share files without running the wizard, click here** in the **Network sharing and security** section. If the **Network Setup Wizard** was run instead, **Internet Connection Firewall (ICF)** and **Internet Connection Sharing (ICS)** would be configured (if appropriate) based on your responses to the Wizard's prompts.

5. The **Enable File Sharing** dialog box will open. Select **Just enable file sharing** and then click **OK (Figure 9-2)**.

6. The contents of the **Network sharing and security** section will change. Click **Share this folder on the network** to make the contents of the folder accessible to other users on the network. The name for the share, in this case **General**, will default to the name of the folder **(Figure 9-3)**. Notice that there are very few options available to configure sharing and that you cannot specify different access levels for different users or groups. This is called **Simple File Sharing**. If your computer is a member of a domain or the default sharing configuration has been changed, a more flexible interface is used instead of Simple File Sharing. Click **OK** to close the **General Properties** dialog box. In the following steps you will change the default sharing configuration to enable access to all sharing options.

7. Click **Start**, and then click **Control Panel**. If necessary, click **Switch to Classic View** to display all Control Panel icons.

8. Double-click **Folder Options** to open the **Folder Options** window.

9. Click the **View** tab and scroll to the bottom of the **Advanced Settings** list box **(Figure 9-4)**.

10. Remove the check mark beside **Use simple file sharing (Recommended)** and then click **OK** to close the **Folder Options** window.

11. Close the **Control Panel** and switch back to the **Windows Explorer** window.

12. Right-click the **General** folder and select the **Sharing and Security** command.

13. The **General Properties** window for the **General** folder will open with the **Sharing** tab selected.

Figure 9-2 Enable file sharing confirmation box

Figure 9-3 Sharing tab using simple file sharing

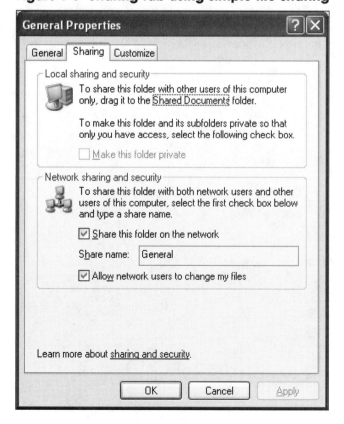

Figure 9-4 Disabling simple file sharing

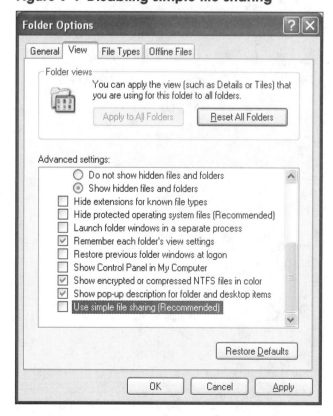

project 9.1

Sharing a Folder (cont'd)

exam objective

Create and remove shared folders.

project steps

14. Observe the options and buttons that are now available to configure the **General** shared folder (**Figure 9-5**). Click **OK** to close the **General Properties** window.
15. Next, you will connect to the **General** shared folder to ensure that users will be able to access it. With the **Windows Explorer** window still open, click the **Tools** menu and select the **Map Network Drive** command.
16. The **Map Network Drive** dialog box will open (**Figure 9-6**). Click the **Browse** button to open the **Browse for Folder** selection window.
17. Expand the **Entire Network**, **Microsoft Windows Network**, and *Workgroup* nodes (where *Workgroup* is the name of the workgroup of which the computer is a member). Find your computer name under the *Workgroup* node and expand it, then select the **General** shared folder and click **OK** (**Figure 9-7**).
18. Notice that the **Folder** selection box now has a **Universal Naming Convention (UNC)** path in it (**Figure 9-8**). A **UNC** path is used to identify network resources and consists of two leading backslashes followed by the name of the server where the resource exists, another backslash and finally the share name for the resource.
19. Click **Finish** to accept the default settings and create a network drive mapping for the **Z:** drive.
20. A new **Windows Explorer** window for the **Z:** drive will open (**Figure 9-9**). This drive mapping will be reconnected each time the current user logs on to the system. Close the **Windows Explorer** window for the **Z:** drive and the original **Windows Explorer** window.

tip

You can also connect to a network resource without the need to map a drive letter by typing its **UNC** name in the **Open** text box on the Run command.

Figure 9-5 Sharing tab with all options available

Figure 9-6 Map Network Drive dialog box

Figure 9-7 Browse for shared folder

Figure 9-8 UNC path to network share

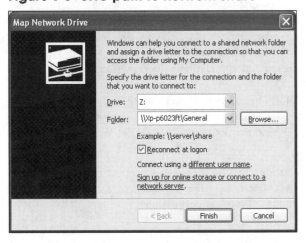

Figure 9-9 Z: drive mapped to the General share

Introducing Types of Permissions for Shared Folders

exam objective

Control access to files and folders by using permissions. Control access to shared folders by using permissions.

overview

When you create shares, you can control the level of access network users have to some extent. As you will see in the next lesson, you have much more latitude in setting the level of control users will have when you use NTFS permissions. For shared folders, there are only three levels of access (**Figure 9-10**):

◆ **Read:** The Read permission allows users to display folder names, file names, file data, and the attributes of folders shared on remote systems. Users can also run programs that are in shared application folders.

◆ **Change:** The Change permission allows users to create folders, add files to folders, modify data in files, add data to files, modify file attributes, and delete files and folders, in addition to the actions permitted by the Read permission.

◆ **Full Control:** The Full Control permission allows full access to the shared folder, including all actions permitted by the Read and Change permissions, and users can change permissions on the share.

These three levels of access are controlled by two conditions: Allow and Deny. The default setting is Allow, which gives users the specific permission for the shared folder. Deny, on the other hand, blocks the permission. The Deny setting should not be used very often, because it supersedes the Allow condition; however, it can be useful in cases where you want to deny a specific user in a group the same level of access granted to the group. It is also possible to grant the Change permission, while at the same time denying the Read permission so that a user will be able to delete files based on the file name, but will not be able to read the file before deleting it. Some important guidelines for assigning shared folder permissionsare listed below:

◆ The default permissions that are assigned to a folder when it is first shared grant the **Everyone** group the **Full Control** permission to the share (**Figure 9-11**).

◆ If you assign a specific permission to a user and the user is a member of a group that has a different set of permissions, then the effective permissions for the user are the combination of the user and group permissions. In other words, you add the two permissions together. For example, if a user has been granted the **Read** permission and is a member of a group that has the **Change** permission, the cumulative effect is the **Change** permission, which includes the **Read** permission.

◆ If you deny a permission to a user, it specifically overrides the Allow condition for that permission. Allow gives users the specific permission for the shared folder. Deny blocks the permission. For example, if a user has been granted the Read permission by virtue of his or her membership in Group A, but he or she also belongs to Group B, which has been specifically denied the Read permission, the user will not be allowed to access the file.

◆ When you copy or move a shared folder to a new location, the shared folder does not remain shared in the new location.

◆ Organize folders with the same security requirements within a single folder. For example, you can store the folders of various applications within a single folder. Then, you can share the folder containing all of the application folders, instead of sharing each application folder individually.

◆ Assign relevant share names to folders to enable users to locate them easily. Share names should also be short so that they are easier to remember and so that other operating systems can use them. MS-DOS, Windows 3.x, and Windows for Workgroups use 8.3 character names.

The Project Manager decides that John Simmons, a Team Leader on the Project Manager's team, must also be allowed to modify the contents of the **General** folder, in addition to just viewing them, so he asks you to assign the appropriate permissions.

tip

In most cases, Administrators will use the default permissions for shared folders which give the Everyone group Full Control, and then control user and group access through NTFS permissions.

Figure 9-10 Shared Folder Permissions

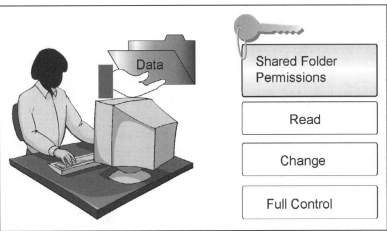

Figure 9-11 Default share permissions

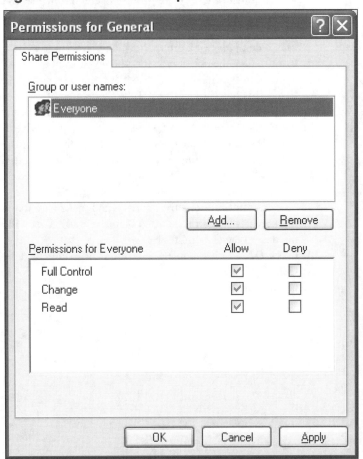

project 9.2

Introducing Types of Permissions for Shared Folders (cont'd)

exam objective

Control access to files and folders by using permissions. Control access to shared folders by using permissions.

learning objective

After completing this project, you will know how to assign shared folder permissions.

specific requirements

◆　Administrative rights on a Windows XP Professional computer.
◆　Completion of Project 9.1.
◆　A user account named **John Simmons**.

estimated completion time

15 minutes

project steps

Assign shared folder permissions.

1. In the **Windows Explorer** window, right-click the General folder in the C: drive, and click the **Properties** command on the shortcut menu to open the **General Properties** dialog box.
2. In the General Properties dialog box, click the **Sharing** tab.
3. Click **Permissions** to open the **Permissions for General** dialog box.
4. By default, the **Everyone** group is selected in the **Group or user names** list. Click **Remove** to remove this group from the list.
5. Then click **Add** to open the **Select Users or Groups** dialog box. Here you can select a user, a computer, or a group to which you want to assign shared folder permissions.
6. Confirm that the object type for which you want to assign permissions, in this case Users, appears in the **Select this object type** text box, and that the location is correct in the **From this location** text box. Type the names of the users for whom you want to assign permissions, for example, **Administrator**; **John Simmons**, separated by semicolons, in the **Enter the object names to select** text box **(Figure 9-12)**.
7. Click **OK** to select the users that have been entered and close the **Select Users or Groups** dialog box. The **Group or user names** list displays the user names you added.
8. Select **Administrator** from the list and place a check mark in the **Allow** check box beside the **Full Control** permission **(Figure 9-13)**.
9. Select **John Simmons** from the list and make sure that the **Allow** check box next to the **Change** permission is selected **(Figure 9-14)**. This will allow John Simmons to change the data in the General folder.
10. Click **OK** to close the **Permissions for General** dialog box, and again to close the General Properties dialog box.
11. Close Windows Explorer.

tip

The Administrator must be given permission to access shares like any other account; however, the Administrator can always modify permissions for a share even if they do not have permission to access the contents of the share itself.

Figure 9-12 Selecting users to assign permissions

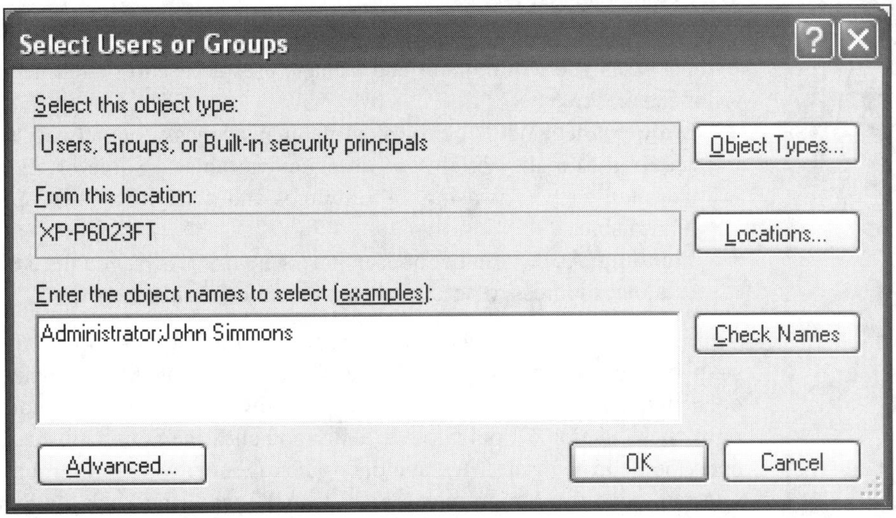

Figure 9-13 Permissions for the Administrator for the General shared folder

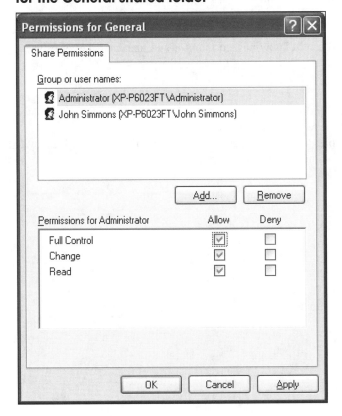

Figure 9-14 Permissions for John Simmons for the General shared folder

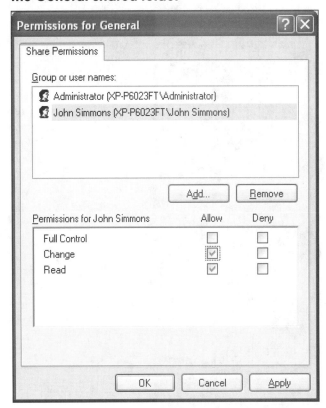

project 9.3

Monitoring Access to Shared Folders

exam objective

Manage and troubleshoot access to shared folders. Monitor, manage, and troubleshoot access to files and folders.

overview

In most cases you will monitor and manage user access to shared network resources for the following reasons:

◆ **Maintenance:** While performing maintenance tasks on network resources, you may be required to make certain resources unavailable to some or all connected users. You can monitor who is using the resources and notify them before making the resources unavailable.

◆ **Planning:** As the number of users on a network grows, you need to monitor the usage of existing resources to be able to plan for future requirements.

Administrators can also use the Shares or Shared Folders nodes in the **Shared Folders snap-in** to contact users when the user limit has been met and another user must access the open file, or the Administrator must shut down the system for maintenance. To do this, right-click either node, point to **All Tasks**, and click the **Send Console Message** command to open the **Send Console Message** dialog box **(Figure 9-15)**. Alternatively, with either node selected, open the **Action** menu, point to **All Tasks**, and click the **Send Console Message** command.

The **General** folder contains a file named **Schedule.doc** that has some information that is relevant to team leaders. The Project Manager wants you to monitor user access to the **General** folder in order to determine the number of users accessing the **Schedule.doc** file. In addition, he wants you to disconnect any team members currently accessing the file so that he can update it.

learning objective

After completing this project, you will know how to monitor and manage access to shared folders.

specific requirements

◆ Administrative rights on a Windows XP Professional computer with the **General** folder shared. This computer will be referred to as the server.

◆ A second Windows XP Professional computer connected with the first computer by a workgroup network. This computer will be referred to as the client.

◆ Completion of Projects 9.1 and 9.2.

estimated completion time

15 minutes

Figure 9-15 The Send Console Message dialog box

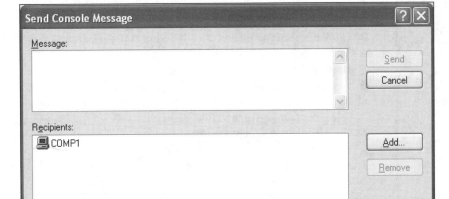

project 9.3

Monitoring Access to Shared Folders (cont'd)

exam objective

Manage and troubleshoot access to shared folders. Monitor, manage, and troubleshoot access to files and folders.

project steps

You will use the **Shared Folders snap-in** to monitor user access to shared resources.

1. On the client computer, log on as the **Administrator**.
2. Right-click **Start** and then click the **Explore** command to open **Windows Explorer**.
3. Click the **Tools** menu and click the **Map Network Drive** command.
4. The **Map Network Drive** dialog box will open. Click the **Browse** button to open the **Browse for Folder** selection window.
5. Expand the **Entire Network**, **Microsoft Windows Network**, and **Workgroup** nodes. Find the name of the server computer under the **Workgroup** node and expand it, then select the **General** shared folder and click **OK**.
6. Click **Finish** to accept the default settings and create a network drive mapping for the **Z:** drive.
7. A new **Windows Explorer** window will open titled **General on 'server_computer' (Z:)**. Double-click **Schedule.doc** to open the schedule file on the General share. *Note that this is not the General folder but is a network connection to the General share.*
8. Close **Windows Explorer**.
9. Switch to the server computer.
10. Click **Start**. Right-click **My Computer** and click the **Manage** command to open the **Computer Management** console.
11. Expand the **Shared Folders** node and click the **Shares** node. A list of shared folders available on the current computer will appear in the details pane of the Shared Folder snap-in.
12. Right-click the **General** folder in the details pane and choose the **Properties** command. On the **General** tab, you can see the number of users who are allowed to concurrently gain access to the folder **(Figure 9-16)**.
13. Click **OK** to close the **General Properties** dialog box.
14. You can view a list of the open files in the shared folders, as well as the users who are accessing the files. To do this, click the **Open Files** node in the **Shared Folders** snap-in. Notice that the **Schedule.doc** file is in use by the Administrator.
15. Administrators can also disconnect users from one open file or from all open files when required. Select **Open Files** in the Shared Folders snap-in.
16. Open the **Action** menu and select the **Disconnect All Open Files** command **(Figure 9-17)**.
17. Click **Yes** when prompted to confirm that you want to close all open resources **(Figure 9-18)**.
18. Close the **Computer Management** console.

tip

The maximum number of concurrent inbound connections supported by Windows XP Professional is 10. However, you can set this to a lower value.

tip

The list of shared folders and open files does not update automatically. To update the list, you must click the Refresh command on the Action menu in the Computer Management window.

Figure 9-16 Determining the user limit

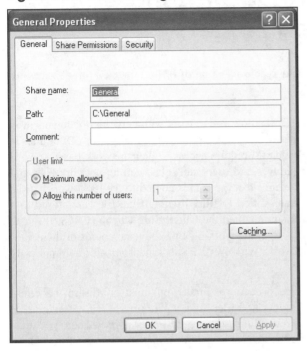

Figure 9-17 The Shared Folders node, disconnecting all open files

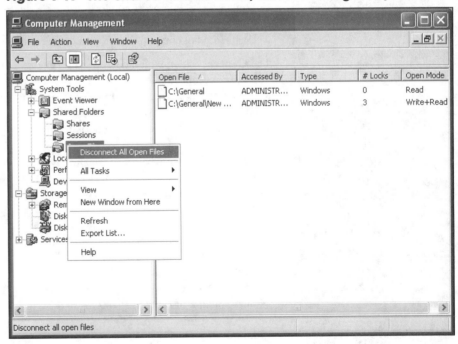

**Figure 9-18 Close all resources
confirmation box**

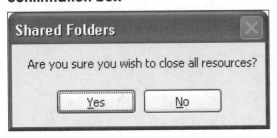

project 9.4

Configuring and Managing Offline Files and Folders

exam objective

Manage and troubleshoot access to and synchronization of offline files. Optimize access to files and folders.

overview

The purpose of offline files and folders is to allow you to work with network documents even when you are disconnected from the network. The most compelling usage for offline files is to support notebook users that travel and still require access to their network based files. If granted permission to do so, Administrators and users can select certain network files and folders to be cached. **Caching** simply means that the data is copied to the local workstation. Network files that are stored locally are called **Offline files**. Offline files are stored in a reserved portion of your system's disk space called the **Client Side Cache (CSC)**. If a user disconnects from the network, they can continue working with the local copies of their files. Then, when they reconnect to the network, Windows XP can synchronize or automatically update the network files.

caution

Offline Files can not be used if Fast User Switching is enabled (**Figure 9-19**).

tip

Offline files are best used for folders that will not be modified by more than one user during the same time period. This will reduce the possibility of lost data when the files are synchronized.

Caching offline folders is a two-stage procedure. First, you must configure the client computer to be able to use offline folders and files. *When **Windows XP Professional** is configured as a member of a domain it has offline folders enabled by default.* Then, you must configure the computer that is sharing the folders to control how the contents of the shared folders will be made available to offline users. The four possible options to control how offline files are cached are listed in **Table 9-1**.

Computers on a Microsoft network use a file-sharing protocol called Server Message Block (SMB) for network communication. This means that non-Microsoft networks, such as Novell NetWare, are not compatible and you cannot set up offline files with them.

The **General** folder, which contains information about client needs, is located on the Project Manager's computer. George Smith must access the **General** folder every other day to update the contents. To be able to do his work even when he is away from the office, George wants you to configure the system so that the contents of the folder will be available to him offline on the local hard disk on his notebook computer.

learning objective

After you have completed this project, you will know how to configure shared folders stored on your computer so that network users can cache them, and will learn how to configure and use offline files from a client computer.

specific requirements

◆ Administrative rights on a Windows XP Professional computer with the **General** folder shared. This computer will be called the server.
◆ A second computer connected to the first by a workgroup network. This computer will be called the client.
◆ Both systems must use the same password for the **Administrator** user account.
◆ Completion of Projects 9.1, 9.2 and 9.3.

estimated completion time

15 minutes

**Figure 9-19 Offline Files can not be used
with Fast User Switching**

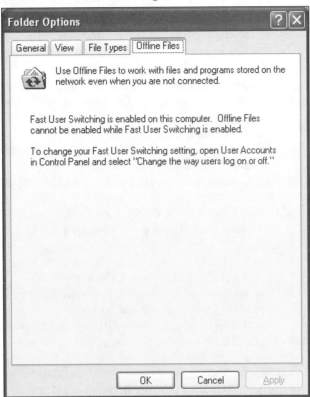

Table 9-1   Caching options for Offline Files

Option	Explanation
Allow caching of files in this shared folder	This check box must be selected to allow any kind of caching to occur.
Automatic caching of documents	This option automatically creates a cached copy of any file that the user opens from this shared folder. If changes are made to either copy of the file, those changes will be synchronized later based on the settings for the Synchronization Manager.
Automatic caching of programs and documents	This option makes offline copies of all files from shared folders that have been read, run, or referenced. Automatic caching for programs enables you to read read-only documents and execute programs that run from the server without connecting to the network. You cannot change the content of these files. Think of this as one way of caching from the server to the client.
Manual caching of documents	This is the default setting, which lets users manually specify the documents they want to be available offline. When you reconnect to the network, any changes that were made to the offline files are updated to the network files.

project 9.4

Configuring and Managing Offline Files and Folders (cont'd)

exam objective

Manage and troubleshoot access to and synchronization of offline files. Optimize access to files and folders.

project steps

Configure a shared folder so that network users can cache the files it contains.

1. Log on to the server computer as the **Administrator**.
2. Using **Windows Explorer**, open the Properties dialog box for the **General** folder and click the **Sharing** tab.
3. Click the **Caching** button.
4. The **Caching Settings** dialog box will open. Ensure that the **Allow caching of files in this shared folder** check box is selected.
5. Choose **Automatic caching of documents** in the **Setting** selection box and click **OK** (**Figure 9-20**).
6. Click **OK** to close the **General Properties** dialog box. The server is now configured to provide automatic caching of offline files.
7. Close the Windows Explorer window.Configure a client computer to use offline files.
8. Log on to the client computer as the **Administrator**.
9. Click **Start**, and then click **My Computer**.
10. Open the **Tools** menu and click the **Folder Options** command.
11. The **Folder Options** dialog box will open. Select the **Offline Files** tab and make sure that a check mark is beside **Enable Offline Files** (**Figure 9-21**).
12. Accept the remainder of the default settings by clicking **OK**. This will configure the client computer to be able to cache offline files and synchronize them with the server.
13. Open the **Tools** menu again and click the **Map Network Drive** command.
14. Select the **G:** drive from the **Drive** selection box.
15. Enter the **UNC** path to the **General** shared folder on the server in the **Folder** selection box. Type two backslashes, the name of the server computer, a backslash and finally the name of the share which is **General** (**Figure 9-22**).
16. Click **Finish** to map drive **G:** to the **General** folder on the server. A **Windows Explorer** window for the new mapping will open.

Test offline files to confirm that it has been properly configured.

17. Double-click **Schedule.doc** to open it and to cache it locally, then close **Schedule.doc**.
18. Log off and disconnect the network cable from the client computer.
19. Log on to the client computer again and open **Windows Explorer**.
20. Right-click the **General on 'server_computer' (G:)** drive and select the **Open** command.
21. A **Windows Explorer** window for the selected drive will open. Examine the details pane at the bottom left corner of the window. The **File System** will be ***NT5CSC** indicating that the **Client Side Cache** is in use.
22. Select the **Schedule.doc** file by clicking it once (**Figure 9-23**). In the details pane the **Status** for **Schedule.doc** will be **offline**.

tip

Offline Files can also be configured by double-clicking **Folder Options** in the **Control Panel** and selecting the **Offline Files** tab.

tip

Offline files stored in the cache will maintain the same NTFS permissions that are set on the files on the server.

Figure 9-20 Enabling Automatic Caching of Documents

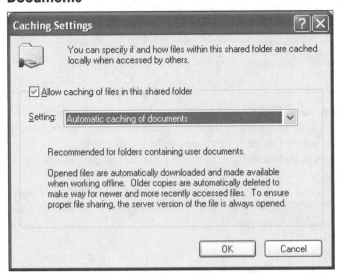

Figure 9-21 Enabling Offline Files

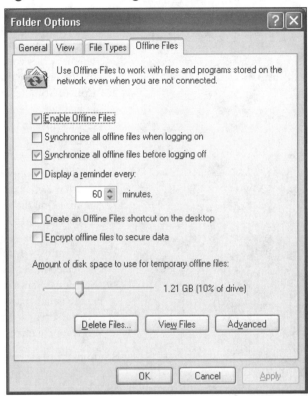

Figure 9-22 Mapping a Network Drive using a UNC path

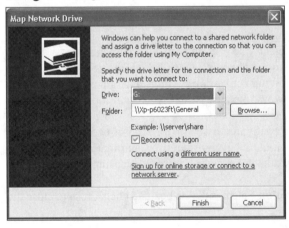

Figure 9-23 Viewing details for an offline file

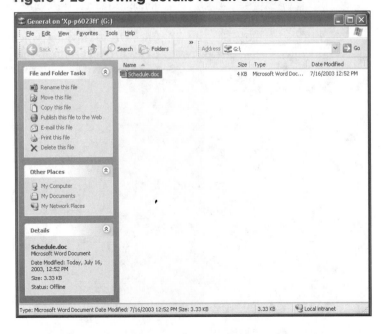

project 9.4

Configuring and Managing Offline Files and Folders *(cont'd)*

exam objective

Manage and troubleshoot access to and synchronization of offline files. Optimize access to files and folders.

project steps

tip

It is wise to always synchronize your files when logging on or off the network.

caution

If a file is modified both on the server and client prior to synchronization, the user will be prompted to choose to keep their version, keep the server version, or rename their version and keep both.

23. Double-click **Schedule.doc**, add a line of text to the file and then save the changes and close the file **(Figure 9-24)**. The changes that were just made were made to the locally cached copy of the file that is stored in the Client Side Cache.
24. On the server computer, open **Schedule.doc** and verify that the file has not changed, then close **Schedule.doc** without saving the file.
25. Log off of the client computer. A **Synchronization Complete** window will open indicating an error in synchronization because you are disconnected from the network. Click **Close** to ignore the error and continue.
26. Reconnect the network cable.
27. Log on to the client computer again. Immediately following the log on process, a **Synchronizing** window will appear **(Figure 9-25)**. This process ensures that any files that have changed on the client are copied to the server and any files that have been modified on the server are copied to the client.
28. Open **Windows Explorer**. Right-click the **General on '*server_computer*' (G:)** drive and select the **Open** command.
29. A **Windows Explorer** window for the selected drive will open. The **File System** indicated in the **Details** pane is now **NTFS**.
30. Select the **Schedule.doc** file by clicking it once. Notice that the **Status** for **Schedule.doc** in the details pane no longer indicates that the file is offline.
31. On the server computer, open **Schedule.doc** and verify that the file is now the same as the copy on the client. Close **Schedule.doc**.

Examine the configuration of the **Synchronization Manager**.

32. Click **Start** and then click **My Computer** to open the My Computer window.
33. Open the **Tools** menu and select the **Synchronize** command to open the **Synchronization Manager Items to Synchronize** dialog box **(Figure 9-26)**.
34. Click the **Setup** button to open the **Synchronization Settings** dialog box **(Figure 9-27)**.
35. Examine each tab. There are three ways to control when synchronization will occur and each tab manages one method.
36. Notice that synchronization can be configured based on the type of network connection in use. This allows synchronization to be configured to automatically run when connected to a Fast Ethernet connection, but not synchronize when using a slower dial-up connection.
37. Click **OK** to close the **Synchronization Settings** dialog box and click **Close** to close the **Items to Synchronize** window.
38. Close the **My Computer** window.

Figure 9-24 Adding text to an offline file

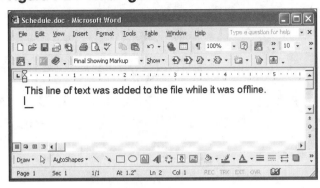

Figure 9-25 Synchronizing offline files

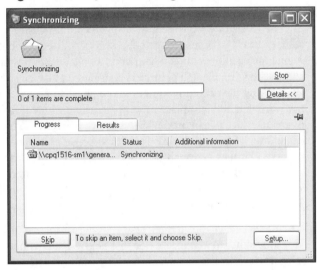

Figure 9-26 Selecting Items to Synchronize

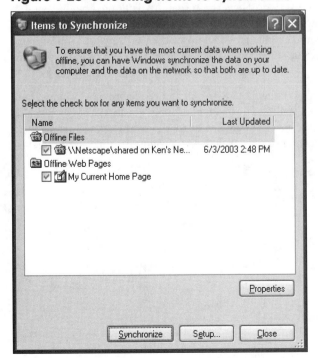

Figure 9-27 Configuring Synchronization Settings

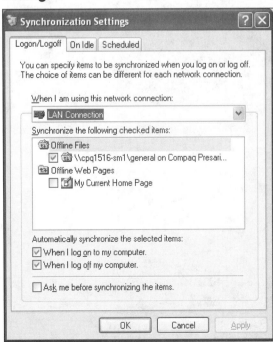

10

Setting Up, Configuring, and Administering Network Printers

Just as you provide accessibility to files and folders and make sure that the correct levels of access are granted, you can also share print resources and assign different levels of access to different sets of users. Although some printing terminology may seem counterintuitive, it can help you to understand how sharing print resources works. In a Windows environment, a **printer** is considered to be the software that delivers the requests for service from the operating system to the physical print device. A **print device** is the physical hardware that actually places the image to be printed onto paper. Because the **printer** is a logical interface to a **print device**, there does not have to be a one-to-one relationship between the **printer** and the **print device**. A single **printer** can service multiple **print devices** and multiple **printers** can send print jobs to a single **print device**. Managing print resources is accomplished through sharing and setting permissions on the **printer**. The ability to configure shared printers is valuable to a business because each client does not need its own expensive hardware print device to be able to print their work.

A **print server** handles the requests for service for a shared **printer**. A print server can send print jobs either to a **print device** that is physically connected to it, or to a network attached **print device** that has its own network interface and network address. In either case, the **print server** receives the print requests, queues them (*stores them in a file on the hard drive*), uses a printer driver to translate the digital documents into printer code, and sends the instructions to the **print device**. Windows XP and 2000 Professional computers, and even Windows 9x computers, can be configured as print servers. However, this ability is limited by the fact that they can, for the most part, only be used on exclusively Microsoft networks. To act as a print server for a network with client computers that are Macintosh, Unix or Netware, or to support more than ten simultaneous clients, you should use Windows 2000 Server or Windows Server 2003 instead.

As a Network Administrator, you must know how to install and configure new printers, how to manage and share print resources, and how to maintain printer security. You should also know how the printing process works, how to monitor user access to network printers, how to ensure the optimum usage of your print resources, and how to troubleshoot printer problems.

Scenario

You are the Network Administrator in charge of a Windows XP network. The Sales Manager of your company has decided that he needs a dedicated color printer for his team. You will add a printer to his computer, share it over the network, and assign appropriate printing permissions to make it accessible to his team.

Lesson 10   Setting Up, Configuring, and Administering Network Printers

Project	Exam 70-270 Objective
10.1 Adding and Sharing a Local Printer	Connect to local and network print devices. Connect to a local print device.
10.2 Connecting to a Network Printer	Connect to local and network print devices. Connect to an Internet printer.
10.3 Assigning Printer Permissions	Control access to printers by using permissions. Monitor, configure, and troubleshoot I/O devices, such as printers, scanners, multimedia devices, mouse, keyboard, and smart card reader.
10.4 Configuring and Managing Printers	Manage printers and print jobs. Monitor, configure, and troubleshoot I/O devices, such as printers, scanners, multimedia devices, mouse, keyboard, and smart card reader.

General Requirements

To complete this lesson, you will need administrative rights on two Windows XP Professional computers connected to a network. You will also need a printer and a user account.

project 10.1	# *Adding and Sharing a Local Printer*
exam objective	Connect to local and network print devices. Connect to a local print device.
overview	The difference between a **Local printer** and a **Network printer** is *not* the way the print device is connected. The real difference is the location of the **print server**. When a **Local printer** is configured, the **print server** resides on the computer where the printer is configured. When a **Network printer** is configured, the **print server** resides on another computer elsewhere on the network. A **Local printer** configured on a computer can be shared with other users on the network who would connect to it from their computers as a **Network printer**.

A **Local printer** can be connected directly to a physical port on a computer such as a parallel (LPT), serial (COM), or USB port, or it can be connected to a network attached print device by means of a network connection. If it is directly attached, and the print device supports Plug and Play, the operating system automatically detects and installs the device when you attach it. Otherwise, if you have a print device that is not Plug and Play, or if you want to add a local printer that is not currently attached to your computer, you must use the **Add Printer Wizard** to create the logical printer; that is, the software interface that delivers the requests for service from the operating system to the physical print device. When you make a request for a print job, the document is spooled (or stored) on the hard drive of the print server where the logical printer has been configured before it is sent to the actual print device. Only members of the local Administrators or Power Users groups can install a local printer.

The Sales Manager prepares a summary report from the weekly sales reports produced by his team. He must present this report to the General Manager. The sales reports generated by the sales team are confidential and also contain a number of color graphics, so the Sales Manager wants to have a dedicated color printer for his team. You must add a printer to his computer and share it over the network to make it accessible to his team. |

tip

Think of a network attached print device as a normal print device with a very long cable.

learning objective	After completing this project, you will know how to add and share a local printer.
specific requirements	◆ Administrative rights on a Windows XP Professional computer connected to a network. ◆ A print device.
estimated completion time	10 minutes
project steps	Add a Plug and Play local printer to your computer. 1. Plug the print device's cable into the appropriate port on your computer. 2. Turn the print device's power on. A **Found New Hardware** information bubble appears from the notification area (**Figure 10-1**). When Windows recognizes the printer, the name is displayed in the information bubble and the necessary printer files are copied. 3. The **Found New Hardware Wizard** dialog box appears to inform you that the software for the print device has been installed. Click **Finish** to complete the installation. An information bubble appears from the notification area briefly stating that your printer is installed and ready to use.

Figure 10-1 Automatic detection of a print device

project 10.1

Adding and Sharing a Local Printer *(cont'd)*

exam objective

Connect to local and network print devices. Connect to a local print device.

project steps

Add a non Plug and Play local printer to your computer.

1. Click **Start** and click **Printers and Faxes** to open the **Printers and Faxes** window.

2. Click the **Add a printer** link under Printer Tasks on the left side of the window to start the **Add Printer Wizard**. The **Welcome to the Add Printer Wizard** screen opens.

3. Click **Next** to open the **Local or Network Printer** screen.

4. The **Local printer attached to this computer** option button and the **Automatically detect and install my Plug and Play printer** check box are selected by default (**Figure 10-2**). Clear the **Automatically detect and install my Plug and Play printer** check box, and click **Next** to open the **Select a Printer Port** screen.

5. The **Use the following port** option button is selected by default. Accept the default port that is selected in the list box, and click **Next**. The **Install Printer Software** screen opens (**Figure 10-3**).

6. Locate and select the manufacturer of the printer you want to install in the **Manufacturer** scrolling list box. Then, locate and select the name of the printer you want to install in the **Printers** scrolling list box.

7. Click **Next** to open the **Name Your Printer** screen. Accept the printer name provided by the Wizard in the **Printer name** text box. If prompted, select the **Yes** or **No** option button depending on whether you want this printer to be your default printer.

8. Click **Next** to open the **Printer Sharing** screen. Select the **Share Name** option button and type a name for the shared printer in the text box. You should record the name that you entered as it will be used in the next project.

9. Click **Next** to open the **Print Test Page** screen. Select the **No** option button under **Do you want to print a test page**?

10. Click **Next** to open the **Completing the Add Printer Wizard** screen, which summarizes the settings you have chosen.

11. Click **Finish** to copy the drivers for the printer and complete the Wizard. The printer you have installed now appears in the Printers and Faxes window.

12. Close the **Printers and Faxes** window.

tip

To configure a network attached print device, use the **Create a new port** option and choose **Standard TCP/IP port**.

Figure 10-2 Choosing the type of printer to create

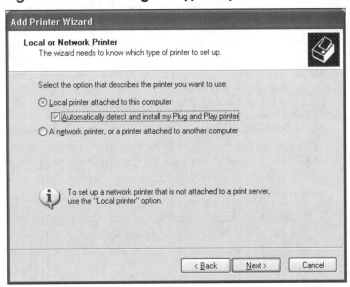

Figure 10-3 Selecting the printer software and driver

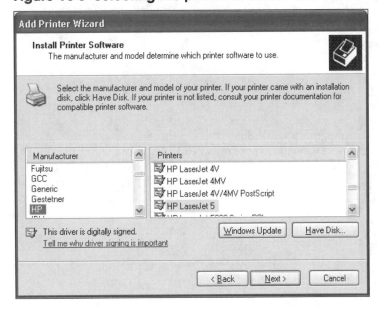

project 10.2

Connecting to a Network Printer

exam objective

Connect to local and network print devices. Connect to an Internet printer.

overview

If you want to access printers that have been shared on other computers on the network (**Table 10-1**), the Add Printer Wizard can be used to connect you to the shared printer by creating a **Network printer** on your computer. You can either enter the UNC pathname for the shared printer, or browse the network to locate the *printservername**sharename* of your choice. You can also use My Network Places to locate and connect to a shared printer just as you would a shared folder, or you can use the Run command on the Start menu and enter the UNC pathname in the Open text box.

If your client is running Windows XP, 2000, NT, or 9x, the computer will automatically install the driver needed to deliver the requests for service from the operating system to the physical print device, as long as a copy of the driver is stored on the print server. Windows 3.x and MS-DOS users will have to manually install the print driver and, if your network includes Macintosh, UNIX, and Netware clients, additional services will have to be installed on the print server.

If you are on an Active Directory network, the Specify a Printer screen will include the **Find a printer in the Directory** option button. When you click Next, a dialog box will open in which you can search the Active Directory for a printer based on its name, location, capability, or comment.

You can also connect to remote printers, such as a printer at a branch office of your company, by connecting to them over the Internet or on your intranet using the **Internet Printing Protocol (IPP)**. As long as you have permission for an Internet printer, you can connect to it using its URL. In this case, on the Specify a Printer page, you will select this option and enter the URL.

The Finance Manager in your company needs to print a cost analysis report that the Sales Manager includes in his monthly sales review. He has asked you to configure his computer so that he can send the cost analysis report to the Sales Manager's printer. You must install a network printer on his computer so that he can print the report.

learning objective

After completing this project, you will know how to connect to a network printer.

specific requirements

◆ Completion of Project 10.1.
◆ Administrative rights on a second Windows XP Professional computer connected to a network with the first Windows XP Professional computer from Project 10.1.

estimated completion time

5 minutes

Table 10-1 Methods of connecting to a network printer

Method	Action to be taken
Add Printer Wizard	Enter the UNC pathname, *printerservername\sharename*, for the shared printer.
Add Printer Wizard	Browse the network to locate the shared network printer.
My Network Places	Connect to the print server and shared printer as you would a shared folder.
Run command	Enter the UNC pathname of the shared printer in the Open text box.
Active Directory	Search Active Directory for a printer using its name, location, capability, or comment as search criteria.

project 10.2

Connecting to a Network Printer
(cont'd)

exam objective

Connect to local and network print devices. Connect to an Internet printer.

project steps

Connect to a network printer.

1. Log on to the second computer as the **Administrator**.
2. Open the **Printers and Faxes** window from the Start menu.
3. Click the **Add a printer** link to start the **Add Printer Wizard**. The **Welcome to the Add Printer Wizard** screen opens.
4. Click **Next** to open the **Local or Network printer** screen.
5. Click the **A network printer, or a printer attached to another computer** option button.
6. Click **Next** to open the **Specify a Printer** screen. This is where you enter the UNC pathname for a share, or the URL for an Internet or intranet print device.
7. Select the **Connect to this printer** option button. In the **Name** text box, type the path for the network printer, following the syntax, *printservername\printername* (**Figure 10-4**). Use the name of the first computer for *printservername* and the share name from project 10.1 for the *printername*. *If you are unsure of the UNC name for a printer, leave the text box blank and click Next to open the Browse for Printer window (Figure 10-5).*
8. Once the UNC name has been entered, click **Next**. The Wizard copies the necessary printer software, and then opens the **Default Printer** screen. Select the **Yes** or **No** option button, depending on whether you want this printer to be your default printer.
9. Click **Next** to open the **Completing the Add Printer Wizard** screen, which summarizes the printer settings you have specified.
10. Click **Finish** to complete the installation of the network printer. An icon for the printer now appears in the Printers and Faxes window (**Figure 10-6**). Close the Printers and Faxes window.

tip

If IIS (Internet Information Services), Microsoft's Web server software, has been installed on the print server that is servicing the request, you can connect to a printer on the intranet by specifying the path of the printer in the URL text box. You can also locate the printer by browsing the network.

Figure 10-4 Specifying the UNC path for a network printer

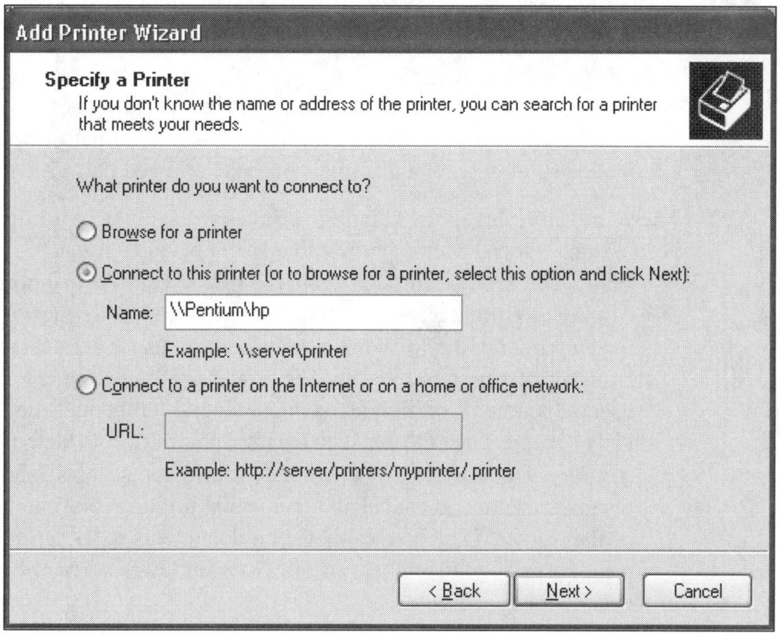

Add Printer Wizard

Specify a Printer
If you don't know the name or address of the printer, you can search for a printer that meets your needs.

What printer do you want to connect to?

○ Bro<u>w</u>se for a printer

◉ <u>C</u>onnect to this printer (or to browse for a printer, select this option and click Next):

Name: \\Pentium\hp

Example: \\server\printer

○ C<u>o</u>nnect to a printer on the Internet or on a home or office network:

URL:

Example: http://server/printers/myprinter/.printer

[< <u>B</u>ack] [<u>N</u>ext >] [Cancel]

Figure 10-5 Browsing to select a UNC path

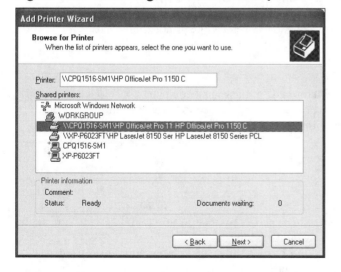

Figure 10-6 Network printer added to the Printers and Faxes window

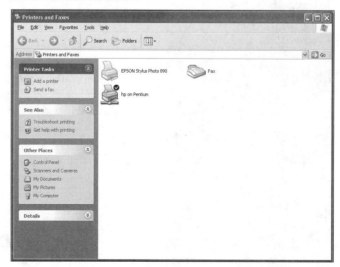

project 10.3 | *Assigning Printer Permissions*

exam objective

Control access to printers by using permissions. Monitor, configure, and troubleshoot I/O devices, such as printers, scanners, multimedia devices, mouse, keyboard, and smart card reader.

overview

When a printer is shared, by default, the Everyone group is granted the Print permission. Since this is the most restrictive print permission that can be assigned, there will generally not be much time spent configuring printer security. However, printer permissions can be used to limit access to a particular printer for certain users, and users who are not Administrators can be allowed to manage a particular printer. Print permissions are set on the **Security** tab in the **Properties** dialog box for the printer. Just like any other permissions, print permissions can be either allowed or denied, and denials override allowed permissions.

There are three levels of standard print permissions. In addition to these standard print permissions, special access permissions may also be assigned.
◆ **Print:** The Print permission enables a user to connect to a printer and send print jobs to it.
◆ **Manage Printers:** The Manage Printers permission grants a user administrative control over a printer. Users with this permission can pause and restart the printer, share a printer, adjust printer permissions, change printer properties, delete a printer, and cancel all other users' documents or all queued documents. Members of the **Administrators** and **Power Users** groups have the Manage Printers permission by default.
◆ **Manage Documents:** The Manage Documents permission enables a user to pause, resume, restart, and cancel all other users' printing jobs but they cannot control the status of the printer. They also cannot send documents to the printer unless they also have the print permission. Members of the **Creator Owner** group have the Manage Documents permission by default.

The Finance Manager is unable to use the shared printer. After giving it some thought, you realize that because the Sales Manager wanted a dedicated printer for his team, you deleted the default Print permission for the Everyone group and only assigned the Print permission to the members of the Sales team. You must assign the Print permission to the Finance Manager so that he can access the printer and print documents.

learning objective

After completing this project, you will know how to assign print permissions.

specific requirements

◆ Administrative rights on a Windows XP Professional computer connected to a network. The computer should be the same computer you used to share the printer in Project 10.1
◆ A user account named **John Simmons**.

estimated completion time

10 minutes

project steps

Assign access permissions for accessing a network printer to a user.
1. Log on to the computer as an **Administrator**.
2. Click **Start** and click **Printers and Faxes** to open the **Printers and Faxes** window.
3. Right-click the printer icon for the printer that was installed in project 10.1. Then, click the **Properties** command on the shortcut menu to open the **Properties** dialog box for the printer.
4. Click the **Security** tab (**Figure 10-7**).

Figure 10-7 Default printer security settings

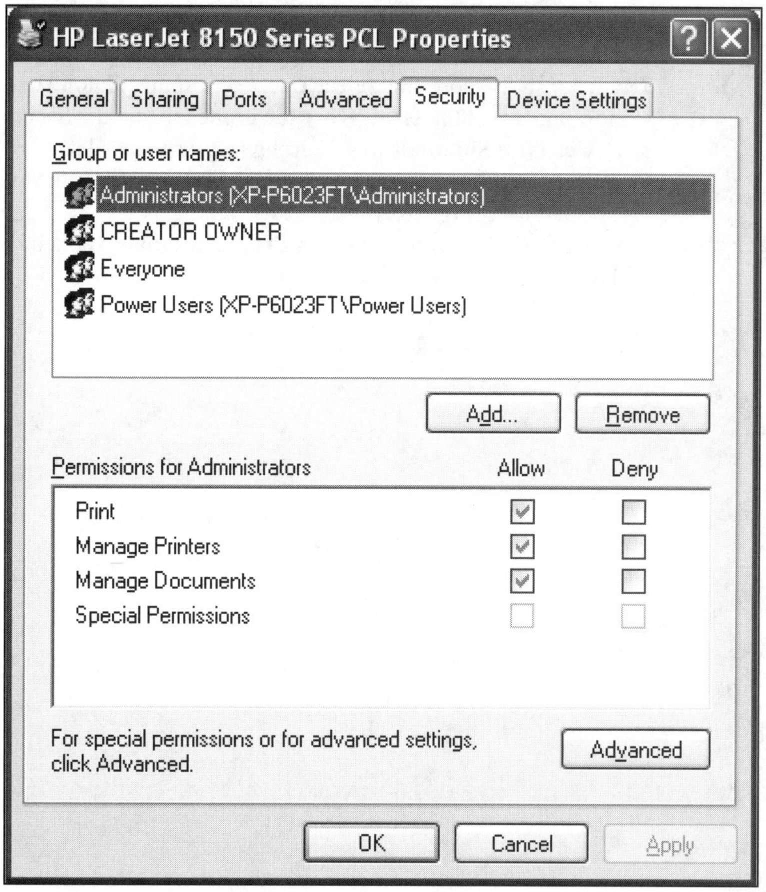

| project 10.3 | *Assigning Printer Permissions (cont'd)* |

exam objective

Control access to printers by using permissions. Monitor, configure, and troubleshoot I/O devices, such as printers, scanners, multimedia devices, mouse, keyboard, and smart card reader.

project steps

5. Click **Add** to open the **Select Users or Groups** dialog box. Make sure that **Users** appears in the **Select this object type** text box, and that the computer on which you are working is listed in the **From this location** text box.
6. Type the user name of the user to whom you want to assign printer access permissions, in this case **John Simmons**, in the **Enter the object names to select** text box (**Figure 10-8**).
7. Click **OK** to close the Select Users or Groups dialog box. The user name you selected now appears in the **Group or user names** list on the Security tab.
8. Select **John Simmons** in the Group or user names list.
9. Select the **Allow** check box for the **Manage Printers** permission to assign it to the selected user (**Figure 10-9**).
10. Click **OK** to close the printer's **Properties** dialog box, and then close the **Printers and Faxes** window.

Figure 10-8 Selecting a user to be assigned printer permissions

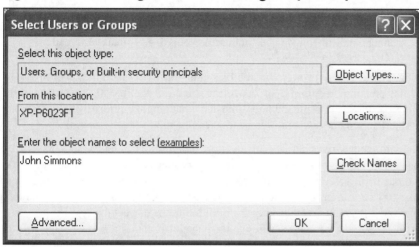

Figure 10-9 Assigning printer permissions to a user

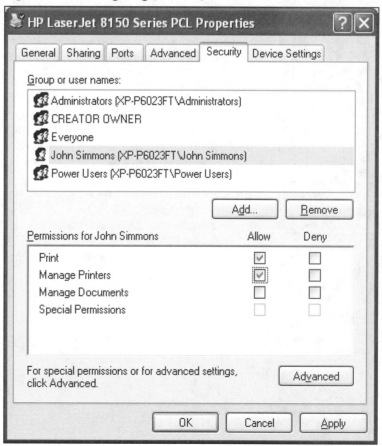

| project 10.4 | *Configuring and Managing Printers* |

exam objective

Manage printers and print jobs. Monitor, configure, and troubleshoot I/O devices, such as printers, scanners, multimedia devices, mouse, keyboard, and smart card reader.

overview

Managing printers and print jobs involves pausing and resuming printing; canceling documents; pausing, resuming, or canceling specific documents; restarting print jobs; scheduling documents to print at a later time; and changing the priority of a document so that the printing requirements of your organization can be met.

Managing printers involves performing a variety of administrative tasks:

◆ **Specifying paper sizes for paper trays:** A printer can have multiple paper trays that hold paper of different sizes; therefore, you can associate a paper size with a specific paper tray for the printer. When a user selects a paper size and gives a print command, Windows XP automatically routes the print job to the correct paper tray.

◆ **Setting a Separator Page:** A Separator page, also called a banner page, is a file that identifies a printed document, usually with the name of the user who requested it, as well as the date and time. It is printed between documents so that you can easily identify the start and end of each print job **(Figure 10-10)**.

◆ **Performing printing tasks:** A user may need to perform a variety of printing tasks such as pausing, resuming, and canceling the printing of documents.

◆ **Sending documents to a different printer:** If a print device is malfunctioning, you might decide to redirect all queued print jobs to a working printer of the same type elsewhere.

◆ **Changing ownership of a printer:** If the owner of a printer (the person who installed it) leaves the organization and you must pass on the administrative responsibility to a new user, you can change its ownership. Users with the Manage Printers permission and members of the Administrators and Power Users groups can take ownership of a printer.

The Sales Manager for your organization needs to print a long document on size A4 paper immediately but does not want to disrupt the printing needs of the other members of his team, who also need the color printer for important jobs. The Sales Manager's document does not contain any color graphics. You decide to use a shared laser printer that is also installed on the Sales Manager's computer instead. You will set the printer to the highest possible priority and configure it to use A4 size paper for the printout.

learning objective

After completing this project, you will know how to:
◆ Set printer priority.
◆ Set the paper size for a paper tray.

specific requirements

◆ Administrative rights on a Windows XP Professional computer with a printer installed.

estimated completion time

10 minutes

Figure 10-10 Setting a Separator Page

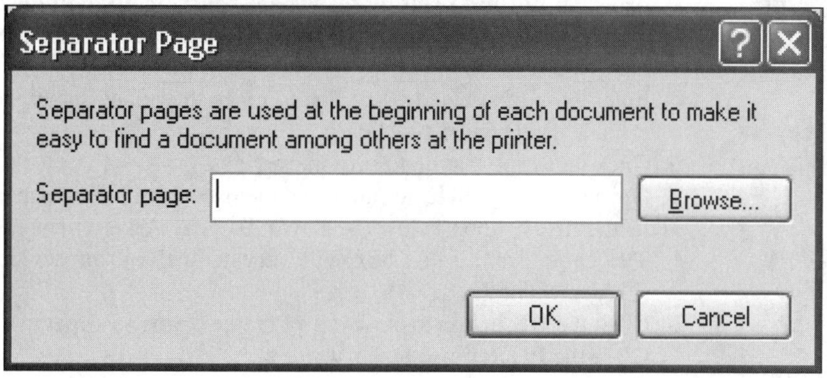

project 10.4

Configuring and Managing Printers
(cont'd)

exam objective

Manage printers and print jobs. Monitor, configure, and troubleshoot I/O devices, such as printers, scanners, multimedia devices, mouse, keyboard, and smart card reader.

project steps

1. Click the **Start** button, and click **Printers and Faxes** to open the **Printers and Faxes** window.
2. Right-click the **<Printer Name>** printer icon for which you want to set the priority, and click **Properties** on the shortcut menu to open the **<Printer Name> Properties** dialog box.
3. Click the **Advanced** tab. By default, the **Always Available**, **Spool print documents so program finishes printing faster**, and **Start printing immediately** option buttons and the **Print spooled documents first** and **Enable Advanced Printing Features** check boxes are selected.
4. Enter **99** in the **Priority** spin box to make the printer the highest priority printer for the print device (**Figure 10-11**).
5. Click the **Apply** button to save the settings.
6. Open the **Device Settings** tab to set the paper size for the paper tray.
7. In the first list box below the **Form To Tray Assignment** node, select the **A4** option. The name for this list box will vary with the print device type and configuration (**Figure 10-12**).
8. Click the **OK** button to close the **<Printer Name> Properties** dialog box.
9. Close the **Printer and Faxes** window.

tip

One is the lowest priority and ninety-nine is the highest priority.

caution

The tabs in the Properties dialog box for a printer may differ from those shown here. For instance, your printer may have an NT Forms tab instead of a Device Settings tab.

Figure 10-11 Setting Printer Priority

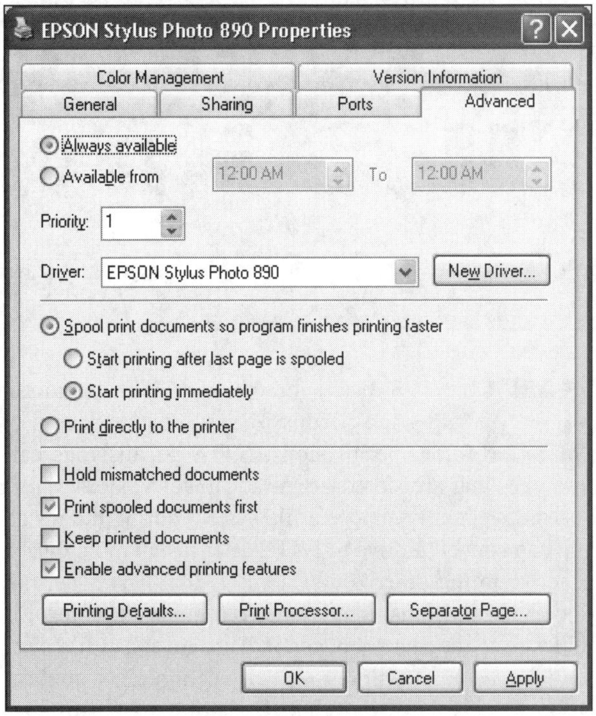

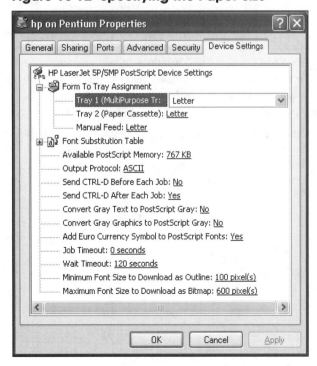

Figure 10-12 Specifying the Paper Size

Working with NTFS Permissions

On NTFS disks, you can use **NTFS permissions**, either alone or in combination with share permissions, to control access to network resources. Unlike shared folder permissions, NTFS permissions can also be used to control access to resources that are stored on the computer where the user is physically logged on. Although you will generally choose a file system during the installation of Windows XP Professional, you can convert a drive to NTFS after installation. One reason that NTFS is considered to be superior to the other file systems is that NTFS permissions can be set for both files and folders, and you have many more options for controlling what users can do with a file or folder once they have opened it. This advanced file system also supports large data storage, long file names, compression, encryption, disk quotas and ownership of files and folders. Because NTFS uses a change journal to ensure that all writes are either completed successfully or rolled back, it is relatively immune to file system corruption. Each file or folder on an NTFS volume has a set of attributes, which include, among others, the compression attribute and the encryption attribute. To see if a volume is using NTFS, right-click the drive in Windows Explorer and click Properties. Also, the Security tab for a file or folder will only appear on an NTFS volume.

The NTFS file system also associates two kinds of **Access Control Lists (ACLs)** with each file or folder. The first is called a **Discretionary Access Control List (DACL)** which identifies the users and groups who are granted or denied access. The second is a **System Access Control List (SACL)** that controls how access to the file or folder is audited. Both lists contain **Access Control Entries (ACE)** that consist of **Security Identifiers (SIDs)** that represent a user or a group along with a set of security permissions for each.

Like share permissions, when permission is Denied, it overrides the Allow condition. By default, the Everyone group is granted the Full Control NTFS permission for the root of a drive, although not for the system subfolders. As with Share Permissions, you will generally remove this permission and set your own according to your organizational needs.

Scenario

You are working as a Network Administrator at Spectrum Computers Ltd. Jessica, the Project Manager for your company, has created a folder named Standards on an NTFS partition. She wants to make its contents available to her team over the network. The files in this folder contain lists of different standards that must be followed by the team members when developing software. Jessica wants you to ensure the security of the Standards folder and its contents by assigning appropriate permissions to all users who will access it.

Lesson 11   Working with NTFS Permissions

Project	Exam 70-270 Objective
11.1 Identifying Types of NTFS Permissions	Basic knowledge
11.2 Assigning NTFS Permissions	Monitor, manage, and troubleshoot access to files and folders. Control access to files and folders by using permissions.
11.3 Using Special Permissions	Monitor, manage, and troubleshoot access to files and folders. Control access to files and folders by using permissions.

General Requirements

To complete the projects in this lesson, you will need a computer with Windows XP Professional installed on a partition or volume formatted with NTFS. The computer must have Simple File sharing disabled and have a user account named John Simmons.

<table>
<tr><td>

project 11.1

</td><td>

Identifying Types of NTFS Permissions

</td></tr>
<tr><td>

exam objective

</td><td>

Basic knowledge

</td></tr>
<tr><td>

overview

tip

When you assign NTFS permissions to a folder, all files and subfolders in the folder inherit the same permissions by default. (This default action can be changed.) On the other hand, NTFS permissions assigned to files cannot be further inherited because files do not contain any object that can inherit these permissions.

tip

You can assign special permissions to both folders and files by clicking the Advanced button on the Security tab of the Properties dialog box for a file or folder.

</td><td>

One of the most important things to remember about NTFS permissions is that they can be configured for both files and folders. While share permissions are configured at the folder level, and any subfolders or files within the folder inherit the shared folder permissions, different NTFS permissions can be assigned to a file than for the folder in which it is stored. File permissions take precedence over folder permissions.

Another important concept is that NTFS permissions, like share permissions, are cumulative, or added together. If a user has the NTFS Read permission granted through membership in one group and the NTFS Modify permission granted through membership in another group, his or her effective permission is Modify.

However, when NTFS permissions are used in combination with share permissions, the most restrictive permission of the two applies. For example, if a user has the Read share permission granted through membership in one group and the NTFS folder Modify permission granted through membership in another group, his or her effective permission when accessing the network share would be Read. Remember, share permissions apply only to users who are connecting over the network, so if users connect to the folder on the computer on which it is being hosted, they will have the NTFS Modify permission locally.

One common way of handling permissions is to create shared folders and leave the default permission, Full Control for the Everyone group, intact. Then, instead of applying any share permissions, use NTFS permissions to secure the resources. Since the most restrictive permission applies, as long as you have fine-tuned your NTFS permissions so that groups have the appropriate level of access, your resources will be secure. Additionally, since NTFS permissions operate locally, you can be confident that security for files and folders is effective whether they are accessed through the network or locally on the computer where the resource resides.

Jessica wants to assign different levels of access to her team members for the Standards folder. To do this efficiently, she needs to brush up on her knowledge of NTFS permissions and their applications. She asks you to prepare a report or presentation on NTFS File and Folder permissions including explaining the effects of combining different NTFS permissions and combining NTFS permissions with share permissions. She also wants you to explain how NTFS permission inheritance works.

</td></tr>
<tr><td>

learning objective

</td><td>

After completing this project, you will be able to explain NTFS File and Folder permissions.

</td></tr>
<tr><td>

specific requirements

</td><td>

◆ Administrative rights on a Windows XP Professional computer with an NTFS volume.

</td></tr>
<tr><td>

estimated completion time

</td><td>

10 minutes

</td></tr>
<tr><td>

project steps

</td><td>

1. Click **Start** and then click **My Computer**. The My Computer window will open.
2. Double-click on the volume that is formatted with NTFS.
3. In the **File and Folder Tasks** section, click **Make a new folder**.
4. A new folder will appear in the right hand pane. In the file name text box for the new folder, type **Standards** and press **[Enter]**.
5. Right-click on the **Standards** folder that you just created and select **Properties**.
6. Select the **Security** tab from the **Standards Properties** dialog box (**Figure 11-1**).

</td></tr>
</table>

Figure 11-1 Standard NTFS folder permissions

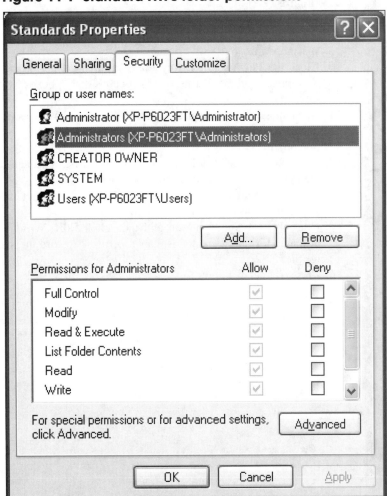

project 11.1

Identifying Types of NTFS Permissions (cont'd)

exam objective

Basic knowledge

project steps

tip

Each standard permission is comprised of one or more special permissions.

7. Record the **standard permissions** that may be assigned to a user or group to control access to a folder.

8. Click the **Advanced** button to open the **Advanced Security Settings** dialog box **(Figure 11-2)**.

9. Select any permission entry in the **Permission entries** list and click **Edit** to display the list of **special permissions** that may be assigned for a folder **(Figure 11-3)**. Record the special permissions.

10. Close the **Permission Entry for Standards**, the **Advanced Security Settings for Standards**, and the **Standards Properties** dialog boxes by clicking the **Cancel** button on each one.

11. Open the standards folder and create a file named **Policies.txt** by clicking the **File** menu in the **Standards Windows Explorer** screen, choosing **New** and then clicking **Text document**.

12. Right-click on the **Policies.txt** file that was just created and select **Properties** to display the **Policies.txt Properties** dialog box.

13. Select the **Security** tab. Which standard permission is not available for files? Record the standard permissions available for files.

14. Click the **Advanced** button and then click **Edit**. Which special permission that is available for folders is not available for files? Record the special permissions available for files.

15. Close all open windows.

Figure 11-2 Advanced Security Settings dialog box

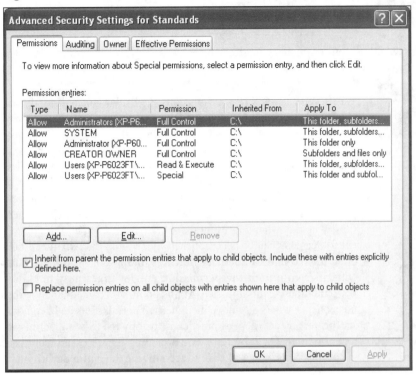

Figure 11-3 Special NTFS folder permissions

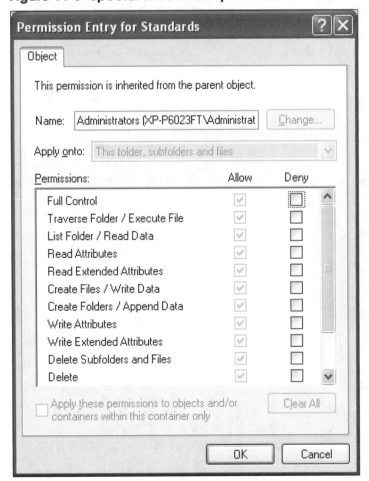

project 11.2   *Assigning NTFS Permissions*

exam objective

Monitor, manage, and troubleshoot access to files and folders. Control access to files and folders by using permissions.

overview

When you assign NTFS permissions, you must not only understand how they work when combined with other NTFS permissions, as well as how they work when combined with share permissions (**Figure 11-4**), but also how they are inherited from the parent folders. By default, whatever permissions you assign to the parent folder are inherited by the subfolders and files stored in that folder. This is true for both share permissions and NTFS permissions. You will know that an NTFS permission has been inherited if it is grayed out and inactive on the Security tab in the Properties dialog box. This indicates that there is no need to assign this permission to the subfolder or file because it has already been inherited. However, for certain files, you may want to prevent the inheritance of some of the permissions granted to the parent folder. This can be accomplished by clicking the **Advanced** button on the Security tab to open the **Advanced Security Settings** dialog box, and then removing the check from the **Inherit from parent the permission entries that apply to child objects** check box at the bottom of the **Permissions** tab. At this point, you can either copy the previously inherited permissions, or you can remove the inherited permissions and keep only those that are explicitly set for the object. The best practice is to copy the existing permissions, because then you can reconfigure the ACL by removing or adding the necessary permissions. If you remove all of the permissions, you will have to reconfigure the entire Security tab.

After you make your presentation on NTFS Permissions, Jessica meets with you and decides upon a strategy for securing the data in the Standards folder. Jessica decides that the members of her team and the team leaders only need to view the contents of the Standards folder so that they can follow the guidelines for developing software. You do this, but Jessica also tells you that clients often create additional standards that apply to their specific application. Therefore, Jessica wants to allow the Project Leader, John Simmons, to append to the standards documents in the Standards folder without granting the ability to change the contents of the folder.

tip

Remember you can assign NTFS permissions to both files and folders, unlike the shared folder permissions, which can be assigned only at the folder level.

tip

The NTFS permissions for a file or folder copied or moved from an NTFS volume to another volume that uses the FAT or FAT32 file system are lost because these file systems do not support NTFS permissions.

learning objective

After completing this project, you will know how to apply standard NTFS permissions and special access permissions.

specific requirements

◆ Administrative rights on a Windows XP Professional computer.
◆ A user account for John Simmons.
◆ A folder named Standards on an NTFS volume or partition.

estimated completion time

10 minutes

Figure 11-4 Combining shared folder permissions and NTFS permissions

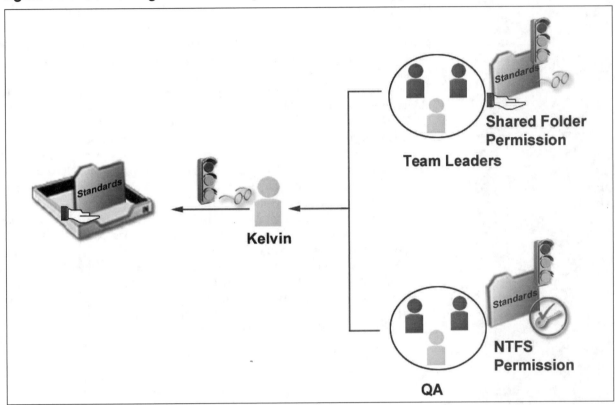

project 11.2

Assigning NTFS Permissions (cont'd)

exam objective

Monitor, manage, and troubleshoot access to files and folders. Control access to files and folders by using permissions.

project steps

Assign the Read and Write NTFS permissions to a user for accessing the Standards folder.

1. Right-click the **Standards** folder, and click the **Properties** command to open the **Standards Properties** dialog box.
2. Click the **Security** tab. (*Note*: If you are working in a workgroup and you do not see a Security tab, simple file sharing is probably enabled on your computer. In Windows Explorer, open the **Tools** menu and click **Folder Options** to open the **Folder Options** dialog box. On the **View** tab, clear the **Use simple file sharing** check box.)
3. Click **Add** to open the **Select Users or Groups** dialog box.
4. Type the user name of the user to whom you want to assign permissions in the **Enter the object names to select** text box.
5. Click **OK** to close the Select Users or Groups dialog box.
6. The user name is added to the **Group or user names** box on the Security tab. The dialog box will show **John Simmons**, the full name you used when you created the account.
7. Select **John Simmons** in the Group or user names list, and select the **Allow** check box for the **Write** permission. The Read & Execute, List Folder Contents, and Read permissions should be selected by default (**Figure 11-5**).
8. Click the **Advanced** button to open the **Advanced Security Settings for Standards** dialog box (**Figure 11-6**). Select the entry for John Simmons. Notice that this entry has not been inherited from a parent object.
9. Click **Edit**. Examine the special permissions that have been assigned. Note the value in the **Apply onto** text box. What objects will be affected by this permission?
10. Click **OK** to close the **Permission Entry for Standards** dialog box.
11. Click **OK** to close the **Advanced Security Settings for Standards** dialog box.
12. Click **OK** to close the **Standards Properties** dialog box.

tip

By default, files and folders that are contained in another folder will inherit any permissions set on the parent folder.

Figure 11-5 Adding a user to an Access Control List

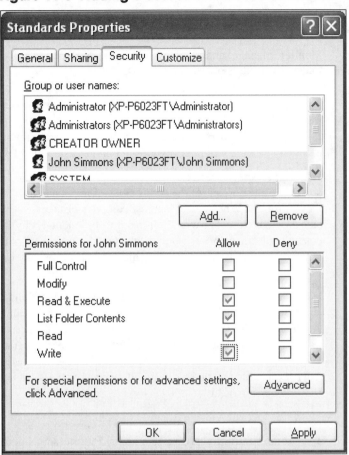

Figure 11-6 Viewing special permissions

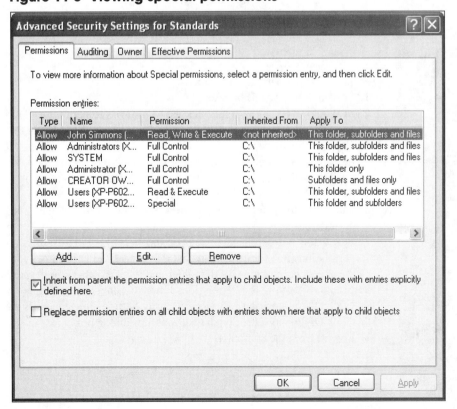

project 11.3 | *Using Special Permissions*

exam objective

Monitor, manage, and troubleshoot access to files and folders. Control access to files and folders by using permissions.

overview

As you have learned, on an NTFS volume, you can precisely control what level of access users will have to both files and folders. For most common day to day tasks, the standard NTFS permissions are sufficient. However, there are a few circumstances where it may be necessary to use special permissions to obtain the required level of control.

When a user creates a file or folder, they become the owner of that object. The owner of an object can always control the permissions of the object and can therefore manage access to it for other users. When a user leaves a company or takes on different responsibilities, the files that they have created will often need to be managed by a different user. While it is not possible for an Administrator to change the owner of a file, they can assign the **Take Ownership** permission to the file which will allow the new user to make themselves the file's owner.

Jessica has been promoted to a new position and John Simmons will take over her responsibilities. He has asked you to make it possible for him to manage access to the files in the Standards folder. You will assign him the Take Ownership special permission and then walk him through the process of becoming the owner of a file.

tip

The Take Ownership permission can be assigned only by the owner of the object, an Administrator, or a user with the Full Control permission for that object.

learning objective

After completing this project, you will know how to assign special access permissions such as Take Ownership of files.

specific requirements

◆ Administrative rights on a Windows XP Professional computer.
◆ A user account named John Simmons (The password for this account was set in project 8.4).
◆ Completion of project 11.2.

estimated completion time

15 minutes

project steps

Set special access permissions for a user.
1. Log on as the **Administrator**.
2. In Windows Explorer, right-click the **Standards** folder on the C: drive of your computer, and then click the **Properties** command to open the **Standards Properties** dialog box.
3. Click the **Security** tab.
4. Select **John Simmons** in the **Group or user names** list, and then click **Advanced** to open the **Advanced Security Settings for Standards** dialog box.
5. Select **John Simmons** in the Permission entries list on the Permission tab.
6. Click **Edit** to open the **Permission Entry for Standards** dialog box. A list of the special permissions appears.
7. Select the **Allow** check boxes for the **Change Permissions** and **Take Ownership** permissions in the **Permissions** list (**Figure 11-7**). This allows John Simmons to change the access permissions for the folder and to take ownership of the folder.
8. Click **OK** to close the Permissions Entry for Standards dialog box.
9. Click **OK** to close the Advanced Security Settings for Standards dialog box.
10. Click **OK** to close the Standards Properties dialog box.
11. Log off from the computer.

Figure 11-7 Assigning special access permissions

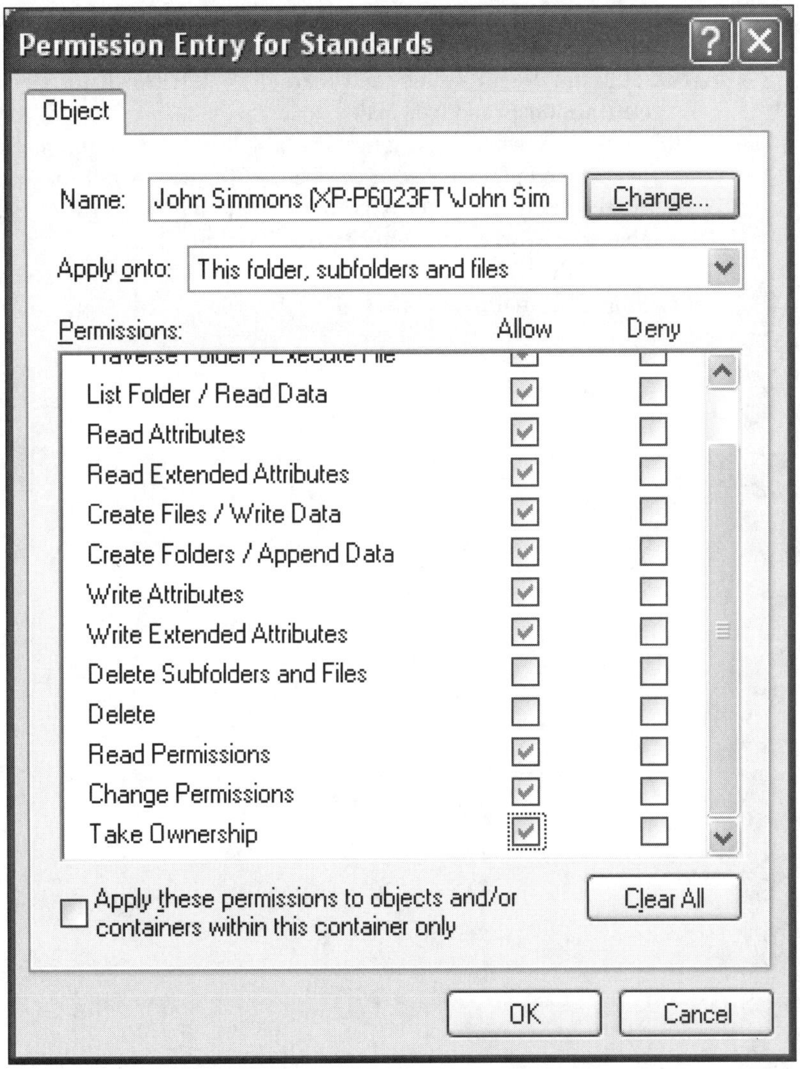

project 11.3

Using Special Permissions (cont'd)

exam objective

Monitor, manage, and troubleshoot access to files and folders. Control access to files and folders by using permissions.

project steps

Take ownership of a folder.

12. Log on as **John Simmons** using the password assigned for this account.

13. In Windows Explorer, right-click the **Standards** folder on the C: drive of your computer, and then click the **Properties** command to open the **Standards Properties** dialog box.

14. Click the **Security** tab, and then click **Advanced** to open the **Advanced Security Settings for Standards** dialog box.

15. Click the **Owner** tab (**Figure 11-8**). Select **John Simmons** from the **Change owner to** list box and place a check mark beside **Replace owner on subcontainers and objects**.

16. Click **OK** to close the **Advanced Security Settings for Standards** dialog box and change the owner of the folder to **John Simmons**.

17. Click **OK** to close the **Standards Properties** dialog box.

18. Log off from the computer.

Figure 11-8 Taking ownership of a folder

Setting group policies is another important part of your overall network security strategy. Group policies are used to manage many different settings for both computers and users, including the desktop appearance, the allocation of software applications, and password limitations. Group policies require a domain-based network that combines Windows 2000 or 2003 Servers that provide the Active Directory to Windows 2000 and XP Professional clients. Group policies can be set for sites, domains, and OUs (organizational units). In addition, local policies can be configured on each computer. Since Windows XP Professional can only be used to set up a peer-to-peer or workgroup network, when you are studying this topic, the emphasis is on setting group policies for individual computers. Group policies for local computers that do not use Active Directory are set using the Local Security Policy console and the Group Policy MMC snap-in. The Local Security Policy console includes account policies, local policies, public key policies, IP security policies, and software restriction policies.

Account policies consist of the password policy and the account lockout policy. These policies are only effective when configured locally or at the domain level. Password policies are used to implement specific rules for how all users who log on to a computer must structure their passwords, the frequency with which they must change them, and the length of time they can use their passwords before they must be changed. These policies are not set individually. They apply to all users on a local computer. Account lockout policies are used to set how many invalid logon attempts will be allowed before the account is barred from use. You can also set a specific time period during which the account will remain locked out or configure the policy so that an Administrator must unlock it.

Local policies are divided into three categories: audit policies, user rights assignments, or security options. For example, you can set a security option to prevent the name of the last user that logged on to the computer from displaying in the logon dialog box. User rights assignments prescribe what actions a user can execute. For example, the Increase quotas and Load and Unload device drivers user rights are assigned to the built-in Administrators group by default. You can add a user to this group so that they can perform these and other administrative tasks, or you can create your own groups and assign specific rights to them for interacting with the operating system.

Public key policies include the Encrypting File System (EFS) recovery policy. Files and folders are encrypted using a security algorithm and a file encryption key to change the contents into unreadable characters. Either the user who encrypted the file or a user who has been designated as the recovery agent can recover an encrypted file. When other users try to access an encrypted file, they will receive an Access Denied message.

IPSec (Internet Protocol Security) policies are used to protect data as it travels on a TCP/IP network. IPSec policies ensure the security of data packets by encrypting them before sending them to another computer on a public network.

While all of these policies can be configured individually on separate computers, Security templates can simplify the administration of your security policies. Instead of having to set many different policies on each workstation, you can use a security template to apply a group of security settings all at once. Security templates can be used in a workgroup or domain environment to ensure consistent sets of policies are applied to all applicable workstations.

Scenario

You are the Administrator of a peer-to-peer network at Tech Financials Corp., which provides financial advice to various companies. There are a large number of documents related to financial matters stored on Richard Desmond's computer. You need to safeguard his computer from security breaches.

Lesson 12   Configuring Local Security Policies

Project	Exam 70-270 Objective
12.1 Configuring Password Policy	Configure, manage, and troubleshoot account policy.
12.2 Enhancing Computer Security Using Account Lockout Policy	Configure, manage, and troubleshoot account policy.
12.3 Configuring Security Options	Configure, manage, and troubleshoot a security configuration and local security policy.
12.4 Increasing Security Using EFS (Encrypting File System)	Configure, manage, and troubleshoot Encrypting File System (EFS).
12.5 Recovering Encrypted Files Using Recovery Agents	Configure, manage, and troubleshoot Encrypting File System (EFS).
12.6 Securing Data on a Network Using IPSec Policies	Configure, manage, and troubleshoot a security configuration and local security policy.
12.7 Working with Security Templates	Configure, manage, and troubleshoot a security configuration and local security policy.

General Requirements

To complete the projects in this lesson, you will need administrative rights on a Windows XP Professional computer with an NTFS volume. You will also need a file named Wages.doc stored in the Employees folder and a file named Metadata.doc stored in the Data folder. Both folders must be saved on an NTFS volume. The exercises will assume this is the C: drive. Substitute the correct drive letter in the exercises if necessary. You will also need a file named Accountinfo that was created on the NTFS drive with a Standard or Restricted User account.

| project 12.1 | *Configuring Password Policy* |

exam objective

Configure, manage, and troubleshoot account policy.

overview

Account policies are used to set the user account properties that control the logon process. They include password policies and account lockout policies. **Password policies** are used to supplement the security of your computer by requiring users to change their passwords at specific time intervals, requiring passwords to be a certain length, and by making users keep a password history so that they cannot simply switch back and forth between two passwords. Password policies for a local computer are set on the computer itself. However, if the local computer is a member of a domain, the domain password policies will apply to the local computer. **Table 12-1** lists the password policy options that may be set.

Richard Desmond wants to set a new password policy for all users who access his computer. He wants to set a password with a minimum of 14 characters to increase the complexity of the password. You need to set up Mr. Desmond's computer so that it will not accept passwords with less than 14 characters and so that all users must change their passwords every 60 days. He also wants to ensure that recently used passwords cannot be reused.

learning objective

After completing this project, you will know how to set a password policy.

specific requirements

◆   Administrative rights on a Windows XP Professional computer.
◆   A limited user account.

estimated completion time

10 minutes

project steps

Set a password policy that requires users to set passwords with at least 14 characters.

1. Open the **Start** menu, click **All Programs**, point to **Administrative Tools**, and click **Local Security Policy** to open the **Local Security Settings** console.
2. Double-click the **Account Policies** node under the Security Settings node, then double-click the **Password Policy** node under the Account Policies node to list the password policies (**Figure 12-1**).
3. Double-click the **Minimum password length** option to open the **Minimum password length Properties** dialog box.
4. In the Local Security Policy Setting dialog box, enter **14** in the **Password must be at least** spin box to set a password policy that requires users to set passwords with at least 14 characters (**Figure 12-2**).
5. Click **OK** to save the password policy and close the **Minimum password length Properties** dialog box.

Table 12-1 Password policy options

Option	Description
Enforce password history	Used to set the number of passwords that will be stored in a password history. You can store up to 24 old passwords to prevent users from repeating old passwords.
Maximum password age	Used to set the maximum number of days users can keep a particular password. This can range from a value of 0 which indicates that a password will never expire, to a maximum of 999 days.
Minimum password age	Used to set the minimum number of days during which users must keep the same password. This is often set to a value a little less than the Maximum password age to prevent a user from defeating the password history by cycling through a number of passwords to reuse a 'favorite' password.
Minimum password length	Used to set the minimum number of characters a password must have. You can set the minimum password length as high as 14 characters.

Passwords must meet complexity requirements	Disabled by default, should be enabled when you want to require users to select secure passwords. The restrictions that are enforced by this setting are listed below:
	• Passwords must be at least 6 characters in length.
	• Passwords must contain characters from three of the following four categories:
	   • English uppercase characters (A through Z)
	   • English lowercase characters (a through z)
	   • Base 10 digits (0 through 9)
	   • Non-alphanumeric characters (e.g., !, $, #, %)
	• Passwords can not contain all or part of the user's account name.

Store password using reversible encryption for all users in the domain	Used to store a reversibly encrypted password for all users. This policy should only be enabled if support is required for applications that use protocols that need to use the user's password for authentication. It is basically the same as storing plaintext versions of passwords. It should not be enabled unless application requirements are more important than password protection.

Figure 12-1 Managing Password Policies

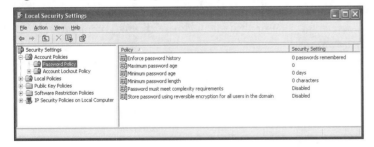

Figure 12-2 The Minimum password length Properties dialog box

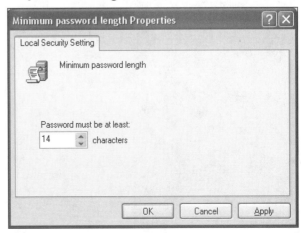

project 12.1

Configuring Password Policy (cont'd)

exam objective

Configure, manage, and troubleshoot account policy.

project steps

6. Double-click **Enforce password history**. Enter **15** in the **Keep password history for** spin box (**Figure 12-3**).
7. Click **OK** to save the password policy and to close the Enforce password history Properties dialog box.
8. Double-click **Minimum password age**. Enter **20** in the **Password can be changed after** spin box.
9. Click **OK** to save the password policy and to close the Minimum password age Properties dialog box.
10. Double-click **Maximum password age**. Enter **60** in the **Passwords will expire in** spin box (**Figure 12-4**).
11. Click **OK** to save the password policy and to close the Maximum password age Properties dialog box. The policies will take effect when you close the console and save the settings.
12. Close the **Local Security Policy** console.
13. Log off from the computer and log on as a normal Limited user.
14. Open the **Control Panel** and if **Category view** is the current view, click the **User Accounts** link, otherwise if the current view is **Classic View** double-click the **User Accounts** icon.
15. Click **Change my password** in the **Pick a Task** window (**Figure 12-5**).
16. The **Change your password** window will open (**Figure 12-6**). Type the user's current password in the first text box. Type **Short#1** in the **Type a new password** input box and also in the password confirmation box.
17. Click **Change Password**. Because the password that was entered did not meet the minimum requirements that were set in the password policy, the error message box shown in **Figure 12-7** appears.
18. Click **OK** to acknowledge the message and return focus to the **Create a password for your account** window.
19. Type **14LetterPasswd** in both password input boxes and click **Create Password**.
20. Close the **Pick a Task** screen for the user account and log off from the computer.
21. Close the Control Panel window.

caution

If the user account has a blank password, the dialog boxes will be different than shown here.

Figure 12-3 The Enforce password history Properties dialog box

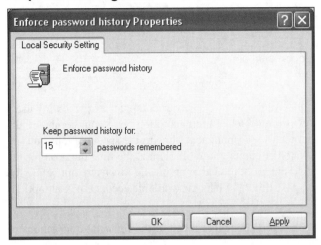

Figure 12-4 The Maximum password age Properties dialog box

Figure 12-5 The Pick a Task user account window

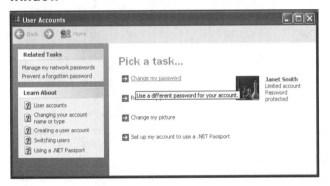

Figure 12-6 The Change your password window

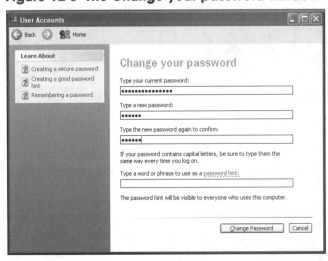

Figure 12-7 The password does not meet policy requirements error message

project 12.2

Enhancing Computer Security Using Account Lockout Policy

exam objective

Configure, manage, and troubleshoot account policy.

overview

Account lockout policy is used to enhance the security of your computer by preventing users from trying to guess passwords. If a user repeatedly attempts to log on to your computer, the computer can automatically lock out the user account according to the specifications you set. You can set the number of invalid logon attempts you will tolerate, the time duration for the account lockout, and the time duration that must pass after an invalid logon attempt before the bad logon attempt counter is reset to 0. **Table 12-2** lists the available account lockout options and their usage.

Richard Desmond has highly confidential documents related to the financial transactions of the company stored on his computer. To ensure the security of these documents, he wants to make sure that unauthorized users will have great difficulty attempting to logon. He wants you to set a security policy that will lock out accounts after two invalid logon attempts and that will only allow an Administrator to unlock them.

learning objective

After completing this project, you will know how to set an account lockout policy.

specific requirements

◆ Administrative rights on a Windows XP Professional computer.

estimated completion time

10 minutes

project steps

Set an account lockout policy so that a user account is locked out after three invalid logon attempts.

1. Open the **Local Security Policy** console.
2. Double-click the **Account Policies** node under the Security Settings node, and then double-click the **Account Lockout Policy** node under the **Account Policies** node. The account lockout policies are listed in the right pane of the window.
3. Double-click the **Account lockout threshold** option in the Policy heading in the right pane of the window to open the **Account lockout threshold Properties** dialog box.
4. Type **3** in the **Account will lock out after** spin box to specify that the account should be locked after three invalid logon attempts (**Figure 12-8**).
5. Click **OK** to open the **Suggested Value Changes** dialog box (**Figure 12-9**). The Suggested Value Changes window shows the suggested values for the **Account lockout duration** and **Reset account lockout counter after** policies.
6. Click **OK** to apply the settings, and close the Suggested Value Changes and Account lockout threshold Properties dialog boxes.
7. Close the **Local Security Policy** console.

tip

The Suggested Value Changes window appears each time the Account lockout duration is changed to or from zero[0]. It will also appear when the Account lockout duration is set to a number lower than the Reset lockout counter after value, or when the Account duration or Reset lockout duration after value is changed from Not Defined.

Table 12-2 Account lockout options

Option	Description
Account lockout duration	Used to set the time duration (minutes from 0 to 99,999) during which you want the account to be disabled after the Account lockout threshold has been exceeded. You can set the value to 0 to lock the account indefinitely until the Administrator unlocks it.
Account lockout threshold	Specifies the number of invalid logon attempts a user can make, after which the account will be locked and the user will be prevented from making further logon attempts. The default value for this option is 0, meaning that the account will never be locked no matter how many invalid logon attempts are made. You can set the account lockout threshold between 0 and 999. A common range for this value is between 3 and 5.
Reset account lockout counter after	Sets the time duration that must elapse after an invalid logon attempt before the account lockout counter is reset to 0. You can reset the bad logon attempt counter between 1 and 99,999 minutes. This value prevents occasional failed logon attempts from causing an unnecessary account lockout.

Figure 12-8 The Account lockout threshold Properties dialog box

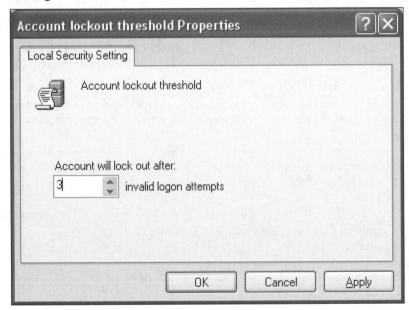

Figure 12-9 The Suggested Value Changes dialog box

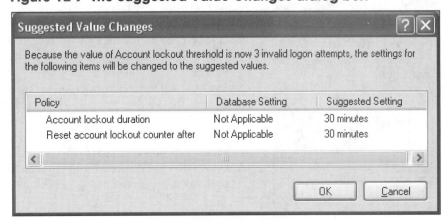

<table>
<tr><td>

project 12.3

</td><td>

Configuring Security Options

</td></tr>
<tr><td>

exam objective

</td><td>

Configure, manage, and troubleshoot a security configuration and local security policy.

</td></tr>
<tr><td>

overview

</td><td>

There are many security options you can configure to further enhance the security of your computer.

The **Security Options** node, which is found under the **Local Policies** node in the Local Security Settings console, is used to set about 60 types of security options for your computer (**Figure 12-10**). You can set restrictions such as denying unknown connections to your computer, logging off users when the logon time expires, and prompting users to change passwords before the password expires.

The **User Rights Assignment** node is used to specify what actions specified groups are able to perform on the system (**Figure 12-11**). You can control actions like who can log on locally to the system, perform a shutdown, backup and restore files, and change the system time. Built-in groups gain many of their characteristics from the rights that are assigned to them by default in User Rights Assignment.

Due to the highly confidential nature of some of Mr. Desmond's files, his computer needs to be further protected from users who might attempt to hack into it. By default, the last user name that signed on to the computer will display in the Windows Security or Log On to Windows dialog box. This will allow an unauthorized user to see a valid user account name on the screen so that all he or she will have to do is attempt to guess the password. You plan to set a security option policy so that the last user name will not display in the logon dialog box.

You have also learned that there are utilities that will allow a person to read files from an NTFS partition without any security restrictions. These tools work outside of the Windows XP Professional operating system and so you have decided to prevent regular users from shutting down the system.

</td></tr>
<tr><td>

caution

By default, Windows XP Professional does not require users to log on in order to shut down the computer. You must open the Shutdown: Allow system to be shut down without having to log on Properties dialog box for this policy, and select the Disabled option button to prevent unauthorized users from shutting down the system.

</td><td></td></tr>
<tr><td>

learning objective

</td><td>

After completing this project, you will know how to set a security option policy so that the last user name will not appear in the Windows Security or Log On to Windows dialog box.

</td></tr>
<tr><td>

specific requirements

</td><td>

◆ Administrative rights on a Windows XP Professional computer.
◆ A limited user account.

</td></tr>
<tr><td>

estimated completion time

</td><td>

15 minutes

</td></tr>
<tr><td>

project steps

</td><td>

Set the **Do not display last user name in logon screen** security option.
1. Open the **Local Security Policy** console, if necessary.
2. Double-click the **Local Policies** node under the Security Settings node. Then, double-click the **Security Options** node to display the security options in the right pane of the window.
3. Double-click the option **Interactive logon: Do not display last user name** in the right pane of the window, to open the **Interactive logon: Do not display last user name Properties** dialog box.
4. Click the **Enabled** option button to program the computer not to display the last user name on the logon screen (**Figure 12-12**).
5. Click **OK** to set the security option and close the **Interactive logon: Do not display last user name Properties** dialog box.

</td></tr>
</table>

Figure 12-10 Security options

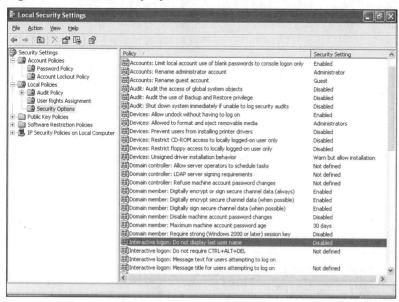

Figure 12-11 User Rights Assignment options

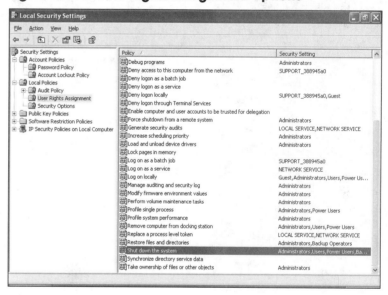

Figure 12-12 The Interactive logon: Do not display last user name Properties dialog box

project 12.3

Configuring Security Options (cont'd)

exam objective

Configure, manage, and troubleshoot a security configuration and local security policy.

project steps

Force authorized users to log on to be able to shut down the system and disable shutdown for the **Users** group.

6. Double-click **Shutdown: Allow system to be shutdown without having to log on** in the right hand pane.

7. The **Properties** dialog box for this option will open. Select **Disabled** to ensure that the system cannot be shutdown unless a user logs on first (**Figure 12-13**).

8. Click **OK** to save the setting.

9. Expand the **User Rights Assignment** node and double-click **Shut down the system** (**Figure 12-11**).

10. The **Shut down the system Properties** box will open (**Figure 12-14**). Select the **Users** group from the list and click **Remove**.

11. Click **OK** to save the changes and then close the **Local Security Policy** console.

12. Log off from the computer. Notice that the **Shutdown** command no longer appears on the **Welcome to Windows** screen.

13. Log on as a limited user. Notice that the **Shutdown** command is missing from the **Start** menu.

14. Log off from the computer.

15. Log on as the **Administrator**. Notice that the **Shutdown** command appears on the **Start** menu.

tip

Certain rights are granted to particular groups by default, but no rights are granted explicitly to any particular user account.

Figure 12-13 Forcing users to log on before shutting down the system

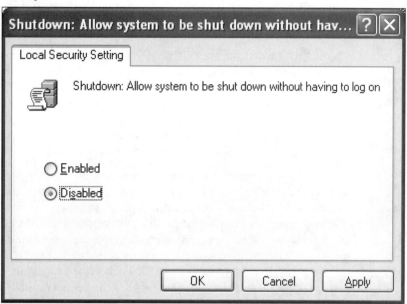

Figure 12-14 Preventing the Users group from performing a shutdown

| project 12.4 | *Increasing Security Using EFS (Encrypting File System)* |

exam objective

Configure, manage, and troubleshoot Encrypting File System (EFS).

overview

As you have learned, the most effective way to protect local resources is to use NTFS permissions. However, NTFS permissions can be bypassed if the computer is started with an alternate operating system such as DOS, and then a utility such as NTFSDOS is used to read the files on the drive. In organizations where security is of primary concern, the Encrypting File System (EFS) can be used to rule out this possibility. Using EFS, files stored on NTFS partitions can be encrypted so that they are only readable for users with the decryption key. Other users will not be able to access the encrypted files even if they have access to your computer.

When a file is encrypted with EFS, the file's contents are encrypted using a **File Encryption Key (FEK)**. This key is based on a symmetric algorithm where the same key used to encrypt the data is also used to decrypt the data. In order to protect the FEK from unauthorized access that would result in compromise of the encrypted file's data, the FEK is itself encrypted. The asymmetric algorithm used is based on a cryptographic key pair that consists of a public key and a private key. When data is encrypted using one of the keys, it can only be decrypted using the other key in the key pair. The FEK is encrypted using the user's public key and the resulting cipher is stored with the encrypted file in a header called the **Data Decryption Field (DDF)**. Because only the user has a copy of their private key, only they can decrypt the DDF to obtain the FEK which is then used to decrypt the file's contents. In Windows XP Professional, it is possible for multiple DDFs to be associated with an encrypted file, which allows shared access to the file. All authorized access to an encrypted file is handled by NTFS and is completely transparent to the user.

In order to provide a 'back door' to prevent loss of data if the user who encrypted a file deletes his or her certificate, or has his or her user account deleted, another user, who is designated as the recovery agent, can open the file. While previous versions of EFS required a recovery agent to be defined, Windows XP Professional does not. It is suggested, however, that a separate account be created only for use as the data recovery agent. The public key for the data recovery agent is used to encrypt the FEK and is stored in a file header named the **Data Recovery Field**.

Richard Desmond wants to make sure that users who access his computer cannot view the confidential financial data on his computer. He asks you for suggestions and you tell him that the best method is to encrypt the folder and its files.

tip

EFS is most applicable for systems that cannot be physically protected from unauthorized access like notebook computers.

caution

While EFS does protect the security of your data, it also poses a risk. If all private keys associated with an encrypted file are lost, the data will be virtually unrecoverable.

tip

Once a file is encrypted, it will remain encrypted even if it is moved or copied as long as it remains on an NTFS volume.

learning objective

After completing this project, you will know how to encrypt files in a folder using EFS from Windows Explorer.

specific requirements

◆ Administrative rights on a Windows XP Professional computer.
◆ A folder named Data containing a file named Metadata.doc.

estimated completion time

15 minutes

project steps

Encrypt a folder.
1. Right-click **Start** and click **Explore** to open Windows Explorer.
2. Locate and then double-click the **Data** folder to open it. The **Metadata.doc** file appears.
3. Right-click the **Metadata.doc** file and click **Properties** to open the **Metadata.doc Properties** dialog box (**Figure 12-15**).

Figure 12-15 The Properties dialog box for the Metadata file

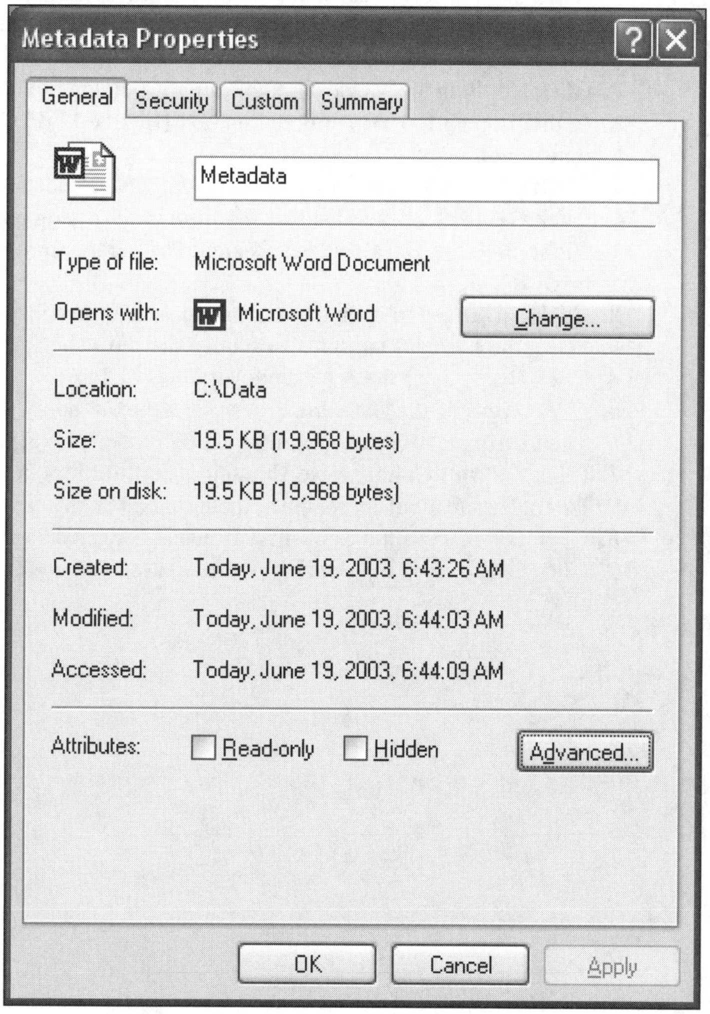

project 12.4

Increasing Security Using EFS (Encrypting File System) (cont'd)

exam objective

Configure, manage, and troubleshoot Encrypting File System (EFS).

project steps

tip

If you are encrypting a folder that contains subfolders or files, the Confirm Attribute Changes dialog box informs you that you are about to encrypt a folder. Click the appropriate option button to encrypt only the selected folder or all subfolders and files in the folder. All new files that are added to an encrypted parent folder are automatically encrypted.

tip

Encrypted files appear in green by default in windows explorer.

4. Click **Advanced** to open the **Advanced Attributes** dialog box. In this dialog box, you can set the encryption attribute for the Metadata.doc file.
5. Select the **Encrypt contents to secure data** check box to encrypt the contents of the **metadata.doc** file (**Figure 12-16**). Note that if you select this check box, you cannot select the **Compress contents to save disk space** check box to compress the data in the file. An encrypted file cannot be compressed, nor can a compressed file be encrypted.
6. Click **OK** to close the **Advanced Attributes** dialog box.
7. Click **Apply** in the Metadata.doc Properties dialog box to apply the attribute.
8. In the **Encryption Warning** dialog box (**Figure 12-17**), click the **Encrypt the file only** option button.
9. Click **OK** to close the Encryption Warning dialog box.
10. Click **OK** to close the Metadata.doc Properties dialog box.
11. Right-click the **Data** folder and click **Properties** to open the **Data Properties** dialog box.
12. Click **Advanced** to open the **Advanced Attributes** dialog box.
13. Select the **Encrypt contents to secure the data** check box.
14. Click **OK** to close the Advanced Attributes dialog box.
15. Click **Apply** in the Data Properties dialog box to apply the encryption attribute.
16. The **Confirm Attribute Changes** dialog box opens (**Figure 12-18**).
17. Click the **Apply changes to this folder**, **subfolders**, **and files** option button to encrypt the folder and all of its contents, including all subfolders and files.
18. Click **OK** to close the Confirm Attribute Changes dialog box.
19. Click **OK** to close the Data Properties dialog box, and then close Windows Explorer.

Figure 12-16 Encrypting a file

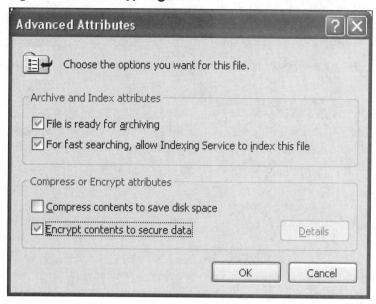

Figure 12-17 The Encryption Warning dialog box

Figure 12-18 The Confirm Attribute Changes dialog box

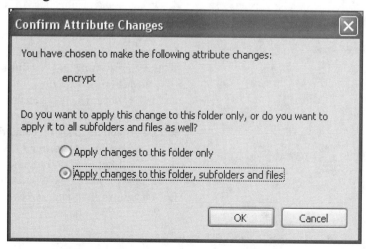

project 12.5

Recovering Encrypted Files Using Recovery Agents

exam objective

Configure, manage, and troubleshoot Encrypting File System (EFS).

overview

Files encrypted using EFS can only be opened and used by the user who encrypted them, other users that have been granted permission to share access to the encrypted file, or by an account that has been designated as the **recovery agent**.

The recovery agent has a file recovery certificate, which is used to decrypt the **Data Recovery Field (DRF)** to access the FEK for the file. If your Windows XP Professional is a standalone computer, or is in a workgroup, you should create a recovery agent for the machine. In a domain environment, a single domain account is normally designated as the recovery agent for all machines in the domain.

Sara, Richard Desmond's assistant at Techno Financials Inc., is on a vacation. An important file that she maintains urgently needs to be sent to a client. Sara has used EFS to encrypt the file. You need to recover the encrypted file. As the Administrator of the local PC, you have been configured as the recovery agent.

tip

It is best to assign a recovery agent before any files are encrypted. Files encrypted prior to the definition of the recovery agent will not be accessible by the recovery agent.

learning objective

After completing this project, you will know how to recover an encrypted file.

specific requirements

- Administrative rights on a Windows XP Professional computer.
- A user account named **user1** and another named **user2**.

estimated completion time

15 minutes

project steps

Recover a file.
1. Log on to your computer as **user1** (or any other standard or restricted user account you have created on your computer). Create and save a file named **Accountinfo** on the C: drive of the computer (this must be an NTFS disk). Encrypt the file.
2. Log off and log back on as **user2** (or any other standard or restricted user account you have created on the computer).
3. Open **Windows Explorer**. Double-click **My Computer**. Double-click the **C:** drive in the contents window. Locate the **Accountinfo** file. Right-click **Accountinfo** and click **Properties**.
4. On the **General** tab, click **Advanced** to open the **Advanced Attributes** dialog box. Clear the check from the **Encrypt contents to secure data** check box in the **Compress or Encrypt attributes** section. Click **OK**.
5. Click **OK** to close the Accountinfo Properties dialog box.
6. The **Error Applying Attributes** dialog box opens to inform you that access has been denied **(Figure 12-19)**.
7. Click **Ignore**. The Advanced Attributes dialog box and the Accountinfo Properties dialog box both automatically close. Close Windows Explorer.
8. Log off and log back on using the local Administrator account.
9. Open the command prompt and type: **cipher /r:filename**.
10. You will be prompted to enter a password to protect the two files that are going to be generated. Enter a password and press **[Enter]**.
11. You will be prompted to reenter the password. Reenter the password and press **[Enter]**.

tip

If you are not the owner of an encrypted file, the designated recovery agent, or have not been granted permission to share the encrypted file, you will receive the message shown in **Figure 12-20** when you attempt to open the file.

Figure 12-19 The Error Applying Attributes dialog box

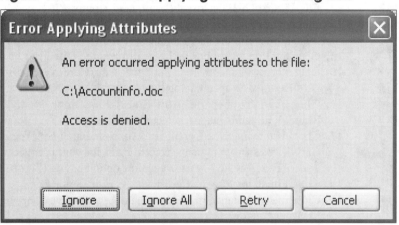

Figure 12-20 User does not have access privileges message

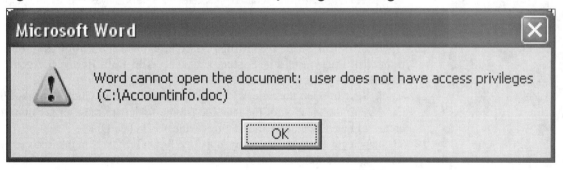

project 12.5

Recovering Encrypted Files Using Recovery Agents *(cont'd)*

exam objective

Configure, manage, and troubleshoot Encrypting File System (EFS).

project steps

12. A message displays to confirm that two files have been created, a .CER file and a .PFX file (**Figure 12-21**). Close the command prompt.
13. If you do not want the local Administrator account to be the recovery agent, log off and log back on with the user account you want to be the recovery agent.
14. Open the Run dialog box and type **mmc** in the **Open** text box.
15. Open the **File** menu and click the **Add/Remove Snap-in** command to open the **Add/Remove Snap-in** dialog box.
16. Click **Add** to open the **Add Standalone Snap-in** dialog box. In the **Available Standalone Snap-ins** list, select **Certificates**.
17. Click **Add** to open the **Certificates snap-in** dialog box. You can create an MMC with the Certificates snap-in to manage certificates for your user account, for the computer, or for a service. Select the **My user account** option button (**Figure 12-22**).
18. Click **Finish** to close the Certificates snap-in dialog box.
19. Close the Add Standalone Snap-in and Add/Remove Snap-in dialog boxes. Save the new MMC as **Certificates**.
20. Expand the **Certificates - Current User** node. Right-click **Personal**, point to **All Tasks**, and select **Import** to start the **Certificate Import Wizard**.
21. Click **Next** to open the **File to Import** screen. Enter the path to the **.pfx** file. The two files were saved by default in the Documents and Settings folder for the user account you used when you ran the cipher /r: command.
22. Click **Next** to open the **Password** screen. Enter the password you created to secure the two files and click **Next**.
23. On the **Certificate Store** screen, select the **Automatically select the certificate store based on the type of certificate** option button (**Figure 12-23**).
24. Click **Next** to open the Completing the Certificate Import Wizard screen. Click **Finish**. The **Certificate Import Wizard** message: The import was successful displays. Click **OK**.
25. Close the Certificates console and save the settings.
26. Open the **Local Security Settings** console, expand the **Public Key Policies** node, right-click **Encrypting File System** and select **Add Data Recovery Agent** to start the **Add Recovery Agent Wizard**.
27. Click **Next** to open the **Select Recovery Agents** screen. Click **Browse Folders** and navigate to the location of the **.cer** file (in the folder for the user account you used to create it in the Documents and Settings folder) and click **Open**.
28. The new recovery agent is displayed as USER_UNKNOWN in the Recovery Agents list box (**Figure 12-24**).
29. Click **Next** to open the **Completing the Add Recovery Agent Wizard** screen and click **Finish**. The user account you used to log on has now been designated as the recovery agent for all encrypted files on the computer. Close the Local Security Settings console.
30. To recover the **Accountinfo** file, you would open the **Accountinfo Properties** dialog box, click **Advanced** to open the **Advanced Attributes** dialog box and remove the check from the **Encrypt data to secure contents** check box, and click **OK**. However, it should be noted that a recovery agent that is added to the local security policy only has access to files that are encrypted after the agent is added. If you are the recovery agent and did not have access to the encrypted file before, you are still not going to have access unless you encrypt it again after having added the recovery agent.

tip

If you use the Browse option to locate the .pfx file, you will need to change the setting in the Files of type drop-down list box to Personal Information Exchange (*.pfx, *.p12) in order to find the file.

Figure 12-21 Using the cipher command to create a .CER file and a .PFX file

Figure 12-22 Creating the Certificates MMC to manage the certificates for the user account

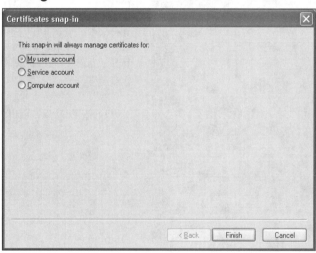

Figure 12-23 The Certificate Import Wizard

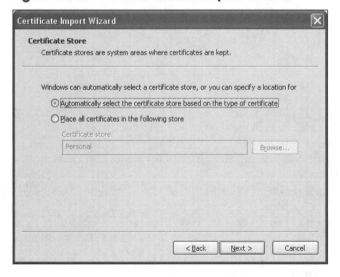

Figure 12-24 The Select Recovery Agents screen in the Add Recovery Agent Wizard

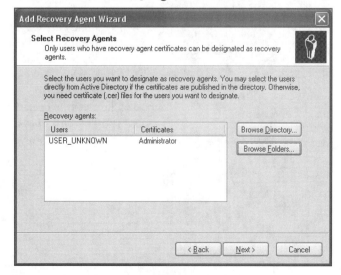

project 12.6	*Securing Data on a Network Using IPSec Policies*

exam objective	Configure, manage, and troubleshoot a security configuration and local security policy.

overview

tip

The default policy options are designed to operate in an Active Directory domain environment because they are configured to use Kerberos for authentication.

Internet Protocol Security (IPSec) policy settings are used to protect confidential data transmitted on a network. Data packets are encrypted before they are sent to a destination computer in order to make sure that they are secure and cannot be intercepted, stolen, or modified in transit. IPSec policies are only available on a **Transmission Control Protocol/Internet Protocol (TCP/IP)** network.

The three default IPSec policy options you can choose from are listed in **Table 12-3**. While additional policies can be created, and the default policies can also be modified, only a single policy can be assigned or in use on a computer at a time.

Richard Desmond needs to transfer certain files from his computer to other computers on the network. The files are encrypted on an NTFS volume using EFS but he has learned that when a file is sent across the network, it is decrypted by EFS, transmitted and then, if appropriate, re-encrypted again by the destination file system. He is concerned that his confidential files could be intercepted as they are transmitted and thus compromised. You decide to set an IPSec policy to enable secure communications between his computer and the others on the network.

learning objective

After completing this project, you will know how to add a new IP Security policy setting.

specific requirements

◆ Administrative rights on a Windows XP Professional computer that is connected to a domain-based network.

estimated completion time

20 minutes

project steps

Assign the **Client (Respond Only)** IPSec policy and add a new security rule to the policy.
1. Open the **Local Security Policy** console.
2. Double-click the **IP Security Policies on Local Computer** node. The IPSec policy options appear in the details pane.
3. Right-click the **Client (Respond Only)** policy option and click **Assign** to assign the policy (**Figure 12-25**).
4. Right-click the **Client (Respond Only)** policy and click **Properties** to open the **Client (Respond Only) Properties** dialog box. You can also open the Client (Respond Only) Properties dialog box by double-clicking the Client (Respond Only) policy option.
5. Click **Add** to initiate the **Security Rule Wizard (Figure 12-26)**. The Security Rule Wizard is used to add a new IP security rule.
6. Click **Next** to open the **Tunnel Endpoint** screen.
7. The **This rule does not specify a tunnel** option button is selected by default. Click **Next** to open the **Network Type** screen.

tip

The IP Security Monitor snap-in reports statistics and allows monitoring of IPSec activity.

Table 12-3 *Default IPSec policy options*

Option	Description
Client (Respond Only)	Sent packets are encrypted only if the server requests encryption, otherwise unencrypted communications will occur.
Server (Request Security)	Attempts secure communication by requesting client computers to encrypt sent packets. If the client will not use encryption, unencrypted communications will occur.
Secure Server (Require Security)	All packets must be encrypted or no communication will occur.

Figure 12-25 Assigning the Client (Respond Only) IPSec policy

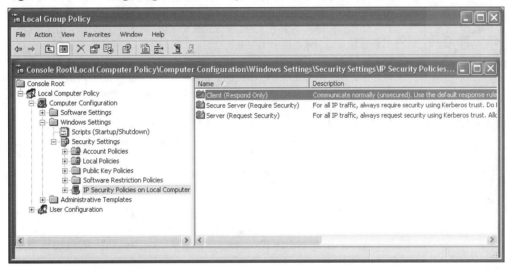

Figure 12-26 The Client (Respond Only) Properties dialog box

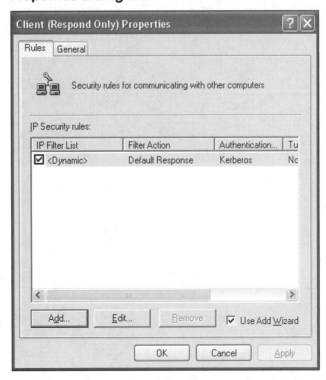

project 12.6

Securing Data on a Network Using IPSec Policies (cont'd)

exam objective

Configure, manage, and troubleshoot a security configuration and local security policy.

project steps

8. In the **Select the network type:** section, click the **Local area network (LAN)** option button to apply the security rule to computers on the local area network (LAN) only **(Figure 12-27)**.

9. Click **Next** to open the **Authentication Method** screen.

10. The **Active Directory default (Kerberos V5 protocol)** option button is selected by default. Click Next to open the **IP Filter List** screen.

11. In the **IP filter lists:** section, click the **All IP Traffic** option button to apply the security rule to all IP traffic. The IP filter list shows the list of IP traffic, such as all ICMP (Internet Control Message Protocol) or all IP traffic. The IP security rule applies to the IP traffic that is selected on the IP filter list.

12. Click **Next** to open the **Filter Action** screen.

13. Click the **Request Security (Optional)** option in the **Filter Actions** section **(Figure 12-28)** to provide secure communication by requesting security from clients.

14. Click **Next** to move to the last screen of the Security Rule Wizard.

15. Click **Finish** to save the settings and exit the Security Rule Wizard.

16. Click **Apply** to apply the rule. Click **OK** to close the Client (Respond Only) Properties dialog box.

17. Close the **Local Security Policy** console.

Additional exercises:

1. If possible, repeat all project steps on a second Windows XP Computer in the domain.

2. Use the ping command to send packets between the two computers.

3. Use the IP Security Monitor snap-in to confirm that the IPSec connection has been established.

caution

Kerberos is only used for network authentication on a domain-based network. If you are on a workgroup network, a Warning dialog box to this effect will open. Click Yes to continue and save the rule properties. You will have to remove the rule after you complete the exercise.

Figure 12-27 The Network Type screen in the Security Rule Wizard

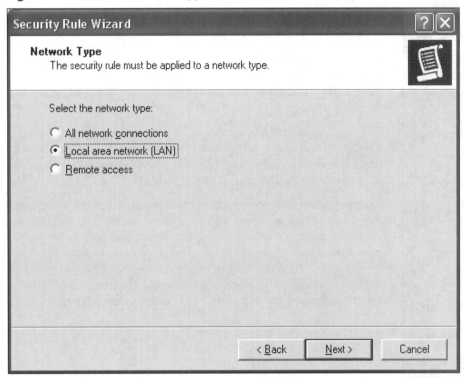

Figure 12-28 The Filter Action screen in the Security Rule Wizard

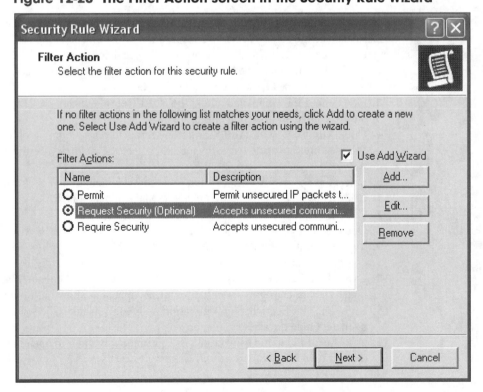

project 12.7

Working with Security Templates

exam objective

Configure, manage, and troubleshoot a security configuration and local security policy.

overview

Security templates are valuable because rather than configuring your local security policies and local group policies one by one, you can use a security template to apply a set of standardized security configuration settings all at once. You can create a custom MMC with the **Security Templates** and **Security Configuration and Analysis** snap-ins to provide a centralized tool for the management of Security Templates.

tip

To force an immediate update of local or group policies that apply to a computer, execute the **gpupdate** command.

Security Templates can be applied to a standalone or workgroup computer using the **Security Configuration and Analysis** snap-in or by using the command line **Secedit** utility. In a domain environment, Security Templates can be imported into a group policy that is applied to computers at the site, domain or OU level.

You plan to increase the security on the computers that you administer by creating a security template and then applying it to all of the computers. To begin, you plan to compare the current security settings on a computer with a pre-defined Security Template provided by Microsoft.

learning objective

In this project you will learn how to use the Security Templates snap-in and the Security Configuration and Analysis snap-in to manage Security Templates.

specific requirements

◆   Administrative rights on a Windows XP Professional computer.

estimated completion time

25 minutes

project steps

Create a custom Security Templates console and use the Security and Configuration Analysis tool to analyze the current security configuration of the local computer. Customize one of the predefined security templates and apply it to the local computer.

1. Click **Start** and click the **Run** command to open the **Run** dialog box.
2. Type **mmc** in the **Open** text box and click **OK** to open the **Console Root** window.
3. Open the **File** menu and click the **Add/Remove Snap-in** command to open the **Add/Remove Snap-in** dialog box.
4. Click **Add** to open the **Add Standalone Snap-in** dialog box. Scroll down the **Available Standalone Snap-ins** list to locate and select the **Security Templates** snap-in. Click **Add**.
5. Select the **Security Configuration and Analysis** snap-in and click **Add**.
6. Click **Close** to close the Add Standalone Snap-in dialog box.
7. Click **OK** to close the Add/Remove Snap-in dialog box.
8. Open the **File** menu and click the **Save** command to open the **Save As** dialog box.
9. Type **Security Templates** in the **File name** text box and click **Save**. By default, the console will be saved in the Administrative Tools folder.
10. Expand the **Security Templates** node. Expand the **%systemroot%\security\templates** node. The pre-configured security templates appear as shown in **Figure 12-29**.
11. Right-click the **Security Configuration and Analysis** node and select **Open database** to open the **Open database** dialog box.
12. Type **Local PC** in the **File name** text box and click **Open** to open the **Import Template** dialog box.

Figure 12-29 The predefined security templates

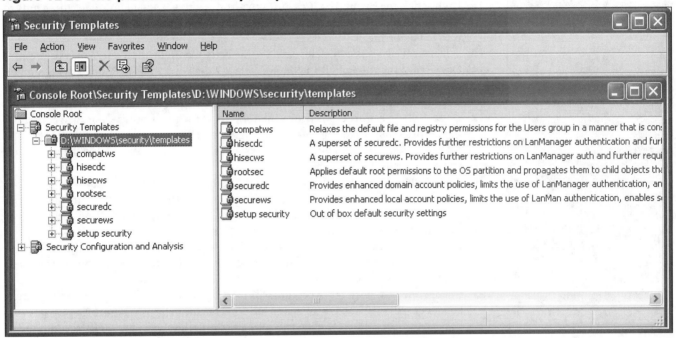

project 12.7	*Working with Security Templates*
	(cont'd)

exam objective

Configure, manage, and troubleshoot a security configuration and local security policy.

project steps

13. Select **securews.inf** in the contents window and click **Open** to open the template for a high-security workstation.
14. Right-click the **Security and Configuration Analysis** node and select the **Analyze Computer Now** command. Click **OK** in the **Perform Analysis** dialog box to confirm the path to the log file.
15. When the analysis is complete, open the **Security Configuration and Analysis** node.
16. Open the **Account Policies** node and select **Password Policy**. Policies with a green check mark indicate that the local computer policy meets the requirements for a high security workstation. Policies with a red X do not (**Figure 12-30**).
17. Double-click **Enforce password history** to open the **Enforce password history Properties** dialog box. The current setting is for 15 passwords to be remembered. The database setting for a high-security workstation is 24. Click **OK** to close the dialog box and maintain the setting in the database.
18. Double-click **Minimum password length**. In the **Password must be at least** spin box, enter 14 to make the policy setting in the database match the current computer setting (**Figure 12-31**). Click **OK**. Note that there are four password policies on the computer that still do not match the database setting.
19. Click the **Account Lockout Policy** node. Double-click **Account lockout threshold**.
20. Note that the current computer setting allows 3 invalid logon attempts, while the database setting for a high-security workstation allows 5 invalid logon attempts.
21. Change the setting in the **Account will lock out after** spin box to match the current computer setting. Click **OK** to define the policy in the database (**Figure 12-32**).
22. Expand the **Local Policies** node and select **Audit Policy**. Open the **Audit account logon events Properties** dialog box. Remove the check mark from the **Define this policy in the database** check box, and click **OK** to remove this policy setting from the database. You will be configuring this audit policy in the next lesson.
23. Select the **Security Options** node. Double-click **Interactive logon: Do not display last user name in logon dialog box**. Click the **Enabled** option button and click **OK** to define this policy in the database. Note that there are a number of security options that do not meet the requirements for a high-security workstation.
24. Right-click the **Security Configuration and Analysis** node and select the **Configure Computer Now** command. In the **Configure System** dialog box, click **OK** to confirm the path to the log file. The system is configured with the custom template you designed in the exercise.
25. Right-click the **Security and Configuration Analysis** node and select the **Analyze Computer Now** command. Click **OK** in the **Perform Analysis** dialog box to confirm the path to the log file. You will now be able to view the information in the database and compare it with the new computer settings.
26. Expand the **Account Policies** node and select **Password Policy**. Notice that now the current computer settings match the database settings for all of the password policies (**Figure 12-33**).
27. Expand the **Local Policies** node and select **Security Options**. Note that all of the computer settings now match the database settings for the custom high-security workstation template you designed in the exercise.
28. Close the Security Templates console and save the console settings.

Figure 12-30 Performing a security analysis

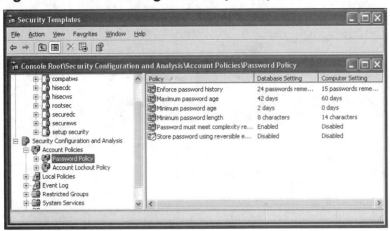

Figure 12-31 The Minimum password length Properties dialog box

Figure 12-32 The Account lockout threshold Properties dialog box

Figure 12-33 Password policies configured using the custom security template

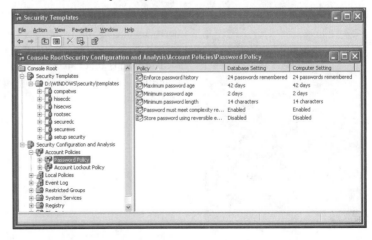

13 Monitoring Events and Resources

A Network Administrator's job includes making sure that the computers on the network function optimally, that resources are secure, that the proper people are accessing the correct resources, and that users who should not be accessing resources are not doing so. Auditing is used to observe and record the events that occur on the network, including logons—both successful and unsuccessful—and access to files, folders, the Registry, and printers. These events are recorded in the Security event log, which you can view using the Event Viewer snap-in in the Computer Management console. These tools are used to keep Administrators informed of such occurrences as a user who is attempting to access a computer by repeatedly guessing account names and/or passwords, users who are accessing files at unusual times of the day, and users who are accessing resources that they should not have access to.

Auditing does not take place automatically. You must configure a local security policy to track the events that you think are important, given your environment and the specifics of your situation. Then, you must decide whether you want to track the success or failure of the events. The events you choose will be recorded in the Security event log. The entries in the log will identify the events that are occurring, the users who are performing the actions, and the success or failure, or both, of the events, depending on what you have chosen to record. As a general rule of thumb, you will want to monitor unsuccessful events if you are concerned about possible security breaches, and successful events if you are evaluating the capacity or overall functioning of your system.

In addition, Administrators need to monitor the performance of the computers on a network and take corrective actions if the performance is not up to par. The System Monitor in the Performance console is used to display data from current activity on the network or from log files, so that you can evaluate the day-to-day usage of the system. Administrators can monitor the usage of memory, measure the processor load, find out if the disks are operating optimally, and evaluate overall network performance by monitoring how well the network cards are functioning and what volume of traffic they are able to handle.

The Performance console is also used to create logs that record information about the performance of the resources on a computer, and to configure alerts that perform certain actions based on the captured data. Performance logs are very helpful in creating baseline measurements that can later be compared to current system loads for the purpose of capacity planning. Alerts can notify an Administrator of conditions that need attention without the need for a person to continually check the status of those conditions.

Scenario

You are the Network Administrator at Stocks and Bonds Inc. The organization has 500 employees and deals in trading stocks and bonds. The head office of Stocks and Bonds Inc. is in New York, with branch offices in Atlanta and Los Angeles. John Thomas is the Managing Director of the organization. He suspects that confidential data is being accessed by unauthorized individuals.

Lesson 13   Monitoring Events and Resources

Project	Exam 70-270 Objective
13.1 Introducing Auditing	Configuring, managing, and troubleshooting security. Configure, manage and troubleshoot auditing.
13.2 Auditing Access to Files and Folders	Configuring, managing, and troubleshooting security. Configure, manage and troubleshoot auditing.
13.3 Managing Auditing	Configuring, managing, and troubleshooting security. Configure, manage and troubleshoot auditing.
13.4 Monitoring System Performance	Monitor, optimize, and troubleshoot performance of the Windows XP Professional desktop. Optimize and troubleshoot processor utilization. Optimize and troubleshoot memory performance. Optimize and troubleshoot disk performance.
13.5 Configuring Alerts	Monitor, optimize, and troubleshoot performance of the Windows XP Professional desktop. Optimize and troubleshoot memory performance.

General Requirements

To complete the projects in this lesson, you will need administrative rights on a Windows XP Professional computer. You will also need a folder named Reports stored on the C: drive.

project 13.1 *Introducing Auditing*

exam objective

Configuring, managing, and troubleshooting security. Configure, manage and troubleshoot auditing.

overview

Auditing is used to track user activities and object access on the computers on a network to ensure the security and seamless functioning of the systems.

Before enabling auditing, the first step is to determine which events need to be audited on each computer. Auditing is not a 'one size fits all' type of solution. Each network will need to be analyzed to determine which events are significant enough to be recorded in that environment. Because events are recorded on the systems where they occur, auditing must be set up for each computer. This can be done for an entire domain through group policies or on standalone or workgroup workstations by applying security templates or by using the Local Security Policy console.

Auditing can be used to track events such as exactly who logged on to a computer and when, what files were accessed or folders were created, what printers were used, and what Registry keys were accessed. **Table 13-1** describes the events that may be audited. In order to audit who is accessing which objects and what actions they are performing on those objects, you must first activate the audit object access policy. Once it is activated you can audit object access for files and folders that are stored on NTFS volumes and partitions as well as audit access to printers.

The reason that auditing is only available on NTFS volumes and partitions is that NTFS provides the **System Access Control List (SACL)** that is associated with every file and folder. This list contains **Access Control Entries (ACEs)** that specify what type of auditing will be performed and for which user or group, represented by their **Security Identifier (SID)**, in the list. Refer to Lesson 11 for more information regarding NTFS.

Auditing is primarily used to help prevent security breaches by allowing you to track unauthorized attempts to log on or access folders. Auditing is also used to track resource usage for the computers on your network. This information can be used for resource planning and to distribute operating costs for resources to the appropriate cost center in your organization.

Audited events are stored in the **Security event log**. You can view the Security log using the **Event Viewer** snap-in in the Computer Management console.

tip

Auditing is simply recording Who, did What, When.

caution

Auditing increases the overhead on a computer. It takes processor time and creates I/O activity to record events and also disk space to store them. In addition, the security logs need to be managed by someone so that they do not run out of space. Therefore, you need to decide which events are important to track for your situation.

learning objective

In this project you will learn how to enable auditing on a Windows XP Professional computer.

specific requirements

Administrative rights on a Windows XP Professional computer.

estimated completion time

5 minutes

Table 13-1   Events that can be audited

Event	Description
Account Logon Events	Determines whether to audit logon or logoff attempts, where this computer is used to validate the account. If this is enabled on a domain controller, an entry is logged for each user who is validated against that domain controller, regardless of which computer in the domain they use to log on to. Event ID 680 is generated in the Security Log by this event.
Account Management	Generated when an account or group is created, deleted, or modified, or a user account is renamed, has a new password set, or was activated or disabled.
Directory Service Access	This event only occurs on domain controllers. It is undefined for workstations and member servers. Events occur when an Active Directory object, such as a computer, user account, printer or domain, is accessed. In a domain, objects in the Active Directory are frequently accessed. Because this can generate a huge number of entries in the security log, it is wise to use caution when auditing this event.
Logon Events	Records each instance of a user logging on to, logging off from, or making a network connection to this computer. Event ID 528 is generated in the Security Log by this event. If auditing for both Logon Events and Account Logon Events are enabled on a workgroup computer, both events will be generated by an interactive logon.
Object Access	Must be enabled to audit a user accessing an object such as a file, folder, registry key, or printer that has its own system access control list (SACL) set.
Policy Change	Changes to user rights assignment policies, audit policies, or trust policies generate this event.
Privilege Use	Audits each instance of a user exercising a user right except for usage of the following rights that are not audited: • Bypass traverse checking • Debug programs • Create a token object • Replace process level token • Generate security audits • Back up files and directories • Restore files and directories
Process Tracking	Generated for program execution, process exit, handle duplication, and indirect object access.
System Events	A computer is shut down or restarted or some event that concerns the Security Log has taken place.

project 13.1

Introducing Auditing (cont'd)

exam objective

Configuring, managing, and troubleshooting security. Configure, manage and troubleshoot auditing.

project steps

Set audit policies for logon and object access events on a computer and then test the auditing of successful logon events.

1. Log on as an **Administrator**. If you have not already done so, make the Administrative Tools command appear on the Start menu. Right-click **Start** and select **Properties** to open the **Taskbar and Start Menu Properties** dialog box. Click **Customize** to open the **Customize Start Menu** dialog box. On the **Advanced** tab, in the **Start menu items** list box, scroll to locate **System Administrative Tools**. Select **Display on the All Programs and the Start menu**, and click **OK** to close both dialog boxes.

2. Click **Start**, point to **Administrative Tools**, and click **Local Security Policy** to open the **Local Security Settings** window.

3. Double-click the **Local Policies** folder to access the **Audit Policy** folder.

4. Click the Audit Policy folder to display the list of audit policies in the details pane **(Figure 13-1)**.

5. Double-click the **Audit logon events** audit policy to open the **Audit logon events Properties** dialog box.

6. Select both the **Success** and **Failure** check boxes to track all logon attempts **(Figure 13-2)**.

7. Click **OK** to save the settings and close the Audit logon events Properties dialog box.

8. Double-click the **Audit object access** audit policy to open the **Audit object access Properties** dialog box.

9. Select both the **Success** and **Failure** check boxes to track attempts to access objects on the computer **(Figure 13-3)**.

10. Click **OK** to save the settings and close the Audit object access Properties dialog box. This simply enables auditing object access on the computer. Next, you will have to choose which files and folders you want the operating system to monitor.

11. The Local Security Setting console displays the status of the Audit logon events and Audit object access audit policies as **Success** or **Failure**, respectively **(Figure 13-4)**.

12. Close the Local Security Settings console.

13. Log off and then log back on again as the **Administrator**.

14. Click **Start**, point to **Administrative Tools**, and click **Event Viewer**.

15. Double-click the **Security** node. The top event in the right hand pane should be a Successful Account Logon **(Figure 13-5)**.

16. Double-click the Success Audit event in the right hand pane to open the **Event Properties** screen **(Figure 13-6)**.

17. Examine the details that are recorded for this event. Can you identify which user logged on to the system?

18. Click **OK** to close the **Event Properties** screen and close the **Event Viewer**.

tip

Account logon events and **Logon events** are often confused. **Account logon events** are generated where the account lives (IE: on a domain controller); **logon events** are generated where the logon attempt occurs.

Figure 13-1 Audit policies in the Local Security Settings console

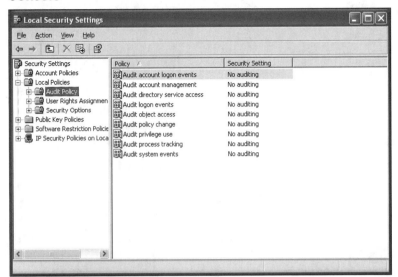

Figure 13-2 The Audit logon events Properties dialog box

Figure 13-3 The Audit object access Properties dialog box

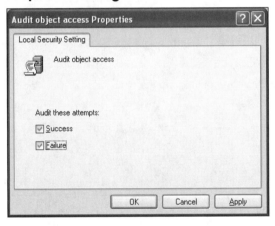

Figure 13-4 Configured audit policies

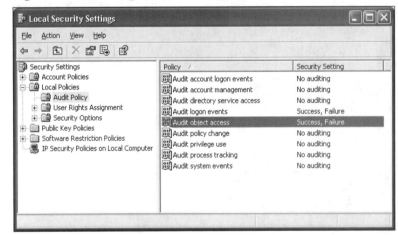

Figure 13-6 Account Logon Event Properties

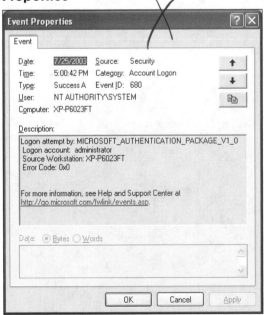

Figure 13-5 Event Viewer displaying recent events

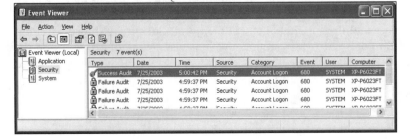

project 13.2	***Auditing Access to Files and Folders***

exam objective

Configuring, managing, and troubleshooting security. Configure, manage and troubleshoot auditing.

overview

Now that you have enabled auditing for object access, you must choose the files, folders or printers that you will audit, the users or groups that you will track, and select the specific events that you want to record for each of the objects.

You can also specify whether or not the subfolders within a folder should inherit the auditing settings. If you are enabling auditing for a subfolder, you can specify whether or not it should inherit the auditing settings of its parent folder. Remember, in order to enable auditing for a file or folder, you must first activate the **Audit object access audit policy** on that computer.

tip

You can enable auditing only for a file or a folder that is stored on an NTFS drive.

John Thomas has several folders on his computer that contain reports of the stock holdings for a number of clients. These folders are stored in a parent folder named Reports on the C: drive of the computer. Some of the files in this folder can be deleted because they are for former clients and one group of users has permission to do so, but recently someone has deleted several current files. You decide to track users who delete files to find out if you have a permissions problem that needs fixing or if unauthorized users are accessing the folder.

learning objective

After completing this project, you will know how to set up auditing for a folder.

specific requirements

♦ Administrative rights on a Windows XP Professional computer.
♦ A folder named Reports on the C: drive.

estimated completion time

15 minutes

project steps

Enable auditing for a folder named **Reports** located on the **C:** drive of your computer. Log an event every time a user in the Everyone group creates or deletes a file in the **Reports** folder.

1. Open **Windows Explorer** to display the files and folders on your computer.
2. Double-click the **C: drive** icon to display the folders on the drive.
3. Right-click the folder for which you want to enable auditing, for example **Reports**, and click the **Properties** command to open the **Reports Properties** dialog box.
4. Click the **Security** tab, and then click **Advanced** to open the **Advanced Security Settings for Reports** dialog box (**Figure 13-7**).
5. Click the **Auditing** tab. The **Inherit from parent the auditing entries that apply to child objects. Include these with entries explicitly defined here** check box is selected by default. This default means that the auditing settings for the parent folder will be inherited by this folder.
6. Select the **Replace auditing entries on all child objects with entries shown here that apply to child objects** check box so that any pre-existing auditing settings on the subfolders in the **Reports** folder will be reset, and will now inherit the settings you are making for the Reports folder (**Figure 13-8**).

Figure 13-7 The Permissions tab in the Advanced Security Settings for Reports dialog box

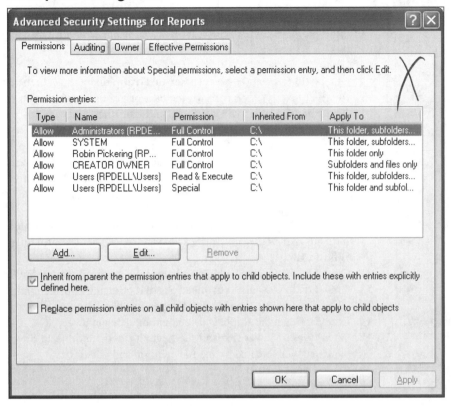

Figure 13-8 The Auditing tab

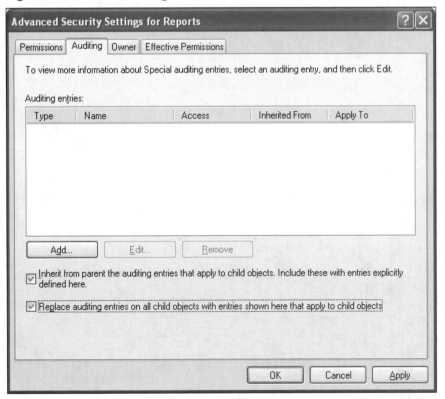

project 13.2

Auditing Access to Files and Folders (cont'd)

exam objective

Configuring, managing, and troubleshooting security. Configure, manage and troubleshoot auditing.

project steps

7. Click **Add** to open the **Select User or Group** dialog box. In the **Enter the object name to select** box, type the name of the user or group for which you want to enable auditing. For example, type: **Everyone**, to indicate that you want to enable auditing for the **Everyone** group **(Figure 13-9)**.
8. Click **OK** to close the **Select User or Group** dialog box and open the **Auditing Entry for Reports** dialog box where you can select the actions to be audited.
9. Select the **Successful** check box next to the **Create Files/Write Data** option to indicate that you want to track each time a file is successfully created, or when data is added to a file.
10. Select the **Successful** check box next to the **Delete Subfolders and Files** option to indicate that you want to track each time a file or subfolder is successfully deleted **(Figure 13-10)**.
11. Click **OK** to save the settings and close the **Auditing Entry for Reports** dialog box.
12. Click **OK** to close the **Advanced Security Settings for Reports** dialog box.
13. Click **OK** to close the **Reports Properties** dialog box.
14. Create a file in the **Reports** folder and then delete it.
15. Open **Event Viewer**, expand the **Security** node and locate the events in the right hand pane that were created by the file creation and deletion.
16. Close **Event Viewer**.
17. Close **Windows Explorer**.

tip

The Everyone group is often selected as the user or group whose actions are to be audited because it encompasses all users no matter how they access the computer or network.

Figure 13-9 Select User or Group dialog box

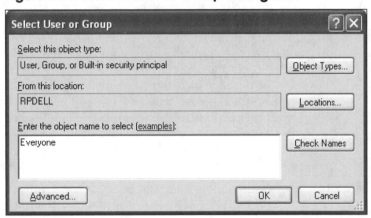

Figure 13-10 Selecting Actions to be audited

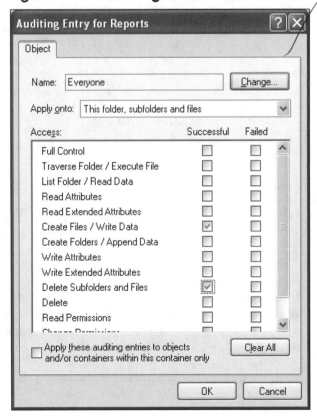

project 13.3

Managing Auditing

exam objective

Configuring, managing, and troubleshooting security. Configure, manage and troubleshoot auditing.

overview

Once you have configured auditing on your systems, you must manage the Security Logs that are generated. Because each Security Log has a fixed maximum size, it can quickly fill with events. It is important that the Security Logs are archived and cleared on a regular basis to prevent the loss of valuable security information. The maximum size of the Security Log should be set large enough so that no events will be lost or overwritten between maintenance intervals. The Security Logs should be reviewed and analyzed for possible patterns of improper usage, unauthorized access or suspected intrusions on a regular basis. Remember, if you have determined that it is worth the overhead to audit for specific events in your environment, it is also worth your time to benefit from that information by reviewing it regularly. Copies of old Security Logs should be stored indefinitely in a secure manner for possible legal purposes as they are often necessary as evidence of any computer crime.

tip

Audit as few events as possible – it can be very difficult to find evidence of an intrusion when it is buried under many irrelevant events.

The hard disk space on John Thomas's computer is becoming inadequate and he is experiencing delays while using certain applications. Rather than immediately upgrading the disk, he has asked you to delete certain applications from his machine. Instead, you find that the Security Log on his computer is occupying excessive disk space. You decide to configure the Security Log on the computer so that all events older than 5 days will be overwritten and the size of the Security Log will not exceed 384 KB.

learning objective

After completing this project, you will know how to set the size of the Security log.

specific requirements

◆   Administrative rights on a Windows XP Professional computer.
◆   A user account.
◆   Completion of projects 13.1 and 13.2.

estimated completion time

15 minutes

project steps

View events in the Security Log of your computer, set the maximum size of the Security Log, and configure the log so that events older than **5** days will be overwritten.

1. Log off of the Administrator account and attempt to log back on as **user1** (or any other user account you have created on the computer). Enter an incorrect user name on your first logon attempt. Enter an incorrect password on your second logon attempt. Log on successfully on your third attempt.
2. Create a file named **Expenses.doc** and save it in the **Reports** folder. Close the file.
3. Log off as user1 and log back on as an **Administrator**.
4. Click **Start**, point to **Administrative Tools**, and click **Event Viewer** to open the Event Viewer window.
5. Select **Security Log** in the left pane of the Event Viewer window to open the events in the Security Log.
6. Scroll down the list and locate the two Failure Audits (**Figure 13-11**). Double-click the first Failure Audit to open the **Event Properties** dialog box to display the details of the selected event (**Figure 13-12**).

Figure 13-11 The Security Log

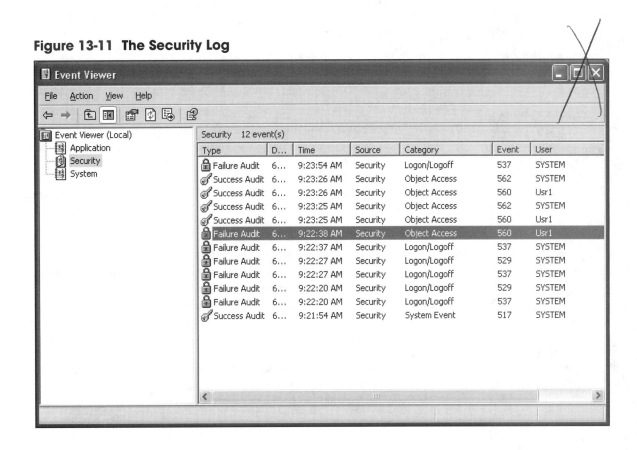

**Figure 13-12 Details of an event recorded in the
Security Log**

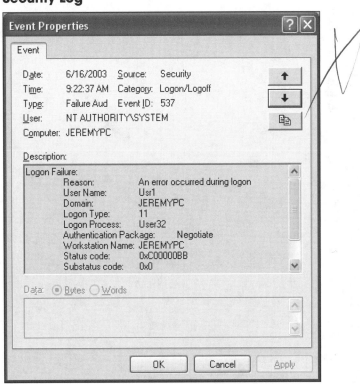

project 13.3

Managing Auditing (cont'd)

exam objective

Configuring, managing, and troubleshooting security. Configure, manage and troubleshoot auditing.

project steps

tip

By default, the newest events are at the top of the list in Event Viewer.

tip

Any value can be entered for the file size, but it will be resized to the closest multiple of 64.

7. Use the up and down arrow buttons to view the next and previous Event Properties dialog boxes for the events in the Security Log. Locate the Event Properties dialog box for the Success Audit in which the Expenses file was saved in the Reports folder.
8. Close the Event Properties dialog box.
9. Right-click **Security Log** and select **Properties** to open the **Security Properties** dialog box.
10. Indicate the maximum size for the log file in the **Maximum log size** text box. For example, type **384**.
11. The **Overwrite events older than** option button is selected by default. To set the number of days old you want events that are overwritten to be, type **5**, in the **Overwrite events older than** text box **(Figure 13-13)**.
12. Click **OK** to save the settings and close the Security Properties dialog box.
13. The Event Viewer message box opens to inform you that the Security log has been reduced in size, and to warn you that the new setting will not take effect until you clear the log. Click **OK**.
14. Right-click **Security** and select **Clear all Events**. The Event Viewer dialog box opens to prompt you to save the log before clearing it. Click **No**.
15. Close the Event Viewer.

Figure 13-13 The Security Properties dialog box

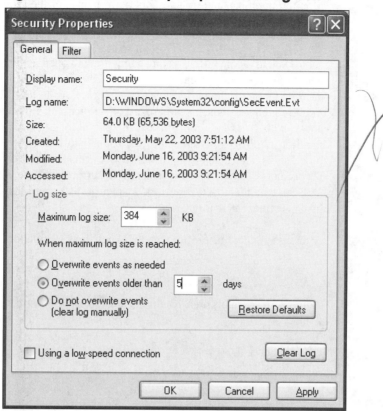

project 13.4 | *Monitoring System Performance*

exam objective

Monitor, optimize, and troubleshoot performance of the Windows XP Professional desktop. Optimize and troubleshoot processor utilization. Optimize and troubleshoot memory performance. Optimize and troubleshoot disk performance.

overview

John Thomas's computer is taking a long time to open applications. Although it is infrequent that the source of a bottleneck is a processor, you suspect that this may be the problem. You decide to monitor the performance of the processor to determine if it needs to be upgraded. You are going to monitor the Processor-%Processor Time counter to see if it is frequently above 80%. This will confirm that the processor is the bottleneck. You are also going to monitor the Processor-Interrupts/Sec counter to find out the average number of times the processor is interrupted by hardware device requests for attention. If the number of interrupts per second is above 1500, it is likely that a hardware failure is causing unnecessary interrupts. You can then identify the network adapter or disk controller card causing the interrupts and install a replacement if necessary.

learning objective

After completing this project, you will know how to monitor resources on a computer.

specific requirements

Administrative rights on a Windows XP Professional computer.

estimated completion time

10 minutes

project steps

Monitor the average time each of the processors in your computer spends processing service requests and the average number of times per second that they are interrupted by device requests. Display the data as a histogram.

1. Click **Start**, point to **Administrative Tools**, and click the **Performance** command to open the **Performance** console **(Figure 13-14)**.
2. Ensure that **System Monitor** is selected in the left pane.
3. Click the **New Counter Set** icon at the top left corner of the right hand pane to clear any existing counters.
4. Click the **+** button to open the **Add Counters** dialog box.
5. Select the **Use local computer counters** option button to indicate that you want to monitor objects on the local computer.
6. **Processor** is selected by default in the **Performance object** list box.
7. Select **%Processor Time** in the **Select counters from list** box.
8. Select the **All instances** option button to monitor all instances of the selected object **(Figure 13-15)**.
9. Click **Add** to add the selected counter.
10. Select **Interrupts/sec** in the **Select counters from list** box.
11. Select the **All instances** option button and click **Add** to add the selected counter to the Performance console.
12. Click **Close** to close the Add Counters dialog box and add the selected counter.
13. The counters can be viewed either as a graph (which is the default), as a histogram or as a report. Click the **View Histogram** button to display the captured data as a histogram. The histogram displays the amount of time all of the processors in your computer have spent processing.
14. Click the **View Report** button and observe the format of data for the active counters.
15. Close the Performance console.

tip

Watch the system monitor as you move your mouse quickly. The number of interrupts per second will increase.

Figure 13-14 The System Monitor in the Performance console

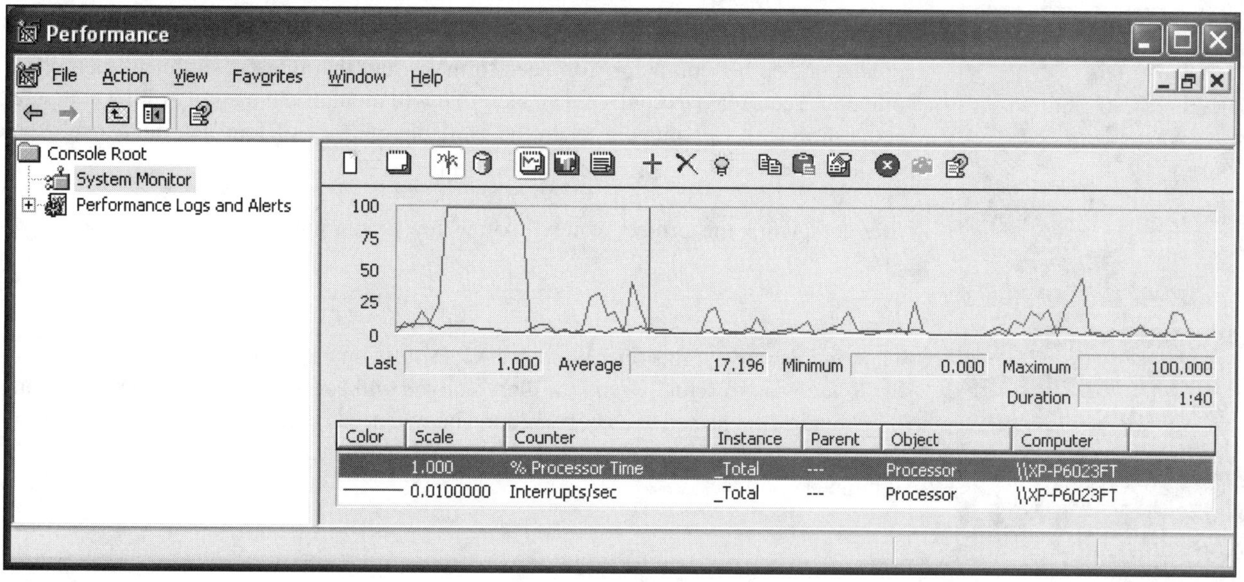

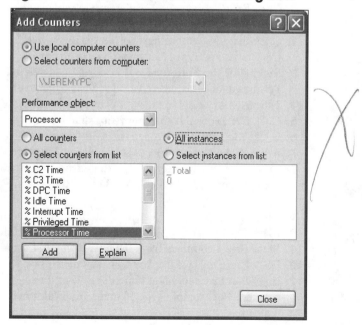

Figure 13-15 The Add Counters dialog box

project 13.5

Configuring Alerts

exam objective

Monitor, optimize, and troubleshoot performance of the Windows XP Professional desktop. Optimize and troubleshoot memory performance.

overview

Joan Peters is a Graphic Artist in the Marketing department. Joan runs several graphics applications on her computer. You need to make sure that there is sufficient memory on her computer. You decide to configure an alert that will monitor the memory of the computer, and send a message to a computer when the available memory of Joan's computer falls below a preset threshold.

learning objective

After completing this project, you will know how to configure an alert.

specific requirements

◆   Administrative rights on a Windows XP Professional computer.
◆   If you want to actually send the alert that you will configure in this project, the computer should be connected to a network, and you will need another computer to send the alert to.

estimated completion time

20 minutes

project steps

Create a counter log to evaluate how much memory your system is using at particular points in time, save it in the PerfLogs folder on the **C:** drive of your computer as a text file that has values separated by commas, set the log file size, manually start and stop the counter log so that you can monitor peak usage times, and configure an alert to send a message to another computer when the available memory falls below **4MB**, the **Pages/Sec exceeds 5**, or the **%Usage** of the page file reaches 99%.

tip

Alerts can be used to notify an Administrator of a potential system problem before it becomes critical.

1.   Click **Start**, point to **Administrative Tools**, and click the **Performance** command to open the **Performance** console.
2.   Click the plus symbol next to the **Performance Logs and Alerts** node to display the **Counter Logs**, **Trace Logs**, and **Alerts** nodes.
3.   Right-click the **Counter Logs** node and click **New Log Settings** to open the **New Log Settings** dialog box where you designate a name for the new log.
4.   Type **Memory Log**, in the **Name** text box to name the new log.
5.   Click **OK** to open the **Memory Log** dialog box.
6.   Click **Add Counters** to open the **Add Counters** dialog box.
7.   In the **Performance object** list box, select **Memory**.
8.   Make sure that the **Select counters from list** option button is selected. Hold down the **Ctrl** key and select the **Available Mbytes** and **Pages/sec** counters in the scrolling list box **(Figure 13-16)**.
9.   Click **Add** to add the selected counters to the counter log.
10. In the **Performance object** list box, select **Paging File**.
11. In the **Select counters from list** box, select, **%Usage** and click **Add**.
12. Click **Close** to close the Add Counters dialog box.
13. Enter the time interval at which you want the log to record the data from the selected counters. For example, type **30** in the **Interval** spin box at the bottom of the Memory Log dialog box.
14. Select the unit of time interval from the **Units** list box. For example, select **minutes** **(Figure 13-17)**.

Figure 13-16 Adding counters for the Memory object

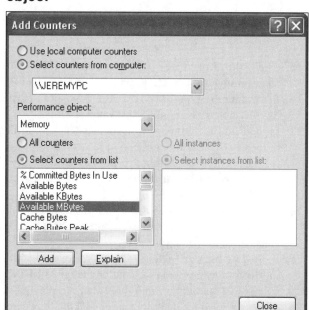

Figure 13-17 Setting the time interval for recording data in the log

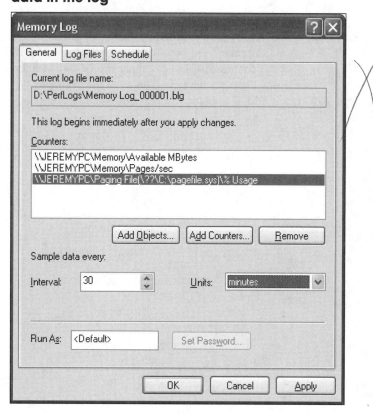

project 13.5

Configuring Alerts *(cont'd)*

exam objective

Monitor, optimize, and troubleshoot performance of the Windows XP Professional desktop. Optimize and troubleshoot memory performance.

project steps

15. Click the **Log Files** tab. Note that the default location for the log file is **%systemdrive%\PerfLogs** which in most cases is **C:\PerfLogs**.
16. In the **Log file type** list box, select **Text File - (Comma delimited)** to indicate that the log file should be a comma-separated text file.
17. In the **End file names with** list box, select **mmddhh** to append the month, day and hour of the day to the name of the log file. You can also append many other different date/time formats or a serial number to the name of the log file, or you can remove the check from the **End file names with** check box to save the counter log with no additional information **(Figure 13-18)**.
18. Click **Configure** to open the **Configure Log Files** dialog box. In the **Location** text box, you can change the default location for saving the log file. In the **File name** text box you can change the name for the log file.
19. In the **Log file size** section, you can select the **Limit of** option button and set a size limit in MB for the log file in the spin box **(Figure 13-19)**.
20. Click **OK** to close the Configure Log Files dialog box.
21. If you accepted the default location and the **PerfLogs** folder has not yet been created, the Memory Log message box will prompt you to create it. Click **Yes**. Click the **Schedule** tab to access the options for scheduling the log file.
22. Select the **Manually (using the shortcut menu)** option button in the **Start log** section to indicate that you will manually start the log.
23. Click **OK** to save the configuration and close the Memory Log dialog box.
24. Right-click the Alerts node and click **New Alert Settings** to open the **New Alert Settings** dialog box.
25. Enter a name for the new alert in the **Name** text box. For example, type **Memory Alert**.
26. Click **OK** to open the **Memory Alert** dialog box.
27. In the **Comment** text box on the **General** tab of the Memory Alert dialog box, enter a message for the alert. The comment will be displayed in the Performance Logs and Alerts snap-in. For example, type: **You need to add memory**.
28. Click **Add** to open the **Add Counters** dialog box.

Figure 13-18 The Log Files tab

Figure 13-19 The Configure Log Files dialog box

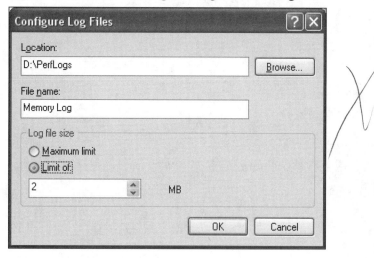

project 13.5

Configuring Alerts (cont'd)

exam objective

Monitor, optimize, and troubleshoot performance of the Windows XP Professional desktop. Optimize and troubleshoot memory performance.

project steps

29. In the **Performance object** list box, select **Memory**.
30. Make sure that the **Select counters from list** option button is selected. Hold down the **Ctrl** key and select the **Available Mbytes** and **Pages/sec** counters in the scrolling list box.
31. Click **Add** to add the selected counters to the alert.
32. In the **Performance object** list box, select **Paging File**.
33. In the **Select counters from list** box, select **%Usage**, and click **Add** to add the selected counter to the alert.
34. Click **Close** to close the Add Counters dialog box. The counters are added to the **Counters** list box on the General tab of the Memory Alert dialog box.
35. Select the **Memory\Available Mbytes** counter in the **Counters** list box. In the **Alert when value is** list box, select **Under**, if necessary. In the **Limit** text box, enter the threshold value **4 (Figure 13-20)**.
36. Select the **Memory\Pages/sec counter** in the **Counters** list box. In the **Alert when value is** list box, select **Over**. In the **Limit** text box, enter the threshold value **5**.
37. Select the **Paging File\%Usage** counter in the Counters list box. In the **Alert when value is** list box, select **Over**. In the **Limit** text box, enter the threshold value, **99**.
38. Click the **Action** tab to display the check boxes that you use to specify the action that the alert should perform.
39. Select the **Send a network message to** check box.
40. Enter the name of the computer to which you want the alert message sent. For example, type **\\Computer1 (Figure 13-21)**.
41. Click the **Schedule** tab to display the options for starting the alert scan.
42. Select the **Manually (using the shortcut menu)** option button to indicate that you will manually start monitoring. **Manually** should also be automatically selected in the **Stop scan** section.
43. Click **OK** to save the configuration and close the Memory Alert dialog box. To start the alert, right-click its name in the details pane of the Performance console and click **Start**.
44. Close the Performance console.

tip

By default, when an alert is generated it will be recorded in the application log of the Event Viewer. After starting your alert try to find the event in the application log.

Figure 13-20 Setting the threshold value for an alert

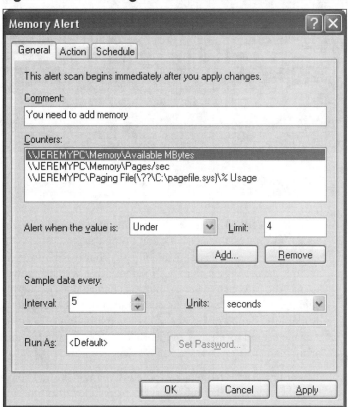

Figure 13-21 The Action tab

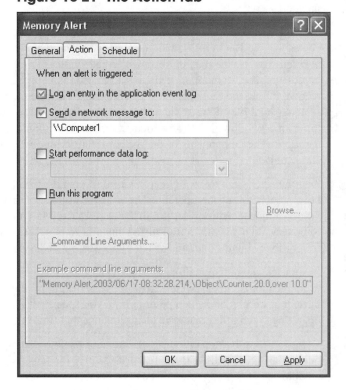

LESSON 14

Backing Up and Restoring Data

A critical area of operations management is ensuring the availability of the necessary network and computer systems and the data stored on them. Many people think of availability as simply a hardware issue—keep the systems running and mitigate risk by using fault-tolerant drive systems, power supplies, battery backups, and so on. And of course when a hardware failure does occur, restore the system to operation as quickly as possible. Beyond hardware failures are many other risks factors that affect availability: denial of service attacks, exploitation of security flaws in an operating system, damage caused by viruses and worms, accidental or intentional loss or corruption of data and many more.

Operating systems today are exposed to many risks and so part of ensuring availability often includes applying the latest service packs, performing regular virus scans, and of course, creating backup copies of the system configuration and any important data. To provide true system availability, users must be able to access the resources and data that they require, when they need to. As an Administrator, you need to have a plan in place to deal with each risk that your systems might face. You need to be familiar with the various tools that can assist you in restoring your systems to a functional state and also how to restore your data in a timely manner.

There are several tools and utilities that are used to protect your data. The **Backup Utility** consists of the **Backup Wizard**, the **Restore Wizard**, and the **Automated System Recovery Wizard**. You use the Backup Wizard to create copies of your data and then store those backup copies in a secure manner. If data is lost or damaged, you can use the Restore Wizard to recover it from the backup copies. You must also back up the **System State** which includes the system's boot files, Registry and COM+ Class Registration Database. These files are required to repair a Windows XP Professional computer if the contents of the system or boot drive are damaged. The components of the System State must always be backed up and restored as a single unit.

Automated System Recovery can be used to quickly rebuild your system if the system files become corrupt, or the operating system will not start. First, it restores all disk signatures, volumes, and partitions on the disks required to start the computer. Automated System Recovery then installs a simplified installation of Windows and automatically starts a restoration using the backup created by the Automated System Recovery Wizard.

In some cases, system malfunctions are caused by changes that have been made to the system or application settings. **System Restore** restores all system and application settings back to those that were in effect at a point in time you specify. It restores key application, driver, and operating system files that have changed since that time but it does not affect data files.

Before making backups, you should create a backup plan so that you can retrieve lost data quickly and efficiently. First, you must identify the data that needs to be backed up and the medium you are going to use. Then, you must decide upon a backup schedule and a backup type. Most disaster recovery plans also define how and where backup media will be stored and usually include the use of offsite storage for some backup copies.

Scenario

Sheffield Financials Inc. is a financial consulting firm located in Houston, Texas. The company has 20 employees offering consulting services to various clients. The consultants are required to back up their work to a floppy disk or Zip drive nightly and to the network server on a weekly basis.

Lesson 14   Backing Up and Restoring Data

Project	Exam 70-270 Objective
14.1 Backing Up Data	Restore and back up the operating system, System State data, and user data. Recover System State data and user data using Windows Backup.
14.2 Restoring Data from a Backup	Restore and back up the operating system, System State data, and user data. Recover System State data and user data using Windows Backup.
14.3 Changing the Default Backup and Restore Options	Restore and back up the operating system, System State data, and user data.
14.4 Performing an Automated System Recovery Backup	Restore and back up the operating system, System State data, and user data.
14.5 Using System Restore to revert to a previous configuration	Restore and back up the operating system, System State data, and user data.

General Requirements

To complete the projects in this lesson, you will need administrative rights on a Windows XP Professional computer with a floppy disk drive or a Zip drive attached. You will also need a folder named Accounts and a folder named AccountsRestore on the C: drive of your computer.

project 14.1

Backing Up Data

exam objective

Restore and back up the operating system, System State data, and user data. Recover System State data and user data using Windows Backup.

overview

When you perform backups, you must decide whether you are going to backup user data, programs, operating system files or System State data. Next, you must choose the media you are going to use and the location where you are going to store the data. Finally, you can either start the backup manually or it can be scheduled to run at a later time.

By default, if there is sufficient free space available on a local NTFS volume, backup creates a volume shadow copy of your data. This is an exact point-in-time copy of the files that have been selected for the backup, including any open files or files that are in use by the system. The backup then copies the contents of the volume shadow copy to the selected backup media. This ensures that applications can continue to write data to the volume during a backup, files that are open are not omitted from the backup, and backups can be performed at any time, without locking out users.

You are one of the 20 consultants working for Sheffield Financials. You are getting ready to go out to lunch and decide that before you leave you should back up an important folder that you are working with.

tip

Volume shadow copy mode is only available on NTFS volumes. There must be enough available free disk space on any of the local NTFS volumes for the shadow copy. If there is not sufficient space on one of the local volumes, the shadow copy will not be created.

learning objective

After completing this project, you will know how to back up data using the Backup Wizard.

specific requirements

◆ Administrative rights on a Windows XP Professional computer with a floppy disk drive or other removable storage media.
◆ A blank formatted diskette.
◆ A folder named Accounts on the C: drive of the computer.

estimated completion time

15 minutes

project steps

Back up the Accounts folder to the floppy drive of your computer.
1. Log on to your Windows XP Professional computer as an **Administrator**. Insert a floppy disk in the floppy disk drive.
2. Click **Start**, click **All Programs**, point to **Accessories**, point to **System Tools**, and click **Backup** to open the **Backup or Restore** Wizard (**Figure 14-1**).
3. Click **Next** to open the **Backup or Restore** screen. Select the **Backup files and settings** option button, if necessary.
4. Click **Next** to open the **What to Back Up** screen. The **My documents and settings** option button is selected by default. This selection will backup the My Documents folder, Favorites, desktop, and cookies. You can also back up everyone's documents and settings, or all data on the computer. Select the **Let me choose what to back up** option button (**Figure 14-2**).
5. Click **Next** to open the **Items to Back Up** screen. Double-click **My Computer** and expand the **C:** drive to select the required folder. Select the check box to the left of the **Accounts** folder (**Figure 14-3**).
6. Click **Next** to open the **Backup Type, Destination, and Name** screen. In the **Choose a place to save your backup** list box, select **3 ½ Floppy (A:)**. In the Type a name for this backup list box, type: **Accounts (Figure 14-4)**.

Figure 14-1 The Backup or Restore Wizard

Figure 14-2 The What to Back Up screen

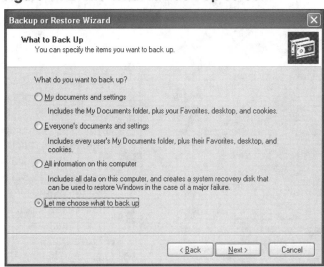

Figure 14-3 The Items to Back Up screen

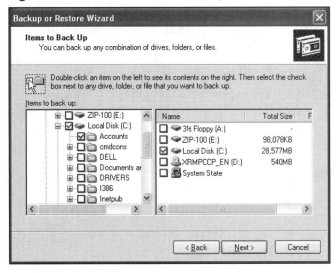

Figure 14-4 The Backup Type, Destination, and Name screen

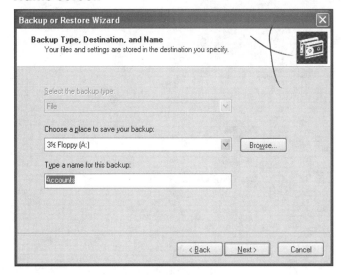

project 14.1

Backing Up Data (cont'd)

exam objective

Restore and back up the operating system, System State data, and user data. Recover System State data and user data using Windows Backup.

project steps

7. Click **Next** to open the **Completing the Backup or Restore Wizard** screen. The backup settings you have chosen are displayed.

8. Click **Advanced** to open the **Type of Backup** screen. A **Normal** backup is performed by default. Remember that in a Normal backup, all selected files and folders are backed up whether they have the Archive attribute or not and the Archive attribute is removed. Click the list arrow and review the four other backup types (**Figure 14-5**).

9. Keep Normal as the backup type, and click **Next** to open the **How to Back Up** screen. Select the **Verify data after backup** option button to verify the integrity of the backed up data after the backup process is complete. The default backup in Windows XP creates a volume shadow copy. A **volume shadow** enables you to create shadow backup copies of all files, including those that are open (**Figure 14-6**).

10. Click **Next** to open the **Backup Options** screen. If the backup medium you are using already contains backups, you can choose to either append this backup to the existing backups or to replace the existing backups. If you replace the existing backups, you can also allow only the file owners and the Administrator to access the backup medium, or any backups appended to the medium. Keep the default selection, **Append this backup to the existing backups**.

11. Click **Next** to open the **When to Backup** screen. You can either perform the backup operation immediately or schedule the backup for a later time. Leave the default selection, **Now**.

12. Click **Next** to open the **Completing the Backup or Restore Wizard** screen.

13. Click **Finish** to begin the backup process. The **Backup Progress** dialog box opens (**Figure 14-7**).

14. Once the backup is complete, click **Report** to open the backup log in Notepad (**Figure 14-8**).

15. Close the backup log file, and click **Close** to close the Backup Progress dialog box.

Figure 14-5 The Type of Backup screen

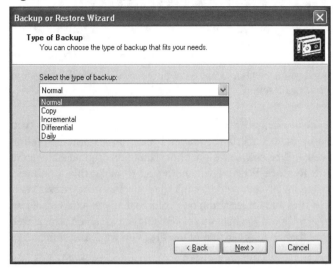

Figure 14-6 The How to Back Up screen

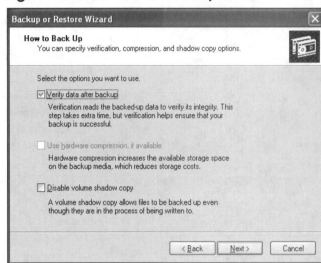

Figure 14-7 The Backup Progress dialog box

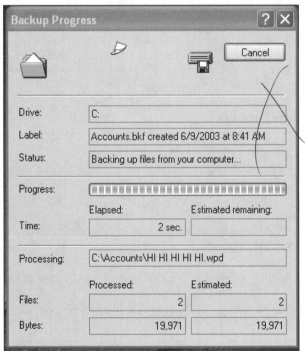

Figure 14-8 A backup log file

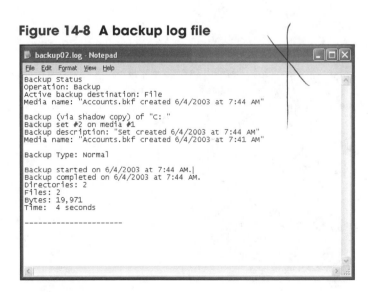

project 14.2 | *Restoring Data from a Backup*

exam objective

Restore and back up the operating system, System State data, and user data. Recover System State data and user data using Windows Backup.

overview

In the event of a hard disk crash, the accidental erasure of data, or damage due to a virus, you will need to restore your backed up data. Experts recommend that you test the restoration process regularly to ensure that you will be able to restore your data to its original state in the event of such a catastrophe. The **Restore Wizard** will help you to make this a painless procedure. You can restore individual drives, folders and files, or an entire backup set. A **backup set** is the compilation of files and folders from one volume that you have backed up and stored in a file, or on one or more tapes. The backup set is displayed as a hierarchical tree that you can use to open drives and folders in order to find the files you want to restore.

You can use the Restore Wizard, or you can manually restore files and folders without using the Wizard. Files and folders that were backed up from an NTFS volume must be restored to an NTFS volume if you want to retain the original NTFS security permissions. To ensure their security, files that have been encrypted using EFS can only be restored to an NTFS volume.

While saving certain files on your computer, you have mistakenly overwritten the files in the Accounts folder. You must now restore the files from the Accounts.bkf file that you created in Project 14.1. You will restore the data to an alternate location in the AccountsRestored folder on the C: drive of your computer.

caution

When restoring data, it is very easy to accidentally overwrite good data with older data. Be sure that anyone who is authorized to restore data has been properly trained and confirms that they are restoring the correct data to the correct location before proceeding.

learning objective

After completing this project, you will know how to restore data from a backup set.

specific requirements

◆ Administrative rights on a Windows XP Professional computer.
◆ A blank folder, AccountsRestored, on the C: drive.
◆ The Accounts.bkf file you created in Project 14.1.

estimated completion time

15 minutes

project steps

Restore the Accounts folder backup.
1. Click **Start**, click **All Programs**, point to **Accessories**, point to **System Tools**, and click **Backup** to open the **Backup or Restore Wizard**.
2. Click the **Advanced Mode** link to open the Backup Utility.
3. Select the **Restore and Manage Media** tab. Expand the **File** node in the left pane of the window.
4. Locate and expand the Accounts.bkf backup set. Expand the C: directory and select the Accounts folder.
5. By default, files and folders will be restored to their original location. Select **Alternate Location** in the **Restore files to** list box at the bottom of the window to choose a new location for the restored files.
6. Type **C:\AccountsRestore** in the **Alternate Location** text box **(Figure 14-9)**.
7. Click **Start Restore** to open the **Confirm Restore** message box **(Figure 14-10)**. Click **Advanced** to open the **Advanced Restore Options** dialog box. By default, the **Restore Security, Restore junction points, and restore file and folder data under junction points to the original location**, and **Preserve existing volume mount points** option buttons are selected **(Figure 14-11)**.

Figure 14-9 The Restore and Manage Media tab in the Backup Utility

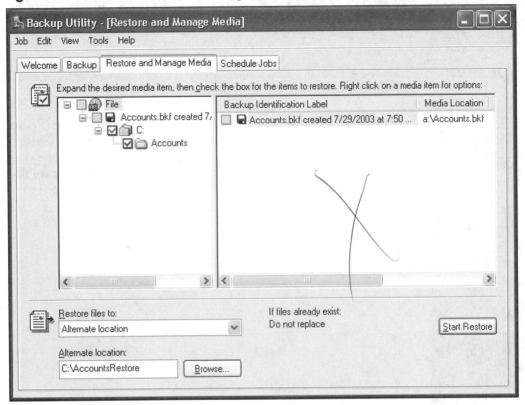

Figure 14-10 The Confirm Restore message box

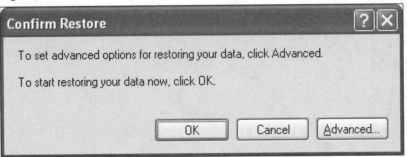

Figure 14-11 The Advanced Restore Options dialog box

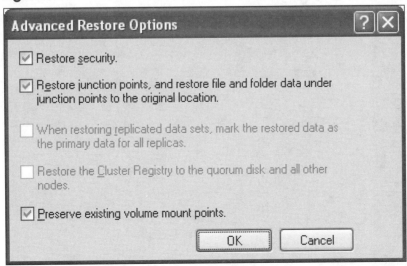

project 14.2

Restoring Data from a Backup (cont'd)

exam objective

Restore and back up the operating system, System State data, and user data. Recover System State data and user data using Windows Backup.

project steps

8. Click **OK** to accept the defaults and close the Advanced Restore Options dialog box.
9. Click **OK** to close the Confirm Restore dialog box and start the restore.
10. The Restore Progress dialog box opens **(Figure 14-12)**. When the process is complete, click **Report** to open the backup and restore log in Notepad **(Figure 14-13)**.
11. Close the report, the Restore Progress dialog box, and the Backup Utility.

Figure 14-12 The Restore Progress window

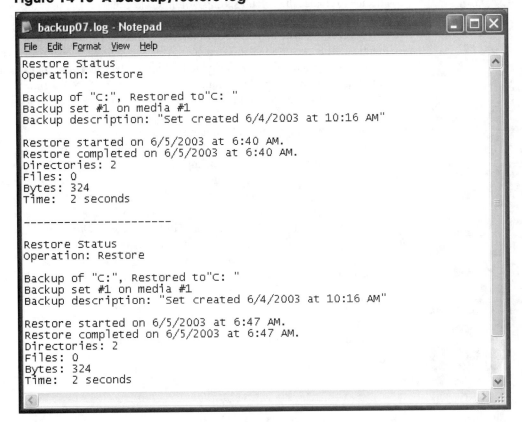

Figure 14-13 A backup/restore log

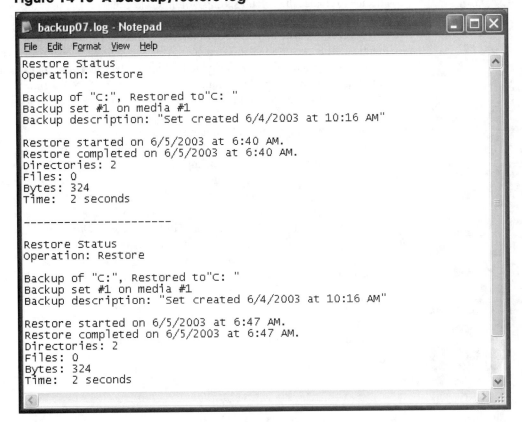

project 14.3

Changing the Default Backup and Restore Options

exam objective

Restore and back up the operating system, System State data, and user data.

overview

You can change the default settings for all backup and restore operations in the **Options** dialog box for the Backup Utility (**Figure 14-14**). The tabs in the dialog box are listed below:

◆ **General:** On this tab, you can change the default status information for the backup and restore processes, as well as send alert messages, verify data, and list the items being backed up by default. The **Compute selection information before backup and restore operations** option estimates the number of files and bytes being backed up, and displays this information before the backup or restore begins. The **Verify data after the backup completes** option checks the backed-up data and the original data on your hard disk to make sure they are identical. If you back up data often on a mounted drive, you should select the **Back up the contents of mounted drives** option to make sure that the data, and not just the path information for the mounted drive, are backed up.

◆ The **Show alert message when I start the Backup utility and Removable Storage is not running** option is used when your main backup medium is tape or other media that you use Removable Storage to manage. If you primarily use some kind of removable disk or if you back up data to a file or a hard disk, you do not need to select this option.

◆ **Restore:** On this tab, you can specify the default setting for how to replace existing files with restored files.

◆ **Backup Type:** On this tab, you can change the default backup type that will be chosen in the Backup Wizard.

◆ **Backup Log:** Here you can specify the amount of information that you want to include by default in the backup log.

◆ **Exclude Files:** Here you can specify the files that you want to exclude from the backup process by default. You can exclude a type of file for a specific user, or all users, for security purposes.

You decide to change the default settings for all backup and restore operations so that you will not have to select options that you want every time you backup and restore files. You always want to check the backed up data against the original data on your hard disk to make sure they are identical. This way, if the data does not match, you will know that there is a problem with either the media or the file you are using to backup the data, and you can use a different media or another file and run the backup again. You also only want to replace the file on a disk with the restored data if the file on the disk is older. Furthermore, you always want to specify detailed information, such as the total size of the backed up data, the start and end time of the backup and restore processes, and the names of all backed up files and folders in the backup and restore logs. You have also decided to use a Normal/Differential backup strategy. Every Monday you will perform a Normal backup, and on Tuesday through Friday you will perform Differential backups. This strategy will take progressively more time to back up each day because each backup will include all data that has changed since the last Normal backup. To restore, only the last Differential backup and the last Normal backup will be required so restoration will be fairly quick. Since you will be running a Differential backup most often, you are going to make Differential the default backup type.

learning objective

After completing this project, you will know how to set default backup and restore options.

specific requirements

Administrative rights on a Windows XP Professional computer.

Figure 14-14 The General tab in the Options dialog box for the Backup Utility

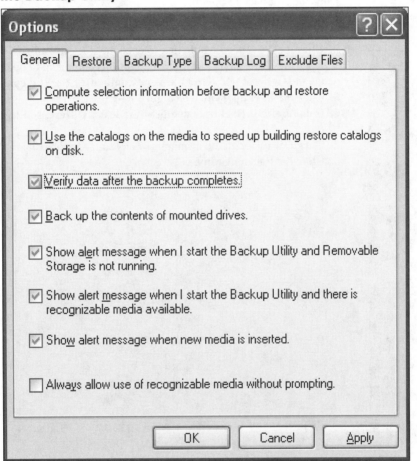

project 14.3

Changing the Default Backup and Restore Options *(cont'd)*

exam objective

Restore and back up the operating system, System State data, and user data.

estimated completion time

5 minutes

project steps

Change default backup options.

1. Click **Start**, click **All Programs**, point to **Accessories**, point to **System Tools**, and click **Backup** to open the **Backup or Restore Wizard**.
2. Click the **Advanced Mode** link to open the Backup Utility.
3. Open the **Tools** menu and click the **Options** command to open the **Options** dialog box.
4. On the **General** tab, select the **Verify data after backup completes** check box.
5. Click the **Backup Type** tab **(Figure 14-15)**.
6. In the **Default Backup Type** list box, select **Differential** to change the default backup type.
7. Click **OK** to accept the changes and close the Options dialog box.
8. Close the Backup Utility.

Figure 14-15 The Backup Type tab

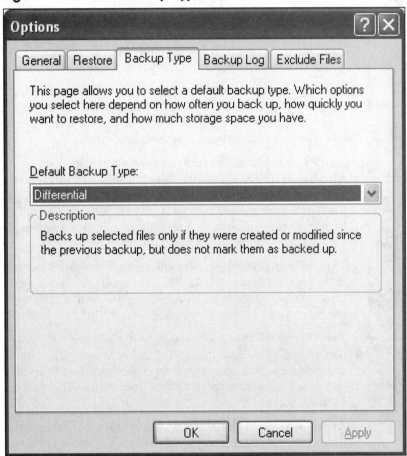

<table>
<tr><td>

project 14.4

</td><td>

Performing an Automated System Recovery Backup

</td></tr>
<tr><td>

exam objective

</td><td>

Restore and back up the operating system, System State data, and user data.

</td></tr>
<tr><td>

overview

</td><td>

A new feature in Windows XP is **Automated System Recovery (ASR) (Figure 14-16)**. ASR is a backup of your system configuration that is designed to enable you to repair your system partition so that you can restart the operating system in the event of a complete malfunction due to a hard drive issue or corrupt system files. When using the other system recovery tools, such as Safe Mode, the Last Known Good Configuration, and the Recovery console are not possible, you can use ASR as a last resort. You can also first try to use the System Restore feature in Windows XP Professional, which is discussed in the next project.

When you use the Automated System Recovery Wizard, the configuration of your system drive is saved to whatever backup medium you choose. When ASR is applied, it formats the system drive. All user data on the system partition will be lost, and you will have to restore all user data, as well as all system partition data.

An ASR backup should be performed immediately following the successful installation of the operating system. The backup should then be updated whenever you modify the system configuration such as when you add a new device driver or use Windows Update to install a patch or service pack. To perform an ASR backup, you will need one floppy disk and a backup storage medium that is sufficient in size to store the operating system files, configuration settings, and System State data.

To perform an ASR restore, you will need the bootable Windows XP Professional CD-ROM or the bootable floppy disk set, the most recent copy of the ASR backup, which is generally saved on tape or another removable storage medium, and the most recent ASR backup media set.

The ASR floppy cannot be used to boot a Windows XP system, but if you can boot the computer using the installation CD-ROM or the setup floppies, you can use the ASR floppy and the ASR backup set to repair the system partition. To create the bootable setup floppies, you must download the necessary files from **www.microsoft.com/xp**. Six disks are needed to create the set.

As part of Sheffield Financials Inc. disaster recovery plan, it has been decided to use the new Automated System Recovery (ASR) tool each time that any system configuration is changed on any computer running Windows XP Professional. Then, if any system suffers a complete loss of its boot or system partitions, it can be quickly restored to service without the need to reconfigure all of the operating system settings. It will be your job to keep the backups current and restore them when there is a need. You will also need to keep separate backups of all user data so that it can be restored if ASR is used to restore a system.

</td></tr>
<tr><td>

learning objective

</td><td>

In this project, you will learn how to create an Automated System Recovery backup.

</td></tr>
<tr><td>

specific requirements

</td><td>

◆ Administrative rights on a Windows XP Professional computer.
◆ A blank formatted diskette.

</td></tr>
<tr><td>

estimated completion time

</td><td>

15 minutes

</td></tr>
</table>

Figure 14-16 The Automated System Recovery Wizard

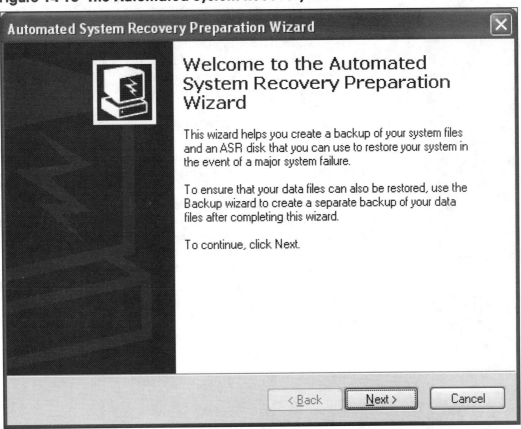

project 14.4

Performing an Automated System Recovery Backup (cont'd)

exam objective

Restore and back up the operating system, System State data, and user data.

project steps

Perform an ASR backup.

1. Click **Start**, click **All Programs**, point to **Accessories**, point to **System Tools**, and click **Backup** to open the **Backup or Restore Wizard**.
2. Click the **Advanced Mode** link to open the Backup Utility.
3. Click the **Automated System Recovery Wizard** button to start the Automated System Recovery Preparation Wizard.
4. Click **Next** to open the **Backup Destination** screen. Enter the path to the backup media and a name for the backup in the **Backup media or file name** text box (**Figure 14-17**). Alternatively, you can click **Browse** and navigate to the removable storage drive on which you are going to save the backup of your system files, and name and save the file in the **Save As** dialog box.
5. Click **Next** to open the **Completing the Automated System Recovery Preparation Wizard** screen.
6. Click **Finish** to create a backup of your system files. The **Backup Progress** dialog box will open. Next, the **Selection Information** message box will open and show you the file and byte estimates (**Figure 14-18**).
7. Once the estimate is complete, the **Backup Progress** dialog box will show how much has been backed up and how long the remaining backup should take (**Figure 14-19**). The entire process can take quite some time. When it is complete, you will be prompted to insert a floppy disk to create the ASR floppy disk.
8. Once the ASR floppy disk has been created, close the Backup program.
9. The backup set and the floppy disk together will be used to restore your system in the event of a complete system failure.

tip

To restore a system using ASR, boot from the Windows XP professional CD, press F2 and provide the ASR diskette when prompted.

Figure 14-17 Specifying the Backup Destination

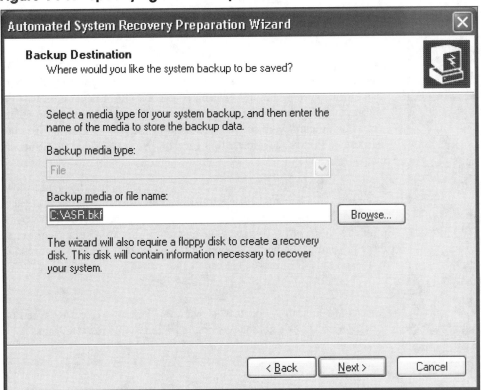

Figure 14-18 Estimating number and size of files in backup

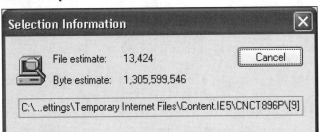

Figure 14-19 Backup Progress window

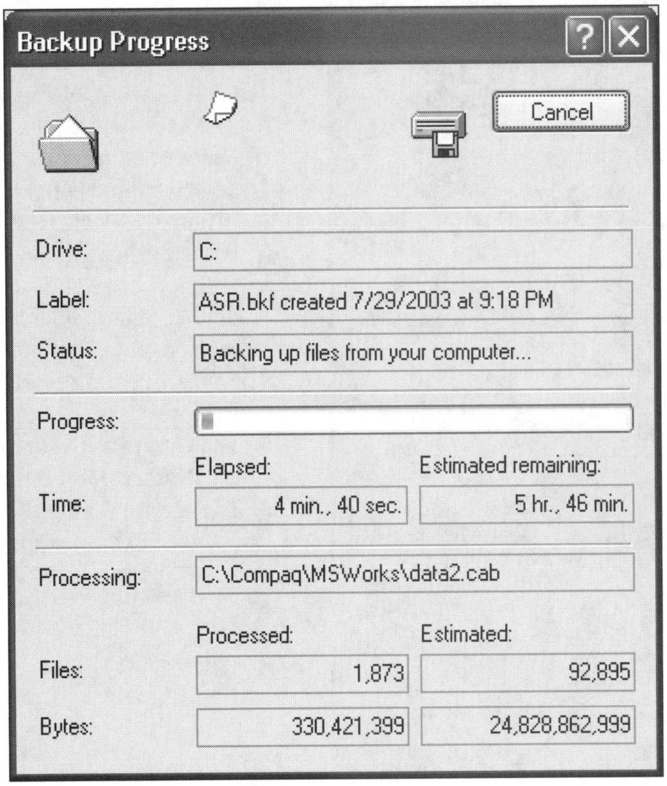

project 14.5

Using System Restore to Revert to a Previous Configuration

exam objective

Restore and back up the operating system, System State data, and user data.

overview

System Restore enables you to roll back the configuration of the operating system to a previous point without losing any user data. It allows you to undo changes that have been made to the system that are causing problems with its operation by restoring the files and settings that were in use at a previous **Restore Point**. Restore Points are automatically created when a significant event occurs, such as when a driver or application is installed, and they are also created daily (assuming that the computer is on). In addition, they can be created manually at any time.

There have been several recent cases where a computer has had to have its configuration restored from a backup because it had become unstable due to some new software that was installed. In some other cases, configuration changes and new drivers have caused similar problems. In an effort to reduce the amount of downtime that users are suffering because of these problems, you intend to attempt to use **System Restore** to correct the problems before you resort to restoring from backup media.

tip

The amount of disk space allocated to store Restore Points can be adjusted by opening the properties for **My Computer**, selecting the System Restore tab and changing the **Disk Space to use** slider control.

learning objective

After completing this project, you will know how to create a Restore Point, and use System Restore to roll back a computer's configuration to that Restore Point.

specific requirements

Administrative rights on a Windows XP Professional computer.

estimated completion time

15 minutes

project steps

Create a Restore Point and examine System Restore settings.

1. Click **Start**, **All Programs**, **Accessories**, **System Tools**, and **System Restore**.
2. The **Welcome to System Restore** screen will open (**Figure 14-20**). Click the *System Restore Settings* link.
3. The **System Properties** dialog box will open with the **System Restore** tab selected (**Figure 14-21**). Review the available options and click **OK** to close the System Properties dialog box. If you have multiple drives available on your system, your screen will appear slightly differently. By selecting the desired drive and then clicking the Settings button, the amount of space allocated to System Restore can be configured for each drive.
4. Select **Create a Restore Point** from the right hand pane of the **Welcome to System Restore** screen and click **Next**.
5. The **Create a Restore Point** screen will open. Type **Before Changing Video Settings** in the **Restore point description** text box (**Figure 14-22**). Click **Create**.
6. The **Restore Point Created** screen will open and will list the date, time and name assigned to the restore point that was just created. Click **Close**.

Figure 14-20 The Welcome to System Restore screen

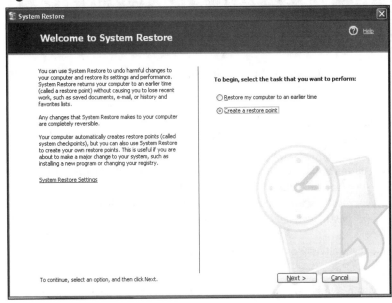

Figure 14-21 The System Restore properties tab

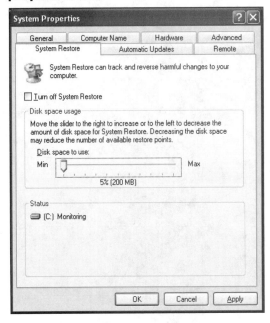

Figure 14-22 Creating a Restore Point

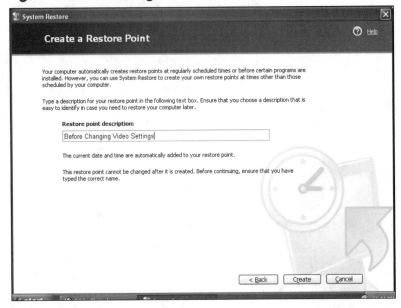

project 14.5

Using System Restore to Revert to a Previous Configuration *(cont'd)*

exam objective

Restore and back up the operating system, System State data, and user data.

project steps

Next, you will make changes to the system configuration.

7. Click **Start**, right-click **My Computer** and select **Properties** from the menu.
8. The **System Properties** dialog box will open. Select the **Advanced** tab.
9. Click the **Settings** button in the **Performance** section to open the **Performance Options** dialog box. Make sure that the **Visual Effects** tab is selected.
10. Select the **Adjust for best performance** option button and click **OK** to save the change (**Figure 14-23**). Observe the changes that have been made to the appearance of the user interface.
11. Click **OK** to close the **System Properties** dialog box.

Now, you will use System Restore to roll back the configuration changes that were just made.

12. Open System Restore again by clicking **Start**, **All Programs**, **Accessories**, **System Tools**, and **System Restore**.
13. Select the **Restore my computer to an earlier time** option button and click **Next** to open the **Select a Restore Point** screen (**Figure 14-24**).
14. Select the most recent **Before Changing Video Settings** restore point from the list and click **Next** to open the **Confirm Restore Point Selection** screen (**Figure 14-25**).
15. If you are using any other applications, make sure that you have saved your work. Click **Next** to revert back to the selected Restore Point. The system will shut down, restore the system and restart.
16. Log on as the **Administrator**. The **Restoration Complete** screen will appear (**Figure 14-26**). Click **OK** to close the screen.
17. Examine the user interface to confirm that it has been returned to its original configuration.

Figure 14-23 Changing Visual Effects for best performance

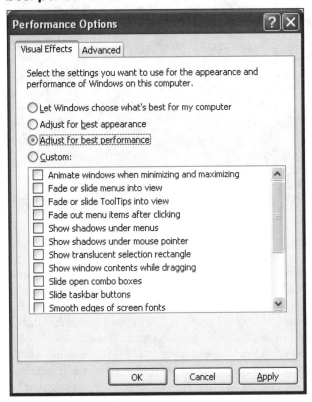

Figure 14-24 Selecting a Restore Point to restore

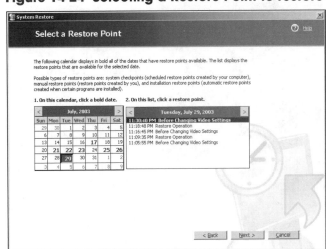

Figure 14-25 Confirming Restore Point Selection

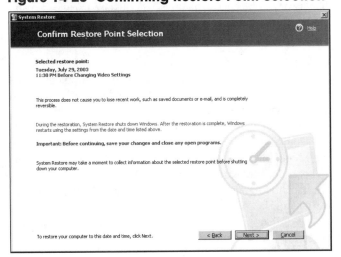

Figure 14-26 The Restoration Complete screen

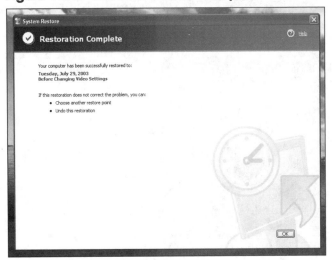

15 Working with the Registry and Boot Process

The Registry is a database that stores hardware and software configuration information. Windows constantly accesses the Registry during operation. Everything from display settings to NIC settings, user profiles, local computer policies, and hardware profile information is stored in the Registry. The Registry is crucially important to the operation of the operating system, functioning in the areas of security, file location, remembering user preferences, tuning parameters, and device configuration. For example, when you make changes to the display settings on your desktop or add new hardware to your computer, Windows XP Professional stores the display settings or the settings for the new drivers in the Registry. When the operating system or an application you are running malfunctions, you may be able to edit the Registry to remedy the problem or restore it to the same version you were using when you last successfully started your computer.

The Registry is organized in a hierarchical structure, which you can view with the Registry Editor. You can access the Registry Editor from the Run dialog box using either of two commands: regedit or regedt32. As with Windows Explorer, you use the plus sign buttons to expand the hierarchical tree to display more branches in the tree. You can also use the Registry Editor to edit information in the Registry such as configuration settings. After you make changes in the Registry Editor, they are immediately saved and applied.

The settings in the Registry file are read during the boot process (the process followed by a computer as it starts). When you are booting your computer and any type of problem occurs that prevents the operating system from starting, you can try to use the Last Known Good Configuration, which is stored in the Registry, to resolve the problem. As its name indicates, the Last Known Good Configuration contains settings saved in the Registry the last time a user successfully logged on to the computer. You can also try to boot the computer in Safe Mode. When you start up in Safe Mode, only the basic drivers and files are loaded and the Registry is activated. You can use Safe Mode to remove corrupt drivers, fix driver conflicts, or uninstall and reinstall applications. If Safe Mode and the Last Known Good Configuration do not work, you can try the Recovery Console. The Recovery Console enables you to start the operating system when all else has failed. It provides you with a set of administrative command-line tools that can be used to repair your Windows XP Professional installation.

Scenario

You are working as an Assistant System Administrator at Riverside Financial Services. Riverside has a Windows 2000 Server domain-based network with 50 Windows XP Professional clients.

Lesson 15 Working with the Registry and Boot Process

Project	Exam 70-270 Objective
15.1 Working with the Registry Editor	Basic knowledge
15.2 Modifying the boot.ini File	Basic knowledge
15.3 Identifying Advanced Boot Options	Troubleshoot system restoration by starting in safe mode. Restore and back up the operating system, System State data, and user data.
15.4 Using the Recovery Console	Restore and back up the operating system, System State data, and user data. Recover System State data and user data by using the Recovery console.

General Requirements

To complete the projects in this lesson, you will need administrative rights on a Windows XP Professional computer.

project 15.1

Working with the Registry Editor

exam objective

Basic Knowledge

overview

Your supervisor asks you to go over the Windows XP Registry with a new intern in your department. You decide that the first thing you will stress is the importance of backing up the Registry before making any modifications. You also want to make sure that the intern understands how values in the Registry can be modified using the Control Panel, which is the safest method, as well as in the Registry itself. Finally you want to make sure that the intern understands how to locate and view Registry data and how certain Registry keys are related.

learning objective

After completing this project, you will know how to:
- ◆ Use the Backup Utility to make a backup of the Registry.
- ◆ Locate and view Registry data.
- ◆ Use the Control Panel to modify Registry settings.
- ◆ Understand the relationship between the HKEY_CLASSES_ROOT and HKEY_LOCAL_MACHINE keys.

specific requirements

Administrative rights on a Windows XP Professional computer.

estimated completion time

20 minutes

project steps

Backup the Registry.
1. Log on to the computer as an **Administrator**.
2. Create a new folder named **RegBackup** on your system drive.
3. Click **Start**, point to **All Programs**, point to **Accessories**, point to **System Tools** and click **Backup** to start the Windows XP Backup utility.
4. The **Welcome to the Backup or Restore Wizard** screen will open. Click the **Advanced Mode** hyperlink to open the **Backup Utility**.
5. Click the **Backup Wizard (Advanced)** button to start the Backup Wizard.
6. The **Welcome to the Backup Wizard** screen will open. Click **Next** to continue.
7. Select the **Only back up System State data** option button and click **Next (Figure 15-1)**.
8. Click the **Browse** button. The **Save As** dialog box will open. Navigate to the **RegBackup** folder you created in step 2. In the **File name** text box, type **Registry.bkf**. Click **Save** to close the **Save As** dialog box and return to the Backup Wizard **(Figure 15-2)**.
9. Click **Next** to open the **Completing the Backup Wizard** screen. Confirm the settings and click **Finish** to backup the Registry.
10. The **Backup Progress** dialog box will display the progress of the backup process.
11. When the backup is complete, click **Report** to make sure there are no error messages. Close the report and the **Backup** utility.

Create a new Registered file type.
12. Open **Control Panel** and if necessary switch to Classic View.
13. Double-click the **Folder Options** icon to open the **Folder Options** dialog box.
14. Open the **File Types** tab. All existing file extensions and the file types with which they are associated display in the **Registered file types** list box **(Figure 15-3)**.
15. Click **New** to open the **Create New Extension** dialog box. Click **Advanced** to expand the dialog box.

Figure 15-1 Selecting to backup the System State

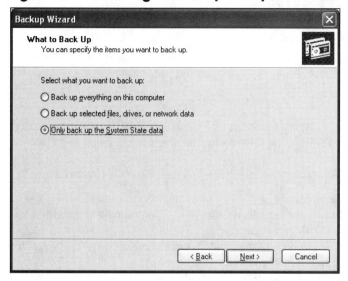

Figure 15-2 Specifying the backup destination

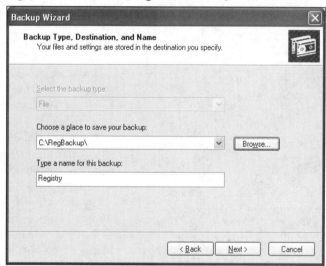

Figure 15-3 The Registered file types list box

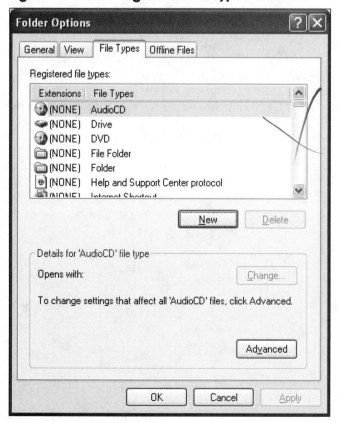

project 15.1

Working with the Registry Editor (cont'd)

exam objective

Basic Knowledge

project steps

16. In the **File Extension** text box, type **new**. In the **Associated File Type** list box, select **Text Document (Figure 15-4)**. Click **OK** to save the new file extension and close the dialog box.
17. Click **Close** to close the Folder Options dialog box and then close the Control Panel.

Search and edit the Registry using regedit.

18. Click **Start** and select **Run** to open the **Run** dialog box. Type **regedit** in the **Open** text box and click **OK** to open the Registry editor.
19. Select **My Computer** in the left pane of the window. Open the **Edit** menu and select the **Find** command to open the **Find** dialog box.
20. In the **Find what** text box, type **.new**. In the **Look at** section, remove the checks from the **Values** and **Data** check boxes. Select the **Match whole string only** check box **(Figure 15-5)**. Click **Find Next**.
21. The .new extension that you just created is located in the HKEY_CLASSES_ROOT key **(Figure 15-6)**. This key contains the file extension and associated application data on the computer. The contents of this key are copied from another Registry key (as you will see later in this project) and can be modified on the File Types tab in the Folder options dialog box as you did in step 16 of this project.
22. Right-click the **.new** extension and select **Delete**. Click **Yes** to confirm the deletion. You can open the Folder Options dialog box to verify that the **.new** extension has been removed.
23. Right-click **HKEY_CLASSES_ROOT**, point to **New** and click **Key**. In the text box for the new key, type **.new** and press **[Enter]**.
24. In the right pane in the Registry editor window, double-click **(Default)** to open the **Edit String** dialog box. Enter **txtfile** in the **Value data** text box **(Figure 15-7)**. Click **OK** to save the key value.
25. In the left pane, scroll up the Registry tree and collapse the **HKEY_CLASSES_ROOT** key.
26. Expand the **HKEY_LOCAL_MACHINE** key. Expand the **SOFTWARE** subkey. Expand the **Classes** subkey. Scroll down and locate the **.new** key.
27. Delete the **.new** file extension and close the **Registry Editor**. You can open the Folder Options dialog box to verify that the **.new** extension has been removed and then close the **Control Panel**.
28. What key are the contents of the **HKEY_CLASSES_ROOT** key copied from?

Figure 15-4 Creating a New File Extension

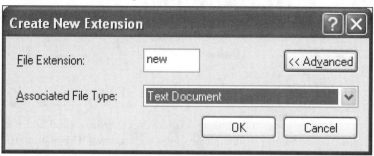

Figure 15-5 Searching the Registry for a key

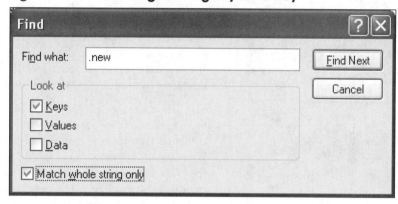

Figure 15-6 The .new file extension in the Registry Editor

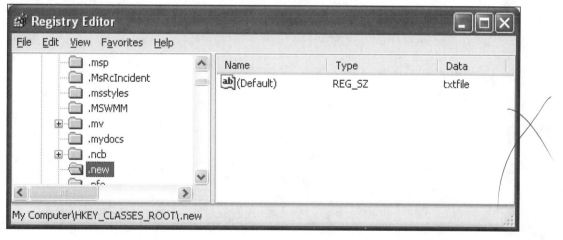

Figure 15-7 Editing the string associated with a Registry key

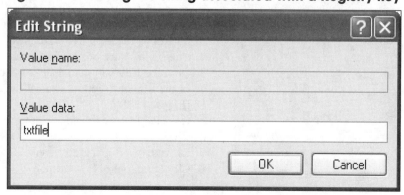

project 15.2   *Modifying the boot.ini File*

exam objective

Basic knowledge

overview

The **boot.ini** file is created during the installation of Windows XP Professional and it is accessed during the selecting the operating system phase of the boot process. The boot.ini file is saved in the root of the system partition, and it tells the computer what OS choices to display during startup. It consists of the **[boot loader]** and the **[operating systems]** sections. The **[boot loader]** section has two entries. First, the **timeout** entry, which defines the number of seconds that the system will wait for operator intervention before loading the default operating system. Second, the **default** entry, which is the Advanced Risc Computing (ARC) path for the default operating system. The **[operating systems]** section follows the [boot loader] section and can have any number of entries under it. Each entry under operating systems is the ARC path to an operating system and a text value that will be displayed on the Operating System Selection screen during the boot process.

Sam Trover's computer has both Windows 95 and Windows XP Professional installed. He needs both versions of the operating system because he has certain demo applications installed on his computer that are only compatible with Windows 95. However, since he most often uses Windows XP, he wants you to speed up the boot process. Presently, unless he is attending to his computer and chooses Windows XP on the Select the Operating System to Start screen, the computer will wait the default 30 seconds before starting Windows XP, which is the default operating system. You decide to edit the boot.ini file so that the timeout period will be only 5 seconds.

tip

Remember that drives and controllers begin with the number 0 and that partitions begin with the number 1 when working with ARC paths.

learning objective

After completing this project, you will know how to edit the boot.ini file using two methods; the Startup and Recovery dialog box or directly editing the file in Notepad. Using the Startup and Recovery dialog box is the recommended method unless you must edit the ARC path either by adding switches or changing the disk numbering.

specific requirements

Administrative rights on a Windows XP Professional computer.

estimated completion time

10 minutes

project steps

Edit boot.ini using the Startup and Recovery dialog box or by directly editing the file in Notepad.

1. Open the Control Panel. Double-click the **System** icon to open the **System Properties** dialog box.
2. Open the **Advanced** tab, and click **Settings** in the **Startup and Recovery** section to open the **Startup and Recovery** dialog box.
3. In the **Time to display list of operating systems** spin box, change the default timeout period to 5 seconds (**Figure 15-8**). Notice that you can also change the default operating system in the **System startup** section of the dialog box. This is the recommended method for editing the boot.ini file for these two settings.
4. Change the value back to 30 to complete the rest of the exercise.
5. Click the **Edit** button to open the boot.ini file for editing with notepad.
6. In the **timeout** section, change the default timeout period of 30 seconds to 5 seconds (**Figure 15-9**).
7. Open the **File** menu and click the Save command to save the setting.
8. Close Notepad.
9. Close the Startup and Recovery and System Properties dialog boxes.
10. Close the Control Panel window.

caution

Always create a backup copy of the boot.ini file before you modify it. Even minor errors in the boot.ini file can result in your computer not booting.

Figure 15-8 The Startup and Recovery dialog box

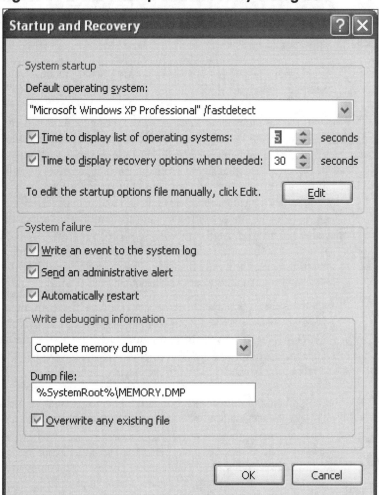

Figure 15-9 Editing boot.ini using Notepad

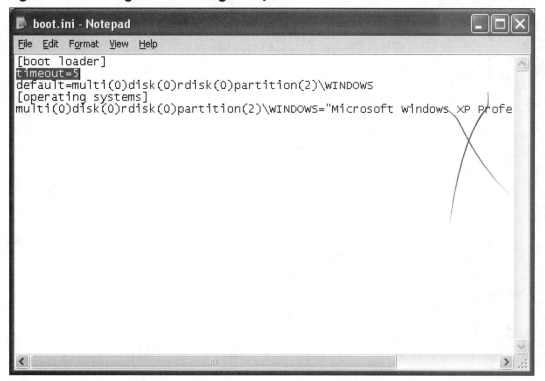

project 15.3

Identifying Advanced Boot Options

exam objective

Troubleshoot system restoration by starting in safe mode. Restore and back up the operating system, System State data, and user data.

overview

If you are having trouble starting the operating system, you can restart and press F8 at boot time to open the **Windows Advanced Options Menu**. You can use the arrow keys on your keyboard to select from several **Safe Mode** commands **(Figure 15-10)**. Safe Mode is used to resolve problems that result from faulty device drivers, faulty programs, system service failures, or services that start automatically. Usually, when you start in Safe Mode, you will be opening the Control Panel so that you can undo whatever setting you recently configured that may be causing the operating system to malfunction at boot time. You can start or stop a system service, uninstall a recently installed program, change a recently instituted display setting, or uninstall a recently installed device driver. When you boot in Safe Mode, the operating system will only load a basic set of files and drivers for the keyboard, mouse, basic VGA monitor, default system services, and disk.

tip

A serial mouse will not function in Safe Mode because serial drivers are not loaded in Safe Mode.

While installing a new software program on his computer, York Sutherland, a junior consultant, changed the resolution of his monitor to 1024 by 768 pixels. As soon as he applied the change, the screen of the computer started to flicker. He shut down and was unable to restart the operating system. You need to start the operating system in Safe Mode and change the resolution back to 800 by 600 pixels.

learning objective

After completing this project, you will know how to restore the computer to proper operation using the Safe Mode option.

specific requirements

Administrative rights on a Windows XP Professional computer.

estimated completion time

10 minutes

project steps

Start your computer in **Safe Mode** and restore the **Display settings**.

1. Shut down and restart your computer.
2. If there is more than one operating system installed, the **Please select the operating system to start** screen will appear. Press the F8 key to open the **Windows Advanced Options Menu (Figure 15-10)**. Use the arrow keys to select **Safe Mode** and press the **[Enter]** key to open the **Please select the operating system to start** screen again. Notice that it indicates **Safe Mode** in blue in the bottom left corner of the screen. Select the operating system to boot and press the **[Enter]** key.
3. If there is only one operating system installed, immediately start pressing the F8 key on your keyboard until the **Windows Advanced Options Menu** appears **(Figure 15-10)**. Use the arrow keys to select **Safe Mode** and press the **[Enter]** key to boot the operating system.
4. When the **Welcome to Windows** dialog box opens, log on as an **Administrator**.
5. The **Desktop** message box informs you that Windows is running in Safe Mode and that some devices may not be available **(Figure 15-11)**.

Figure 15-10 The Windows Advanced Options Menu

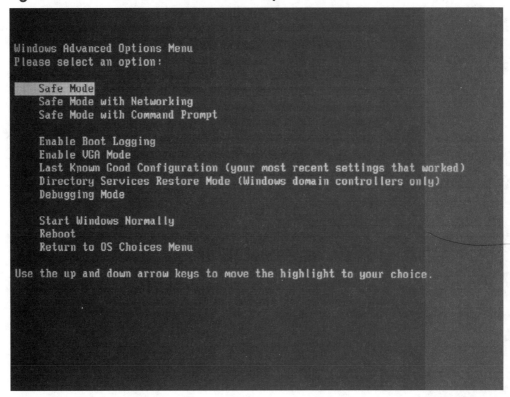

Figure 15-11 The Desktop warning dialog box

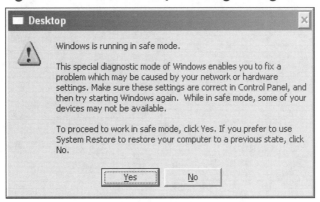

project 15.3

Identifying Advanced Boot Options (cont'd)

exam objective

Troubleshoot system restoration by starting in safe mode. Restore and back up the operating system, System State data, and user data.

project steps

6. Click **Yes** to continue with Startup. When Startup is complete, your desktop will be displayed with no wallpaper and 'Safe Mode' will appear in all four corners of the screen.
7. Click **Start** and click the **Control Panel** command to open the **Control Panel** window. Switch to Classic View if necessary.
8. Double-click the **Display** icon to open the **Display Properties** dialog box and select the **Settings** tab where you can change the screen resolution.
9. Drag the **Screen area** slider to set it at **800 by 600** pixels **(Figure 15-12)**.
10. Click **Apply**. The screen will go black and the new settings will be applied.
11. Click **OK** to close the Display Properties dialog box.
12. Close the Control Panel.
13. Restart the computer.

Figure 15-12 The Display Properties dialog box

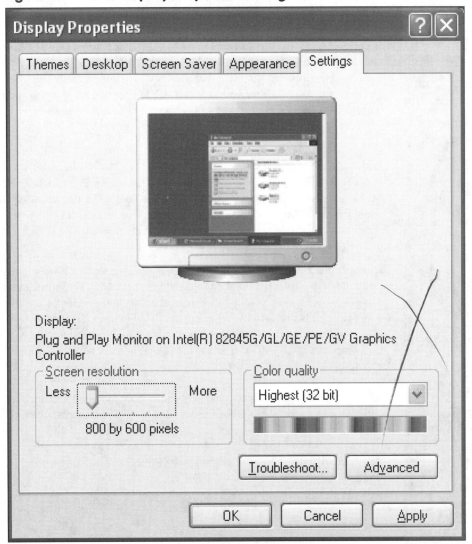

project 15.4

Using the Recovery Console

exam objective

Restore and back up the operating system, System State data, and user data. Recover System State data and user data by using the Recovery console.

overview

If you are unable to fix boot problems using the Last Known Good Configuration, Safe Mode, or a System Restore, the final tool you can turn to is the **Recovery Console**. It is a mini command line operating system that allows you to access the NTFS volumes on your system and perform tasks such as list, copy and delete files, set the startup mode for services, repair corrupt boot sectors and master boot records, and manage partitions.

You start the Recovery Console by booting your computer with a Windows XP Professional CD or from the Windows XP Professional Setup disks. To obtain the Windows XP Professional Setup disks you must download them from Microsoft's web site. You can also pre-install the Recovery Console onto your Windows XP Professional computers so that it can be run simply by selecting it from the **Please select the operating system to start** screen when the computer first boots. The Recovery Console method is recommended only if you are an advanced user or Administrator who can use basic commands to identify and locate problems relating to drivers and files.

Richard Anderson, one of the consultants, is not able to boot his computer. You suspect that a virus may have infected his computer and that the Master Boot Record has been affected. Since you cannot boot his computer using the Last Known Good Configuration or Safe Mode, you will fix this problem by booting from the Windows XP Professional CD-ROM and then using the Recovery Console. However, you want to install the Recovery Console on the rest of the computers in the office first so that it will be easier to repair them if they also become infected.

learning objective

After completing this project, you will know how to install the Recovery Console and start and use it by selecting it from the Windows XP Professional operating system selection screen.

specific requirements

◆   Administrative rights on a Windows XP Professional computer.
◆   A Windows XP Professional CD-ROM.

estimated completion time

15 minutes

project steps

Install and run the Recovery Console.
  1. Insert the Windows XP Professional CD into the CD-ROM drive of your computer.
  2. Click **Start** and click the **Run** command to open the Run dialog box. Enter: **X:\i386\winnt32.exe /cmdcons**, where **X** represents the drive letter for your CD-ROM drive, and click **OK (Figure 15-13)**.
  3. A **Windows Setup** warning dialog box will open to let you know that you can install the Windows Recovery Console as a startup option and that it will require 7 MB of hard disk space **(Figure 15-14)**. Click **Yes** to setup Recovery Console.
  4. First the computer will attempt to perform a dynamic update. Press **[Esc]** to cancel the search for updates. Click **Yes** to cancel the download. This dialog box will appear whether you are connected to the Internet or not.
  5. Select the **Skip this step and continue installing Windows** option button, and click **Next** to open the **Copying Installation Files** screen.

tip

The Recovery Console can also be accessed by booting the computer from the Windows XP Professional CD-ROM and then selecting Repair to run the Recovery Console.

Figure 15-13 Starting the Recovery Console setup

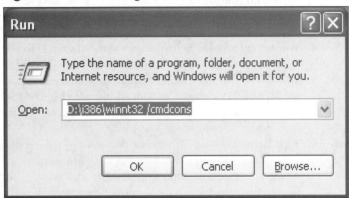

Figure 15-14 Confirming installation of the Recovery Console as a startup option

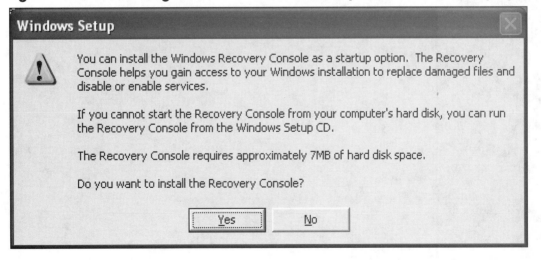

project 15.4

Using the Recovery Console (cont'd)

exam objective

Restore and back up the operating system, System State data, and user data. Recover System State data and user data by using the Recovery console.

project steps

6. In less than a minute, a **Microsoft Windows XP Professional Setup** dialog box will open to inform you that the Recovery Console has been successfully installed. Click **OK**.
7. Restart the computer. When the **Please select the operating system to start** screen opens, select **Microsoft Windows Recovery Console** and press **[Enter]**.
8. You will be asked which Windows installation you would like to log on to; usually there will only be one installation. Type: **1** and press **[Enter]**.
9. You will be prompted to log on using an Administrator password. Enter the password and press **[Enter]** to open a command prompt **(Figure 15-15)**. Even if the computer is a member of a domain, this password is the Local Administrator account password—not the Domain Administrator password.
10. Type **Help**, and press **[Enter]** to view a list of the Recovery Console commands.
11. Press **[Enter]** to scroll down the list of commands.
12. At the command prompt, type **fixmbr** and press **[Enter]** to repair the Master Boot Record that may have become corrupt by a virus. Viruses commonly affect the MBR on the hard drive.
13. Type **Exit** and press **[Enter]** to restart the computer.

Figure 15-15 Logging on to the Recovery Console

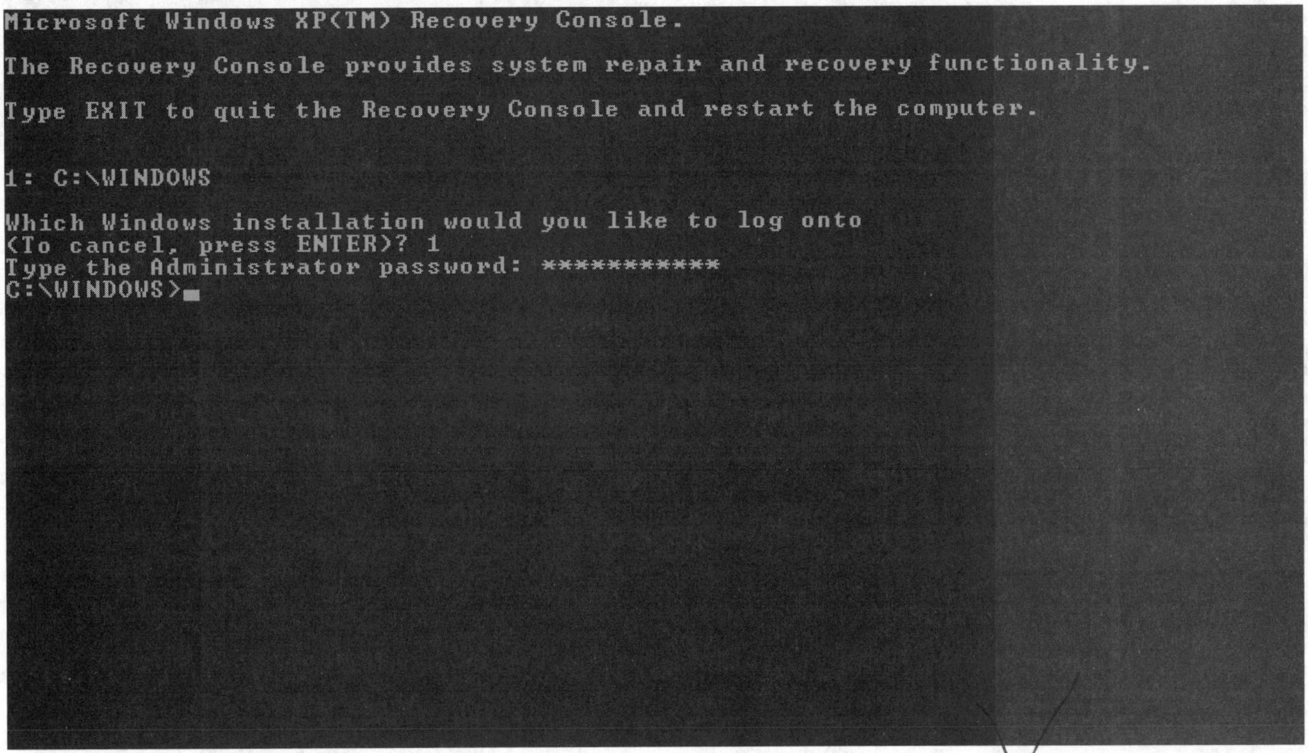

```
Microsoft Windows XP(TM) Recovery Console.

The Recovery Console provides system repair and recovery functionality.

Type EXIT to quit the Recovery Console and restart the computer.


1: C:\WINDOWS

Which Windows installation would you like to log onto
<To cancel, press ENTER>? 1
Type the Administrator password: ***********
C:\WINDOWS>_
```

To support users that are geographically separated, it is necessary to use WAN protocols. Some think that the difference between a LAN and a WAN is the distance involved. While it is often true that WANs are used to cover greater distances than LANs, the real difference between them is the protocols that are used to establish and maintain the data link. While LANs will use OSI Layer 2 protocols like Ethernet and 802.5 (Token Ring), WANs use Layer 2 protocols such as PPP, HDLC and Frame Relay.

These protocols can be used over many different types of physical media. Dial-up connections are commonly made using the Public Switched Telephone Network (PSTN), also referred to as Plain Old Telephone Service (POTS). This is a circuit switched network that establishes a link from the caller to the receiver for the duration of the call and then disconnects the link. Basic Rate Interface (BRI) ISDN also uses switched circuits but provides two 64Kbps digital 'Bearer' channels for communication and one 16Kbps 'Delta' channel for call setup and maintenance. Dedicated digital circuits such as T1 lines provide point to point connectivity at higher speeds. Frame Relay is often cheaper for long distances and relies on frame switches to send frames through a 'cloud' where each frame from a specific source will follow a pre-defined Permanent Virtual Circuit (PVC) to its destination. Asynchronous Transfer Mode (ATM) uses a network that switches fixed size cells at very high speeds and is often used to support voice, video, and data at the same time.

Your Windows XP Professional computer uses dial-up networking or Remote Access Services (RAS), as well as virtual private networks (VPNs) to connect to the other systems using these and other types of physical circuits. For example, you might need to access resources on your PC or on your organization's LAN when you are traveling to another state or country, or you might want to make a resource on your computer available to a branch office or even to a single user in another city or state. Your employees might also need Internet access on your local LAN if you do not yet have a dedicated connection, or they may need to access their e-mail while on the road. Network and Dialup software or Remote Access Services are used to connect to an ISP (Internet Service Provider) or to your company's network. Users dial in to a RAS server, connect to it through a modem, and the RAS server routes the connection to the LAN via a network interface card. Internet Connection Sharing (ICS) is used to share an Internet link with other computers on your LAN so that just one computer on the LAN functions as the gateway to the Web. This is particularly useful for small networks where it may not be feasible to have separate dial-up connections for different computers on a network.

Security is an important consideration when you access resources over a public network. In order to create secure connections, Windows XP Professional supports several protocols that provide security, authentication, and encryption for RAS connections. Virtual private networks (VPNs) are used to create secure connections over an untrusted public network. VPNs use tunneling protocols to create a secure tunnel within the public Internet through which the corporate LAN can be accessed.

Some features new to Windows XP include the ability to set up a basic firewall using an Internet Connection Firewall (ICF), and the ability to establish Remote Desktop sessions with another Windows XP computer. Remote Desktop sessions can be used by telecommuting or traveling employees to access their desktop computers at the workplace. Remote Assistance allows Windows XP users to contact help desk technicians and support personnel, who are also at a Windows XP machine, to obtain help in resolving system difficulties.

Scenario

You are the System Administrator at Tech Systems Inc. located in Houston, Texas. Tech Systems has 50 employees in its main office in Houston and its branch office in Chicago. The Houston employees need to access resources on computers at the Chicago office and on the Internet. At the Houston office, there are 35 Windows XP Professional client computers and several servers. Mark Wendell owns Tech Systems and works in the Texas office. The employees of Tech Systems Inc. often need to access resources on the local network or remote networks.

Lesson 16 Configuring Remote Access and Dial-up Networking

Project	Exam 70-270 Objective
16.1 Creating a Dial-Up Connection to a Remote Access Server	Connect to computers using dial-up networking. Create a dial-up connection to a Remote Access server.
16.2 Connecting to the Internet by Using a Dial-Up Connection	Connect to computers using dial-up networking. Connect to the Internet using dial-up networking.
16.3 Setting Up a VPN Connection	Connect to computers using dial-up networking. Connect to computers using a virtual private connection (VPN).
16.4 Configuring Inbound Connections	Connect to computers using dial-up networking.
16.5 Configuring Internet Connection Sharing	Connect to computers using dial-up networking. Configure and troubleshoot Internet Connection Sharing (ICS).
16.6 Setting Up a Firewall	Connect to computers using dial-up networking. Configure, manage, and troubleshoot an Internet connection firewall (ICF).
16.7 Configuring Remote Desktop and Remote Assistance	Connect to computers using dial-up networking. Configure, manage, and troubleshoot remote desktop and remote assistance.

General Requirements

To complete the projects in this lesson, you will need administrative rights on a Windows XP Professional computer with a modem installed. Two Windows XP Professional computers will be required to fully explore some projects.

project 16.1

Creating a Dial-Up Connection to a Remote Access Server

exam objective

Connect to computers using dial-up networking. Create a dial-up connection to a Remote Access server.

overview

You can create a RAS connection to a local area network (LAN) from a remote location. For example, if you are traveling to another city as part of your job and you need to access resources on your office computer, you can configure a Windows XP Professional computer as a RAS client to use a modem or another device to connect to your RAS server. Using RAS, you simply connect to the LAN by dialing the phone number of the RAS server and provide log on credentials that are authorized for remote access. When you dial in to the RAS server, it receives the data from the modem and sends it to the LAN through the network interface card (NIC). Depending on the Layer 3 protocol in use, the RAS server acts as either a router or a gateway to the rest of the network. When the RAS connection has been established, the remote user can access network resources for which they have permissions in the same way they would if they were logged on to the LAN.

Mark Wendell wants to connect his computer to the network at the Chicago office. He also wants to be the sole user of this connection because the data he will be accessing is confidential. Configure an outbound connection on his computer using a standard modem and make sure that only he can use the connection.

learning objective

After completing this project, you will know how to create a dial-up connection to a remote access server.

specific requirements

◆ Administrative rights on a Windows XP Professional computer with a modem.
◆ The phone number needed to access the RAS server to which you wish to connect.

estimated completion time

15 minutes

project steps

Create a dial-up connection to a RAS.
1. Click **Start**, and then click **Control Panel**. Switch to Classic View if necessary and double-click **Network Connections** to open the **Network Connections** window.
2. In the **Network Tasks** section, click the **Create a new connection** link to start the **New Connection Wizard**.
3. If this is the first time that the **New Connection Wizard** has been run, the **Location Information** dialog box will open (**Figure 16-1**). The information is used by the Telephony API (TAPI) to configure dialing rules for all telephony programs. Select your country from the **What country/region are you in now?** selection box and type your area code in the **What area code (or city code) are you in now?** input box. Click **OK** to open the **Phone and Modem Options** dialog box. Click **OK** to accept the default location.
4. On the **Network Connection Wizard** screen, click **Next** to open the **Network Connection Type** screen. Select the **Connect to the network at my workplace** option button (**Figure 16-2**).

Figure 16-1 Entering TAPI Location Information

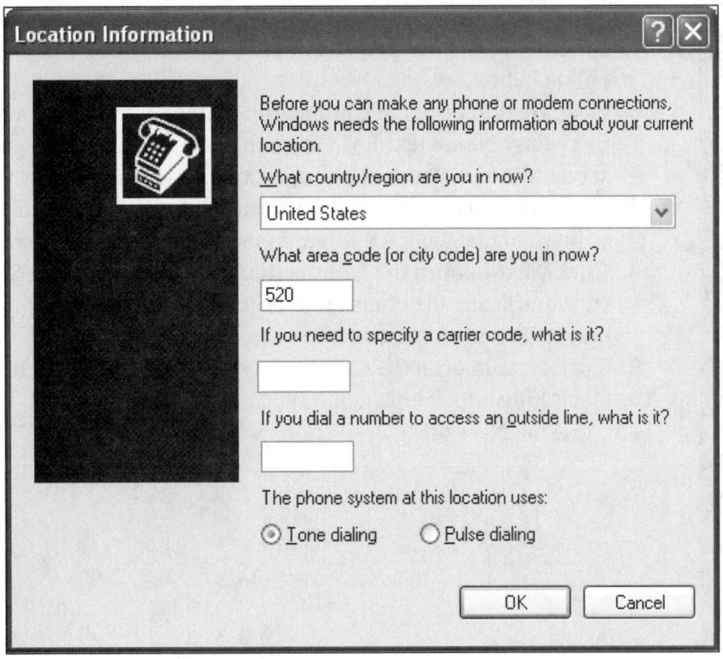

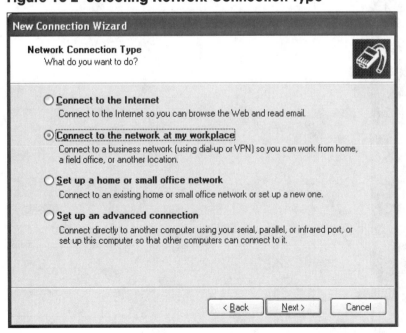

Figure 16-2 Selecting Network Connection Type

project 16.1

Creating a Dial-Up Connection to a Remote Access Server (cont'd)

exam objective

Connect to computers using dial-up networking. Create a dial-up connection to a Remote Access server.

project steps

5. Click **Next** to open the **Network Connection** screen. Select the **Dial-up connection** option button.

6. Click **Next** to open the **Connection Name** screen. Enter a name for the connection in the **Company Name** text box. You can enter the name of your company or the name of the server to which you will be connecting.

7. Click **Next** to open the **Phone Number to Dial** screen. Enter the telephone number you will use to dial the RAS server in the **Phone number** text box.

8. Click **Next** to open the **Connection Availability** screen. Select the **Anyone's use** option button to make the connection accessible to all users **(Figure 16-3)**. (*Note:* this step is only applicable if the computer is a member of a domain.)

9. Click **Next** to open the **Completing the New Connection Wizard** screen.

10. Click **Finish** to complete the Wizard.

11. Close the **Network Connections** window.

tip

You will only be prompted to select the connection availability if your computer is a member of a domain. Connections created on a computer that is a member of a workgroup will always be shared with all users on that computer.

Figure 16-3 The Connection Availability screen

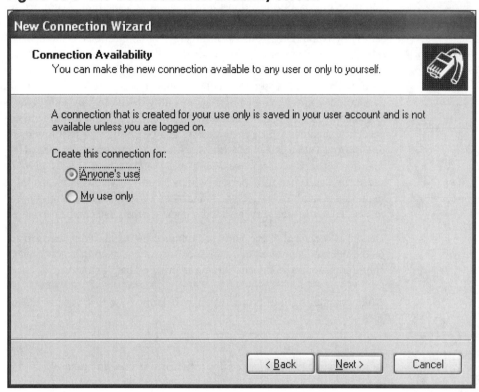

project 16.2

Connecting to the Internet by Using a Dial-Up Connection

exam objective

Connect to computers using dial-up networking. Connect to the Internet using dial-up networking.

overview

You can establish a connection to the Internet using one of several methods. The most common way is through dial-up access using a modem. A connection to an ISP is also commonly made through an ISDN adapter and ISDN line, a cable modem, or a Digital Subscriber Line (DSL). Any of these types of connections to the internet can be shared with other computers on a LAN by using Internet Connection Sharing (ICS). Another method of establishing a connection with the Internet is through a **proxy server**. Proxy servers have two main purposes. First, they provide a connection to the Internet for computers on a LAN. Second, they provide a means for controlling in-coming and out-going requests for service. For instance, a proxy server can be used by an employer to prevent employees from accessing certain Web sites. A proxy server can also be configured to allow or disallow access from unauthorized computers outside the LAN. Many proxy servers also provide caching to improve network performance. Web pages that have been requested by network users will be saved for a specified time period by the caching server. This means that when a second user requests the same Web page, the request can be fulfilled by the proxy server rather than being forwarded to the Web server, so the request for the page can be carried out more quickly.

Debbie Howe, head of the Software Engineering team, often needs to search for information on the Internet. However, her computer does not have an Internet connection. She asks you to configure a dial-up connection to the Internet on her computer.

learning objective

After completing this project, you will know how to create a dial-up connection to the Internet.

specific requirements

Administrative rights on a Windows XP Professional computer.

estimated completion time

15 minutes

project steps

Connect to the Internet using a dial-up modem.
1. Click **Start**, click **Control Panel**, click the **Switch to Classic View** link if required, and double-click **Network Connections** to open the **Network Connections** window.
2. Click the **Create a new connection** link to start the **New Connection Wizard**.
3. Click **Next** to open the **Network Connection Type** screen. Select the **Connect to the Internet** option button.
4. Click **Next** to open the **Getting Ready** screen. Select the **Set up my connection manually** option button. This selection assumes you have chosen your ISP and have the information provided by the ISP that you will need to enter, such as the phone number for the ISP, and your user name and password (**Figure 16-4**).
5. Click **Next** to open the **Internet Connection** screen. Select the **Connect using a dial-up modem** option button (**Figure 16-5**).

Figure 16-4 The Getting Ready screen

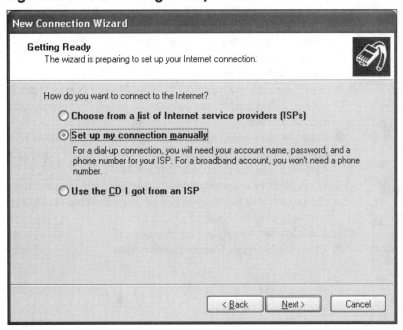

Figure 16-5 The Internet Connection screen

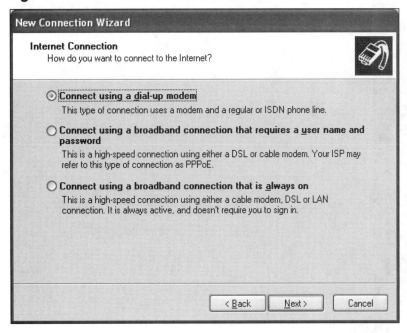

Connecting to the Internet by Using a Dial-Up Connection (cont'd)

exam objective

Connect to computers using dial-up networking. Connect to the Internet using dial-up networking.

project steps

tip

You can also create a desktop shortcut for any connection you create by right-clicking the connection in the Network Connections window and selecting Create Shortcut.

6. Click **Next** to open the **Connection Name** screen. Enter the name of your ISP in the **ISP Name** text box. This name will identify the connection.

7. Click **Next** to open the **Phone Number to Dial** screen. Enter the phone number for the ISP in the **Phone number** text box.

8. If the computer is a member of a domain, click **Next** to open the **Connection Availability** screen. Select the **My use only** option button so that only you will be able to access your Internet account.

9. Click **Next** to open the **Internet Account Information** screen. Enter your **user name** and **password** in the User name and Password text boxes. Reenter your password in the **Confirm password** text box **(Figure 16-6)**.

10. Click **Next** to open the **Completing the New Connection Wizard** screen. Select the **Add a shortcut to this connection to my desktop** check box to add an icon for your ISP connection to the desktop.

11. Click **Finish** to complete the Wizard.

12. Close the **Network Connections** window.

Figure 16-6 The Internet Account Information screen

New Connection Wizard

Internet Account Information
You will need an account name and password to sign in to your Internet account.

Type an ISP account name and password, then write down this information and store it in a safe place. (If you have forgotten an existing account name or password, contact your ISP.)

User name:

Password:

Confirm password:

☑ Make this the default Internet connection

☑ Turn on Internet Connection Firewall for this connection

< Back   Next >   Cancel

project 16.3 | *Setting Up a VPN Connection*

exam objective

Connect to computers using dial-up networking. Connect to computers using a virtual private connection (VPN).

overview

A **Virtual Private Network (VPN)** is an extension of a private network across a shared or public network that is secured by encapsulating and encrypting the data stream. A VPN through the Internet is commonly used as an inexpensive method to connect remote users and offices together.

Suppose you want to connect two distant offices. Before VPN technologies were introduced, you would have had to use dial-up, leased lines, or frame relay to connect them. The costs associated with these connections, especially over long distances were high. Using a VPN, the cost is greatly reduced because you can use the existing infrastructure of the Internet to move your private data.

To configure a VPN, a computer must be configured as the VPN server, which will be the terminus of the secure tunnel. Many different types of computers can be configured as a VPN server, including Windows 2000 and 2003 Server computers, Linux computers, and even a Windows 2000 Professional or Windows XP Professional computer although they only support one concurrent connection. Secure connections in VPNs are created using either **Point-to-Point Tunneling Protocol (PPTP)** or **Layer Two Tunneling Protocol (L2TP)**.

L2TP is the preferred protocol as it has less overhead than PPTP, does tunnel authentication, can be used over any type of packet switched network and relies on **IPSec** to provide encryption. L2TP is only supported under Windows XP Professional, Windows 2000 and Windows 2003. **PPTP** is an older protocol and is therefore more compatible with earlier operating systems and can even be used with Windows 95. PPTP uses Microsoft Point-to-Point Encryption (MPPE) to furnish encryption.

You need to connect the Houston LAN to the Chicago LAN so that users can share resources. You must ensure that data transfers are secure from unauthorized access. You decide to create a Virtual Private Network (VPN) connection between the two networks that will be available to all users in your office.

tip

Remember that VPNs are created across existing network connections. Unless pings have been specifically blocked, you must be able to ping the IP Address of the VPN server to be able to establish a VPN connection with it.

learning objective

After completing this project, you will know how to set up a VPN connection with a remote network.

specific requirements

◆ Administrative rights on a Windows XP Professional computer with a modem installed.
◆ The IP address or domain name of the VPN server that you wish to connect to.

estimated completion time

15 minutes

project steps

Connect to computers using a Virtual Private Connection.
1. Click **Start**, click **Control Panel**, and double-click **Network Connections** to open the **Network Connections** window.
2. Click the **Create a new connection** link to start the **New Connection Wizard**.
3. Click **Next** to open the **Network Connection Type** screen. Select the **Connect to network at my workplace** option button.
4. Click **Next** to open the **Network Connection** screen. Select the **Virtual Private Network** connection option button (**Figure 16-7**).

Figure 16-7 Creating a VPN

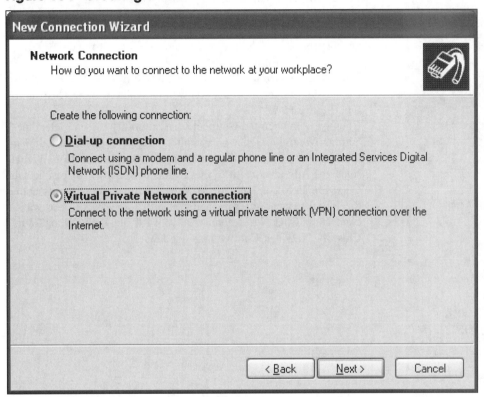

project 16.3

Setting Up a VPN Connection (cont'd)

exam objective

Connect to computers using dial-up networking. Connect to computers using a virtual private connection (VPN).

project steps

5. Click **Next** to open the **Connection Name** screen. Enter a name for the VPN connection in the **Company Name** text box. You can use the name of your organization or the name of the server you will be dialing in to.
6. Click **Next** to open the Public Network screen. Select the **Automatically dial this initial connection** option button and select the name for your Internet connection on the drop-down list **(Figure 16-8)**.
7. Click **Next** to open the **VPN Server Selection** screen. Enter the host name or IP address for the VPN server to which you want to connect in the **Host name or IP address** text box **(Figure 16-9)**.
8. Click **Next** to open the **Connection Availability** screen. Select the **My use only** option button. (*Note:* this step is only applicable if the computer is a domain member.)
9. Click **Next** to open the **Completing the New Connection Wizard** screen. If desired, select the **Add a shortcut to this connection** to my desktop check box.
10. Click **Finish** to complete the Wizard. If you are not currently connected to the Internet the Initial Connection message box opens and asks if you want to create the initial connection. Click **Yes** to connect to your ISP and the VPN, or **No** to cancel.
11. Close the **Network Connections** window.

Figure 16-8 The Public Network screen

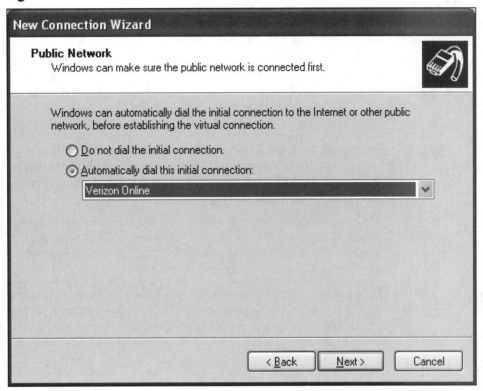

Figure 16-9 The VPN Server Selection screen

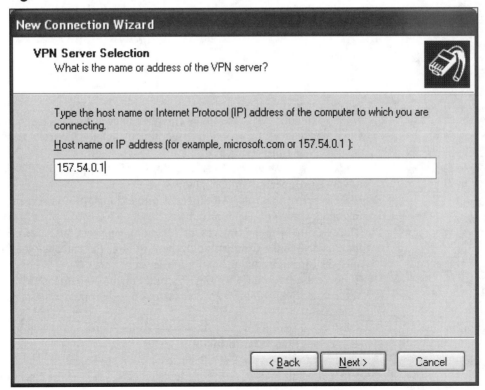

project 16.4

Configuring Inbound Connections

exam objective

Connect to computers using dial-up networking.

overview

Inbound connections are used to allow other computers to connect to yours via either dial-up (modem, ISDN, X.25), VPN (PPTP, L2TP), or direct (serial, infrared) connections. Windows XP Professional computers can accept up to three concurrent inbound connections, one of each type.

Each user that is going to use an inbound connection must have a local user account that has been granted dial-in permission. They will also require the phone number they will dial or the IP address they will use to connect to your computer. For dial-up connections, call back options can be set for each user.

When you configure inbound connections, you can select the networking components, such as the TCP/IP protocol, to be used for the connection. You must also specify the names of the devices, such as the modem, that will be used for the connection and whether or not the computer should allow incoming VPN connections.

Mark Wendell frequently travels and usually takes his laptop with him when he is away from the office. He regularly needs to access his office computer to monitor additions to a confidential folder, which is updated frequently by his executive secretary. He wants you to create an inbound connection on his office computer so that he can access this folder from his laptop when he is traveling.

learning objective

After completing this project, you will know how to configure an inbound connection.

specific requirements

Administrative rights on a Windows XP Professional computer with a modem installed.

estimated completion time

15 minutes

project steps

Configure a Windows XP Professional computer to accept incoming connections.

1. Open the **Network Connections** window and click the **Create a new connection** link to start the **New Connection Wizard**.
2. Click **Next** to open the **Network Connection Type** screen. Select the **Set up an advanced connection** option button.
3. Click **Next** to open the **Advanced Connection Options** screen. Select the **Accept incoming connections** option button.
4. Click **Next** to open the **Devices for Incoming Connections** screen. Select the check box for a modem in the **Connection devices** list box. You can click the **Properties** button to open the Properties dialog box for the device.
5. Click **Next** to open the **Incoming Virtual Private Network (VPN) Connection** screen. You can accept incoming VPN connections if your computer has a publicly accessible IP address.
6. Select the **Do not allow virtual private connections** option button to disallow inbound VPN connections (**Figure 16-10**).
7. Click **Next** to open the **User Permissions** screen. Select the check boxes for the users who will be allowed to access the inbound connection in the **Users allowed to connect** list box (**Figure 16-11**).

tip

When configuring an inbound VPN connection that will use an Ethernet adapter on your computer, the adapter will not appear in the Devices for Incoming Connections list. Do not select any device from the devices list and click Next to continue configuring the VPN.

Figure 16-10 The Incoming Virtual Private Network (VPN) Connection screen

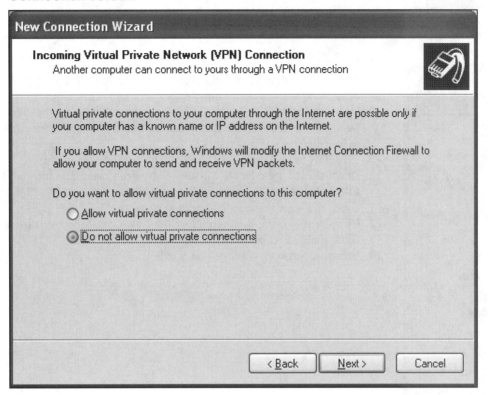

Figure 16-11 The User Permissions screen

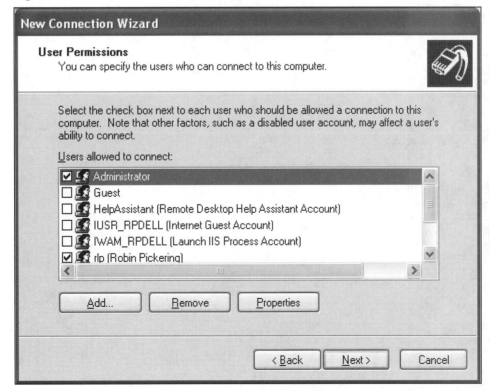

project 16.4

Configuring Inbound Connections *(cont'd)*

exam objective

Connect to computers using dial-up networking.

project steps

8. Select one of these users in the **Users allowed to connect** list box and click **Properties** to open the Properties dialog box for the user.

9. Open the **Callback** tab. Select the **Allow the caller to set the callback number** option button so that they will be able to dial in from different locations and specify the number to be called back **(Figure 16-12)**.

10. Click **OK** to save the callback setting and close the dialog box.

11. Click **Next** to open the **Networking Software** screen. The **Internet Protocol (TCP/IP)**, **File and Printer Sharing for Microsoft Networks**, and **Client for Microsoft Networks** check boxes are selected by default **(Figure 16-13)**.

12. Click **Next** to open the **Completing the New Connection Wizard** screen.

13. Click **Finish** to complete the Wizard.

14. Close the **Network Connections** window.

**Figure 16-12 The Callback tab on the Properties
dialog box for a user**

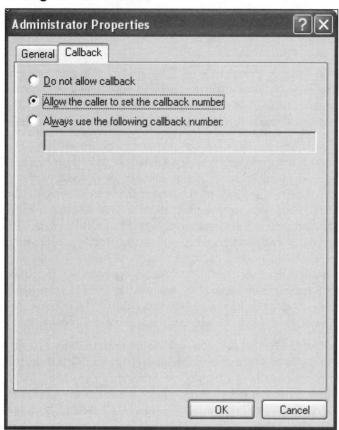

Figure 16-13 The Networking Software screen

project 16.5	*Configuring Internet Connection Sharing*

exam objective

Connect to computers using dial-up networking. Configure and troubleshoot Internet Connection Sharing (ICS).

overview

After you set up an Internet connection on a computer, you can configure **Internet Connection Sharing** so that you can share the link with other computers on your LAN. ICS is most useful for small networks where you want all the computers to be able to access the Internet using a single connection. Any type of Internet connection such as dial-up, DSL or Cable will work with ICS.

The computer on which ICS is configured is assigned a static IP address of 192.168.0.1. Because this address cannot be changed, ICS may not be suitable for networks with an existing IP addressing scheme. All other computers on the LAN must be configured to obtain their IP addresses automatically. Each client computer will obtain an address in the range of 192.168.0.2 through 192.168.0.254 from the ICS computer which acts like a DHCP server. The clients will also be assigned a default gateway address which will be the IP address of the internal network adapter for the computer that is running Internet Connection Sharing. When a client computer attempts to access resources that are on the Internet their data packets will be routed through the computer running ICS to their destination on the Internet. The computer running ICS not only acts as a network router, it also provides basic **Network Address Translation (NAT)** to allow the single Internet connection to be shared with a number of computers on the LAN.

You previously configured a dial-up connection to the Internet on Debbie Howe's computer. She has found the ability to be able to search the Internet so valuable that she wants to make that ability available to all of the members of her Software Engineering Team. Instead of installing and configuring modems and phone lines for each of the other users you have decided to make use of Windows XP Professional's Internet Connection Sharing feature. You will run ICS on Debbie's computer to share her existing Internet connection.

learning objective

At the end of this project, you will know how to configure Internet connection sharing to allow other computers on your network to access the Internet.

specific requirements

◆ Administrative rights on a Windows XP Professional computer.
◆ Completion of Project 16.2.

estimated completion time

15 minutes

project steps

Configure Internet Connection Sharing (ICS).

1. Open the **Network Connections** window.
2. Right-click a connection icon for an Internet connection such as the one created in project 16.2 and select **Properties** to open the Properties dialog box for the connection.
3. Open the **Advanced** tab (**Figure 16-14**). Select the **Allow other network users to connect through this computer's Internet connection** option button.
4. If you enabled the Internet connection only for yourself, the **Network Connections** message box will open to remind you that the user name and password for the connection were not saved for all users (**Figure 16-15**). If you do not change this setting, ICS will only be able to dial the connection when you are logged on. You must save your user name and password for all users in the **Connect** dialog box. Click **OK** to close the message box. To change this, after you have enabled ICS, right click the connection in the Network Connections windows and select **Connect**. Then, select the **Anyone who uses this computer** option button.

Figure 16-14 Enabling Internet Connection Sharing

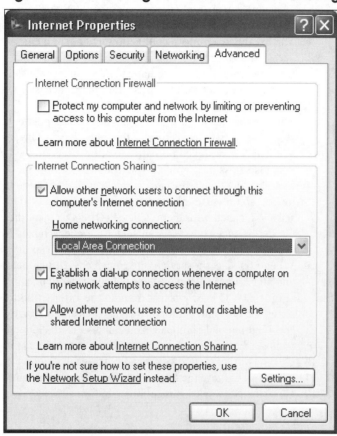

Figure 16-15 The Network Connections message box

project 16.5

Configuring Internet Connection Sharing *(cont'd)*

exam objective

Connect to computers using dial-up networking. Configure and troubleshoot Internet Connection Sharing (ICS).

project steps

5. If you have multiple network adapters installed, a list box will allow you to select which local area connection will represent the LAN that you want to enable connection sharing (**Figure 16-14**). If you have only one LAN connection, the list box will not appear.

6. The **Establish a dial-up connection whenever a computer on my network attempts to access the Internet** option is enabled by default when ICS is enabled. It configures the Internet connection to automatically dial and establish a connection to the Internet when another computer on the LAN attempts to access Internet resources through the ICS computer.

7. Remove the check mark from the **Allow other network users to control or disable the shared Internet connection** so that only you will be able to perform these actions.

8. While ICS is designed primarily to allow users on the LAN to access internet resources, it is also possible to make specific services on the LAN accessible to users on the Internet. Any time a resource is made available on the Internet it can expose the network to risk, so only use this option if you are aware of the dangers and how to mitigate the risks associated with them. Click **Settings** to open the **Advanced Settings** dialog box. On the Services tab, you can select the check boxes for each service running on your network that you want to allow Internet users to access (**Figure 16-16**).

9. When you select a service, the **Service Settings** dialog box will open. Here, you can enter the name or IP address for the computer that is hosting this service on your network (**Figure 16-17**). Any traffic sent to the Internet address of the ICS computer on the specified port and protocol will be forwarded to the selected service running on the specified internal computer. You can also click Add and supply the IP address, protocol and port that will be used to create a customized mapping to a service.

10. Click **OK** to close the **Advanced Settings** dialog box.
11. Click **OK** to close the Properties dialog box for the Internet connection.
12. Close the **Network Connections** window.

caution

Before making any services on the LAN available to users on the Internet, be sure to carefully review the security risks involved and take steps to minimize those risks.

Figure 16-16 Selecting Services to make available to Internet users

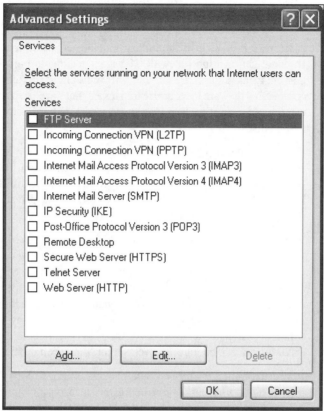

Figure 16-17 Configuring Service Settings

project 16.6

Setting Up a Firewall

exam objective

Connect to computers using dial-up networking. Configure, manage, and troubleshoot an Internet connection firewall (ICF).

overview

A firewall is a security boundary that protects one network from another network. The **Internet Connection Firewall (ICF)** is a new feature in Windows XP. It is a stateful firewall that analyzes network traffic and will only allow packets from the public network into the computer if they are in response to packets that have been sent from the private network out of the computer. Any packets that are received that are not in response to an outbound request will be discarded.

If you use Internet Connection Sharing (ICS) to provide Internet access to your network, ICF should be enabled on the shared Internet connection. ICF should also be enabled on the Internet connection of any computer that is connected directly to the Internet. As shown in **Figure 16-18** all traffic that passes between the private and public networks must pass through ICF for examination.

When you configure ICS, you must decide what types of traffic you are going to block, and what types of traffic you are going to allow. You allow certain types of data packets to pass through the firewall by creating a **port mapping** on the Services tab in the Advanced Settings dialog box. You create a port mapping by associating a specific port on the external IP address of the computer with a port number on an internal IP address. For example, you can forward inbound HTTP traffic to a Web server on your LAN by mapping port 80 on the computer, which is designated as the port for the HTTP service, to the IP address for the Web server. In this way you can configure a Web server to run behind the firewall.

In order to monitor dropped data packets, either to look for potential security threats or to troubleshoot why data is not being received, you can enable ICF logging. When you log dropped packets, all rejected packets, whether they are inbound or outbound, will be recorded in the ICF log file. When you log successful connections, all successful connections, both incoming and outgoing, will be recorded. The default log file size is 4 MB, which can be increased to a maximum of 32MB.

You want to use the Internet Connection Firewall to protect the Internet connection on Debbie's computer that is shared using ICS. You rely on technical support from your Houston office and they would like to be able to use the Remote Assistance feature of Windows XP Professional and also use the application and white board sharing capabilities of Windows Messenger to provide support for your office. By default ICF will block the protocols for both of these services, so you will need to configure Debbie's computer to enable them. Because you will be opening up additional ports on the firewall and thereby increasing the risk of attack, you want to enable logging of rejected packets to determine whether anyone has attempted unauthorized access to your network.

learning objective

At the end of this project, you will know how to protect Internet connections by using the Internet Connection Firewall.

specific requirements

Administrative rights on a Windows XP Professional computer.

estimated completion time

15 minutes

Figure 16-18 Placement of the Internet Connection Firewall

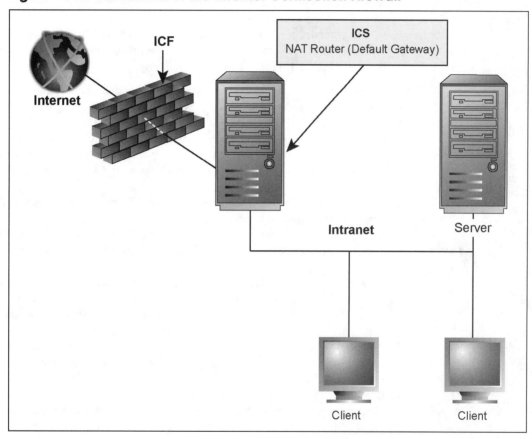

project 16.6

Setting Up a Firewall (cont'd)

exam objective

Connect to computers using dial-up networking. Configure, manage, and troubleshoot an Internet connection firewall (ICF).

project steps

Enable the Internet Connection Firewall.

1. Click **Start**, click **Control Panel**, click the **Switch to Classic View** link if required, and double-click **Network Connections** to open the **Network Connections** window.
2. Right-click an Internet connection and select **Properties**. The properties dialog box for the selected connection will open. Select the **Advanced** tab.
3. In the **Internet Connection Firewall** section check the box beside **Protect my computer and network by limiting or preventing access to this computer from the Internet (Figure 16-19)**.

Create a custom port mapping to allow internet users access to a service on your network.

4. Click the **Settings** button to open the **Advanced Settings** dialog box **(Figure 16-20)**.
5. The **Services** tab will be selected. The settings on this tab control what type of inbound traffic will be allowed through this computer and specifies which computer it will be directed to. This is called port mapping and is more of a function of Internet Connection Sharing than it is of the Internet Connection Firewall. Click **Add** to create a custom port mapping.
6. In the **Description of service** text box type **Windows Messenger White Board** to describe the purpose of this port mapping.
7. Type the IP address for your computer in the **Name or IP address** text box. If you completed project 16.5, ICS will be enabled and therefore your IP address will be **192.168.0.1**.
8. Type **1503** for both the **External** and **Internal port number for this service** and ensure that the **TCP** protocol is selected **(Figure 16-21)**.
9. Click **OK** to save the new port mapping. Notice that **Windows Messenger White Board** now appears with a check mark beside it in the services list.
10. Remote Desktop uses the RDP protocol on TCP port 3389 and allows an authorized support person to remotely control a computer. Select **Remote Desktop** from the services list and click **Edit**. The **Service Settings** dialog box will open.
11. Because this is a pre-defined port mapping, it is only necessary to enter the IP address of the computer that will host the Remote Desktop service. Type **192.168.0.1** in the **Name or IP address** text box and then click **OK** to close the dialog box.

caution

When allowing inbound connections to access services on a computer, make sure that it has the latest security patches, service packs and current anti-virus software.

Figure 16-19 Enabling the Internet Connection Firewall

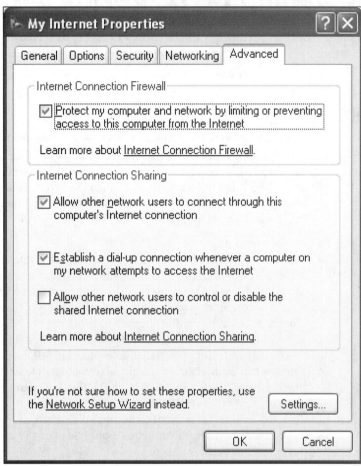

Figure 16-20 The Advanced Settings dialog box

Figure 16-21 Adding a custom port mapping

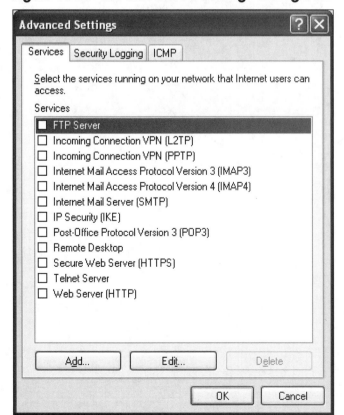

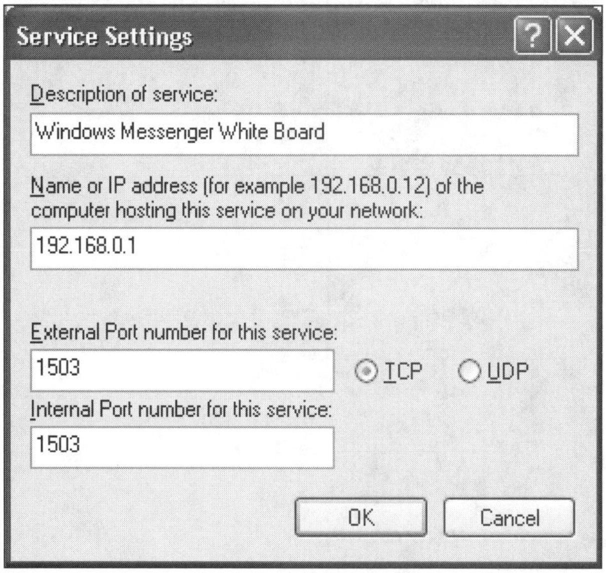

Setting Up a Firewall (cont'd)

exam objective

Connect to computers using dial-up networking. Configure, manage, and troubleshoot an Internet connection firewall (ICF).

project steps

Enable logging of discarded packets and set maximum log file size.

12. In the **Advanced Settings** dialog box select the **Security Logging** tab.

13. In the **Logging Options** section, check the box beside **Log dropped packets**. This setting will record a log entry for any inbound or outbound packet that is discarded by the firewall.

14. In the **Log File Options** section, change the **Size Limit** for the log file to **16384** KB (**Figure 16-22**). This will increase the maximum size of the log file so that there will be less chance of loosing security records generated by ICF.

Enable inbound pings.

15. Click the **ICMP** tab to manage the behavior of the Internet Control Message Protocol (ICMP). ICMP is used for several functions but the best known use is for the **Ping** command. When a Ping command is issued, an ICMP echo request is sent to the target host. That host, in response, sends an ICMP echo reply back to the originator of the Ping command. Pings are commonly used to check connectivity between hosts but attackers will also use ping scans to locate hosts that will then attempt to compromise. For this reason, ICF is pre-configured to disallow most ICMP traffic.

16. You want to enable incoming pings so that the Houston office can verify that the connection is functioning. Check the **Allow incoming echo request** box to enable incoming Pings (**Figure 16-23**).

17. Click **OK** to close the **Advanced Settings** dialog box and save the configuration for ICF.

18. Click **OK** to close the **Properties** dialog box for the connection and then close the **Network Connections** screen.

Figure 16-22 Configuring logging options

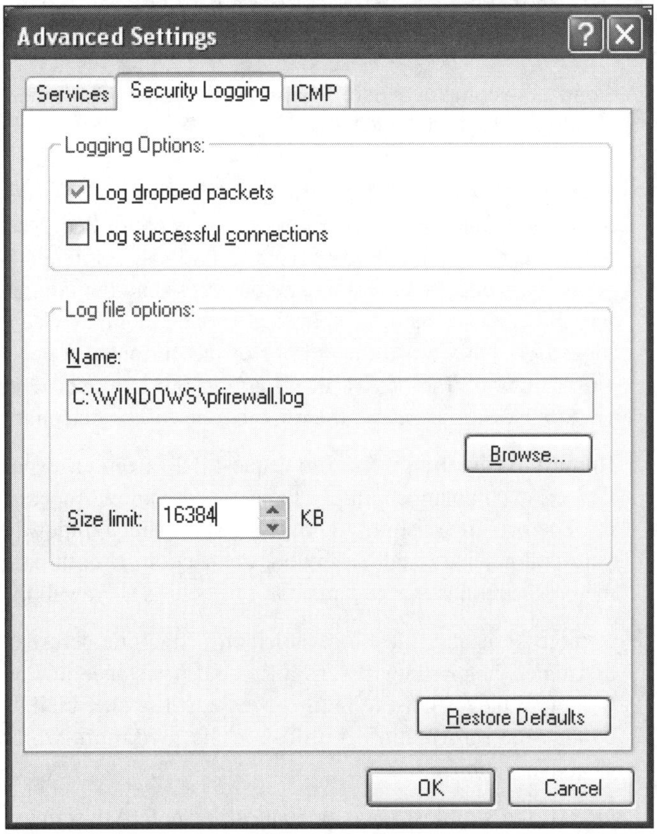

Figure 16-23 Allowing incoming pings

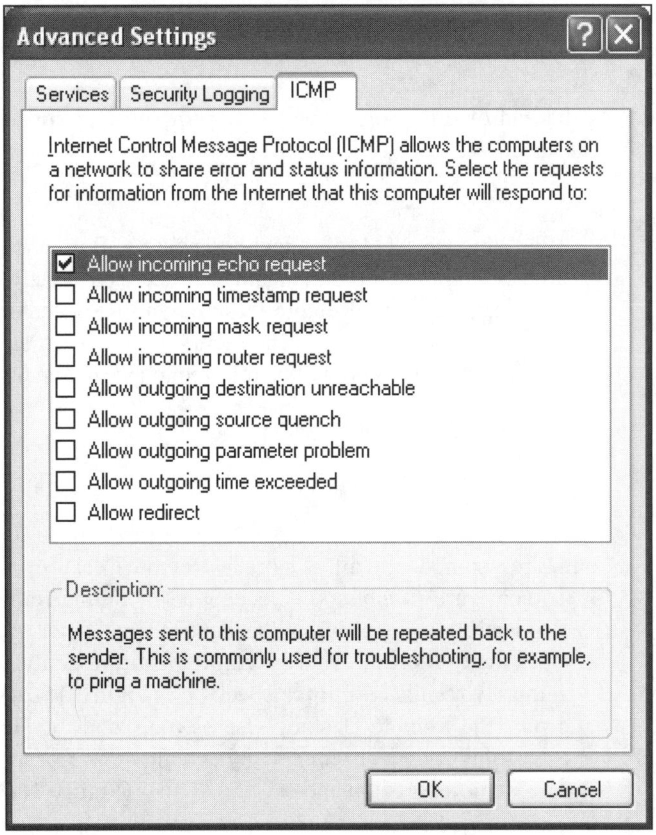

project 16.7 *Configuring Remote Desktop and Remote Assistance*

exam objective

Connect to computers using dial-up networking. Configure, manage, and troubleshoot remote desktop and remote assistance.

overview

Remote Desktop and **Remote Assistance** provide functionality that is based on Terminal Services so that computers can be remotely controlled. **Remote Desktop** functionality allows you to access a remote computer from a local computer to run applications, open files, and access network resources. When you access another computer via Remote Desktop, the desktop is locked so that users physically at the computer cannot use it while you are remotely logged on. Only an Administrator or the currently connected remote user's account will be able to unlock the desktop by logging on. If a user does log on locally while a Remote Desktop session is active, the remote user will be disconnected.

Remote Assistance is used to request help from an expert, help desk support personnel, a network technician, or simply someone who knows more about a particular problem than you do. The person assisting you must be at another Windows XP computer that is accessible by your computer through a network connection. If both parties are connected by the Internet, the person requesting help must not be behind a firewall that is blocking TCP port 3389.

Remote Assistance must be enabled on a computer before it can be used. When a user requires assistance, he or she will send a Remote Assistance invitation through the Help and Support Center, or they can use Windows Messenger or an e-mail to request assistance. The necessary connection information is stored in the invitation, which the recipient opens in order to establish a connection.

One of the simplest ways to request Remote Assistance is for both the person requesting assistance and the expert or technician to be using Windows Messenger. MSN Messenger or a MAPI-compliant e-mail program such as Outlook or Outlook Express can also be used. After the Remote Assistance session is established, the expert or technician can see everything that happens on the other computer, and the two parties can send messages to one another using chat boxes that are launched on each computer.

learning objective

At the end of this project, you will know how to configure remote desktop and remote assistance.

specific requirements

◆　Two Windows XP Professional computers. Both should have Outlook Express configured as their e-mail program and have access to a mail server. The first will be configured to accept incoming Remote Desktop and Remote Assistance connections and will be referred to as *Computer1*. The second will be used as the client computer to connect to the first computer and will be referred to as *Computer2*.

estimated completion time

20 minutes

project steps

Configure a computer to allow inbound Remote Desktop and Remote Assistance connections.
1. To configure *Computer1* to accept an incoming remote connection, open the **System Properties** dialog box from the Control Panel.
2. Open the **Remote** tab. In the **Remote Desktop** section, select the **Allow users to connect remotely to this computer** check box (**Figure 16-24**). Members of the Administrators group, the Remote Desktop Users group, and the HelpServicesGroup will be able to access this computer remotely by default.
3. The **Remote Sessions** message box opens (**Figure 16-25**). Click **OK**.

Figure 16-24 Enabling Remote Assistance and Remote Desktop

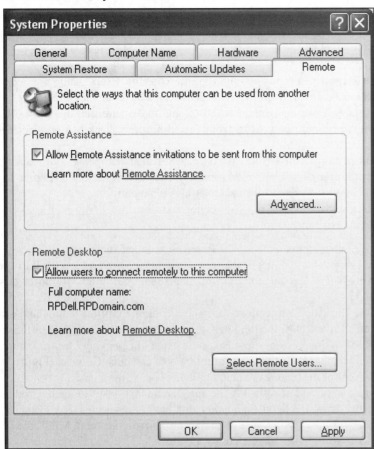

Figure 16-25 The Remote Sessions message box

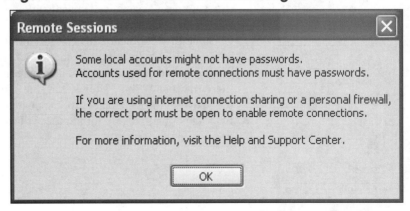

project 16.7

Configuring Remote Desktop and Remote Assistance (cont'd)

exam objective

Connect to computers using dial-up networking. Configure, manage, and troubleshoot remote desktop and remote assistance.

project steps

4. Click **Select Remote Users** to open the **Remote Desktop Users** dialog box where you can add additional users who will be allowed to access the computer remotely.
5. Close the Remote Desktop Users dialog box and make sure that the **Allow Remote Assistance invitations to be sent to from this computer** check box is selected in the **Remote Assistance** section.
6. Click **Advanced** to open the **Remote Assistance Settings** dialog box. Make sure that the **Allow this computer to be controlled remotely check box** is selected (**Figure 16-26**).
7. Click **OK** to close the Remote Assistance Settings dialog box.
8. Click **OK** to close the System Properties dialog box.
9. Log off from the computer.

Remotely control another computer using the Remote Desktop Connection.
10. To configure *Computer2* to initiate a remote connection, click **Start**, click **All Programs**, point to **Accessories**, point to **Communications**, and click **Remote Desktop Connection**.
11. In the **Remote Desktop Connection** dialog box, click the **Options** button and examine the options on all five tabs of the Remote Desktop Connection. Click the **Options** button again to go back to the previous view. Enter the name of *Computer1* for the computer to which you want to connect in the **Computer** text box, and click **Connect (Figure 16-27)**.
12. The logon screen for the remote computer will display.
13. Enter your user name and password in the appropriate text boxes to log on. You can use any account that is available on *Computer1* that has been selected as a member of the Remote Users group or you can use the Administrator account which always has permission to make Remote connections.
14. Test the Remote Desktop connection by running a program from the Start menu.
15. Close the open windows. Click **Start** and select **Log Off** to end the Remote Desktop session. The Log Off option closes all programs, logs off the current user and terminates the Remote Desktop session. The option to Disconnect leaves all of your active programs running and closes the Remote Desktop session. You can reconnect to a disconnected session and resume your work where you left off.

Use Remote Assistance to send a request for help to another user.
16. To configure *Computer1* to send a request for help, click **Start**, click **All Programs**, and select **Remote Assistance** to open the Remote Assistance page in the Help and Support Center.
17. Click the **Invite someone to help you link (Figure 16-28)**. If you do not have Windows Messenger or Outlook Express configured, the invitation can be saved as a file which can then be sent to the support person by other means. If you select the **Save invitation as a file (Advanced)** link, after specifying the logon name and password, you will be prompted for the location to save the invitation.
18. Enter the e-mail address for the user at the *Computer2* in the **Type an e-mail address text** box in the **Outlook Express** section (**Figure 16-29**).

Figure 16-26 The Remote Assistance Settings dialog box

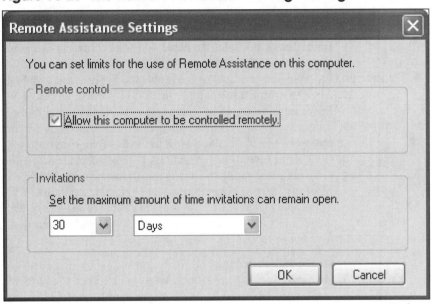

Figure 16-27 The Remote Desktop Connection dialog box

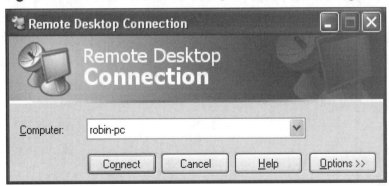

Configuring Remote Desktop and Remote Assistance *(cont'd)*

exam objective

Connect to computers using dial-up networking. Configure, manage, and troubleshoot remote desktop and remote assistance.

project steps

tip

If you send an assistance invitation and you are using a Network Address Translation device, the receiver must save the invitation file, right-click it and select Open With Notepad. Under the RCTICKET attribute, they must replace the private IP address with the public IP address the computer is using. Then, he or she must save the file and double-click it to open the Remote Assistance session.

19. Click the **Invite this person** link to open the **Remote Assistance—E-Mail and Invitation page**. Enter the name you want to appear in the invitation in the **From** text box.
20. Enter a message regarding the problem you need help with in the **Message** list box.
21. Click **Continue**. Enter a time limit during which the recipient can accept the invitation. For example, change the default 1 hour to 30 minutes (**Figure 16-30**).
22. Type the password the recipient must use to connect to your computer in the **Type password** text box and reenter it in the **Confirm password** text box.
23. Click **Send Invitation**. An Outlook Express message box will open to inform you that a program is attempting to send an e-mail message on your behalf. Click **Send**. You should receive a message informing you that your invitation has been successfully sent. Remember that in order to send an invitation using Outlook Express, both the sender and the recipient must have an email account and both systems must be properly configured to send and receive e-mail.

Respond to the help request.
24. On *Computer2*, open Outlook Express and open the message sent as an invitation to assist the user on *Computer1*. Open the attached file, which must be of the MSRC incident type. If prompted to save or open the file, open it unless the sender is using NAT.
25. Next, click **Yes** to accept the invitation, and when prompted to connect to the sender's computer, enter the password that was entered in Step 22 and click **Yes** to connect to your computer.
26. On *Computer1*, a **Remote Assistance** message box will open to inform you that your invitation has been accepted (**Figure 16-31**). Click **Yes**.
27. Remote Assistance windows will open on both computers complete with **Message Entry** and **Chat History** sections to allow you and the technician to interact in order to solve the problem.
28. Click the **Disconnect** button to end the remote assistance session and close the Remote Assistance windows on both computers.

Figure 16-28 Requesting Remote Assistance from the Help and Support Center

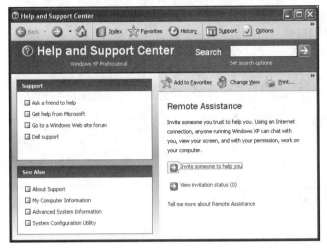

Figure 16-29 Sending an assistance invitation via e-mail

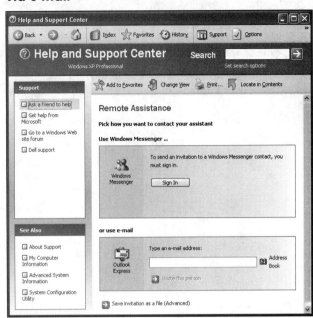

Figure 16-30 The Remote Assistance - E-mail an Invitation page

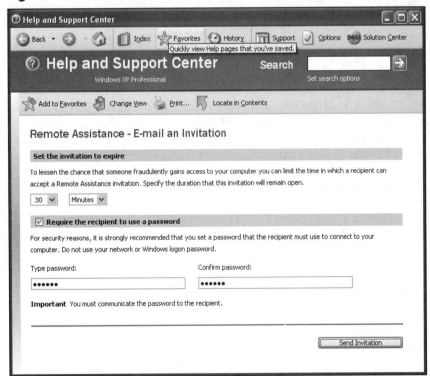

Figure 16-31 The Remote Assistance message box

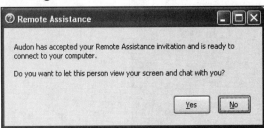

Understanding the Domain Name System (DNS) is crucial to your understanding of how Windows networks function. DNS is the main name resolution service for Windows XP, 2000 and 2003 networks. It is used to locate the IP address for computers on a TCP/IP network by using the Fully Qualified Domain Name (FQDN). This makes it possible for users to connect to other computers using a name that is easy to remember instead of requiring knowledge of each computer's IP address. In an Active Directory domain, DNS is not only used for name resolution. It is also used to define the hierarchical layout of the domain name space. A properly functioning DNS is also critical to find services necessary to log on, change passwords, and locate resources. In a malfunctioning Active Directory domain environment, one of the first troubleshooting steps should always be to confirm the correct configuration and operation of all of the components of DNS. Windows XP Professional participates as a DNS client and must be properly configured to be able to locate a DNS server in order for name resolution to function correctly.

In addition to the Internet, most networks today also make use of Web servers to provide and publish information either for the internal use of an organization or for public distribution. Because the use of Web servers has become so common, one of the responsibilities of a Network Administrator is normally to support and maintain them. Windows XP professional includes Internet Information Services which provides both a Web server and an FTP server. It is important to learn how to configure it securely and administer and maintain it within your environment.

Scenario

You are the Network Administrator for Solutions Inc., an organization that creates business planning, analysis, and management reporting solutions for clients. There are 15 employees and 15 client computers on the network. There is also one server, which functions as the domain controller, the DHCP server, and the DNS name server. A new client computer must be configured as a DNS client and you must create a Web server so that users on your network will be able to access a common policies and procedures manual that you want to publish on your corporate intranet.

Lesson 17 Introducing DNS and Web Server Resources

Project	Exam 70-270 Objective
17.1 Configuring Windows XP as a DNS Client	Basic knowledge
17.2 Managing Web Server Resources	Manage and troubleshoot Web server resources.

General Requirements

To complete the projects in this lesson, you will need a Windows XP Professional computer with TCP/IP configured with access to a server that has the DNS service installed.

project 17.1

Configuring Windows XP as a DNS Client

exam objective

Basic knowledge

overview

In order to use the DNS name resolution process, the client computer must have access to a server that is running either the DNS or the BIND service. After you have configured Transmission Control Protocol/Internet Protocol (TCP/IP) properly, you can configure your Windows XP Professional computer as a DNS client. You can either configure the machine to automatically obtain the address of a DNS server from a DHCP server on the network, or you can manually enter the IP addresses for the preferred and alternate DNS servers that you want the client to use.

Steve Irving, the Accounts Officer of Solutions Inc., has just received a new Windows XP Professional computer. It must be configured as a DNS client so that he can access the network and the Internet.

tip

BIND is the naming service used for most Unix and Linux platforms and is very common on the Internet.

learning objective

After completing this project, you will know how to configure a Windows XP Professional computer as a DNS client.

specific requirements

◆   Administrative rights on a Windows XP Professional computer with TCP/IP configured.
◆   The IP address of a DNS server.

estimated completion time

5 minutes

project steps

Configure a Windows XP Professional machine to be a DNS client.

1. Click **Start** and click **Control Panel**. Double-click the **Network Connections** icon to open the **Network Connections** window.
2. Right-click **Local Area Connection** under **LAN or High-Speed Internet** and select **Properties** to open the **Local Area Connection Properties** dialog box.
3. Select **Internet Protocol (TCP/IP)** in the **This connection uses the following items** box (**Figure 17-1**).
4. Click **Properties** to open the **Internet Protocol (TCP/IP) Properties** dialog box.
5. Select the **Use the following DNS server addresses** option button. You will have to ask the Network Administrator for the IP address for a DNS server on the network.
6. Type the IP address of the primary DNS server for the client in the **Preferred DNS Server** text box. For example, type 135.85.42.2 (**Figure 17-2**).
7. If another DNS server is available on the network you can type its IP address in the **Alternate DNS server** text box. This DNS server will be used if the primary DNS server is unavailable.
8. Click **OK** to save the DNS configuration and close the Internet Protocol (TCP/IP) Properties dialog box.
9. Click **Close** to close the Local Area Connections dialog box.
10. Close the **Network Connections** window.

tip

If you select the **Obtain DNS server address automatically** option, the DHCP server on your network will provide the DNS server addresses that it has been configured with to the client.

Figure 17-1 The Local Area Connection Properties dialog box

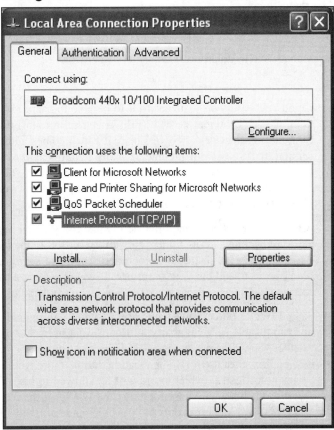

Figure 17-2 Manually configuring DNS server addresses

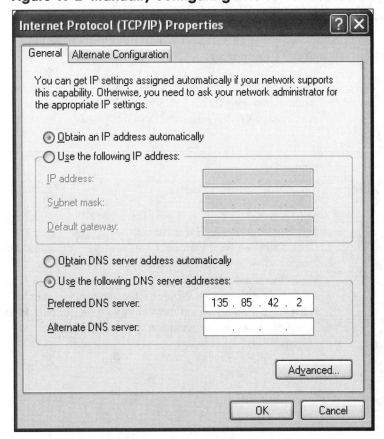

project 17.2

Managing Web Server Resources

exam objective

Manage and troubleshoot Web server resources.

overview

If you want users on your network to be able to share resources with other users who are running Web browsers or FTP (File Transfer Protocol) utilities, you can install **Internet Information Services (IIS)** version 5.1, which comes with Windows XP Professional. This version of IIS does not include as many features as the Windows 2000 and 2003 Server versions. It is intended for use only for small intranets or for a Web site that does not get very much traffic. Sharing Web resources involves publishing your files so they are available via HTTP (Hyper Text Transfer Protocol).

After you install IIS, an icon for the Internet Information Services Manager will be added to the Administrative Tools folder. This utility is used to manage and configure your Web site. By default, an IIS installation includes FrontPage server extensions, the IIS snap-in, the SMTP service, and the WWW service. If you also want a default FTP site, you will have to add the File Transfer Protocol (FTP) Service to the default installation.

caution

Many recent security exploits have involved IIS. Do not allow unauthorized installations of IIS within your organization and make sure that all authorized installations are always kept up to date with the latest security patches and recommended security configuration settings.

Shared Web resources must have access controls configured to keep them secure. One simple tip is to disable services that you do not want users to be able to access. You can specify whether you will allow anonymous connections or whether users must authenticate and what method they must use for authentication. Furthermore, you can limit the number of incoming connections, restrict which users will be allowed to have Operator privileges, and restrict access to the home directory for either the WWW or the FTP service by setting permissions. You can also grant access only to a specific range of IP addresses, or you can deny access for specific IP or DNS addresses, or a range of addresses.

Catherine, one of Solution Inc.'s employees, is in the process of completing a Web site for Solutions Inc. You are the Network Administrator for the organization. Catherine approaches you to install IIS on her computer so that she can manage the site from her computer.

learning objective

After completing this project, you will know how to install IIS on a computer running Windows XP Professional.

specific requirements

◆ Administrative rights on a Windows XP Professional computer.
◆ A Windows XP Professional CD-ROM.

estimated completion time

15 minutes

project steps

Install IIS on Windows XP Professional.
1. Click **Start** and click **Control Panel** to open the Control Panel.
2. Double-click the **Add or Remove Programs** icon to open the **Add or Remove Programs** window.
3. Click the **Add/Remove Windows Components** icon in the vertical menu bar on the left side on the window to start the **Windows Components Wizard (Figure 17-3)**.
4. Select the **Internet Information Services (IIS)** check box in the **Components** list box **(Figure 17-4)**.

Figure 17-3 The Add/Remove Windows Components window

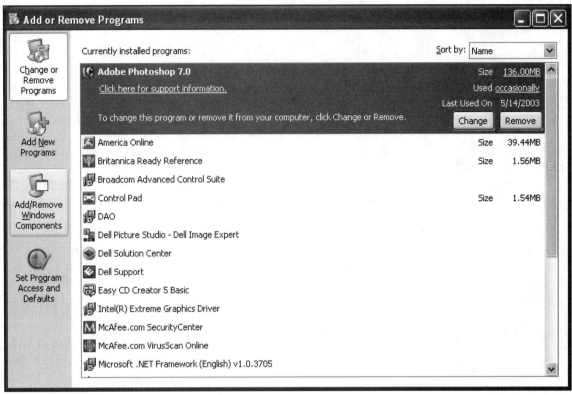

Figure 17-4 Installing IIS on a computer

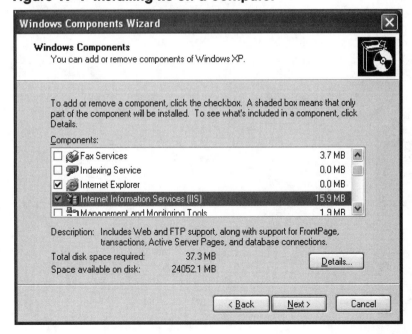

project 17.2

Managing Web Server Resources (cont'd)

exam objective

Manage and troubleshoot Web server resources.

project steps

5. Double-click **Internet Information Services (IIS)** to open the Internet Information Services dialog box. The components that are checked are the default installation for IIS. If you want a default FTP site to be created, select the File Transfer Protocol (FTP) Service. Click **OK** to close the Internet Information Services dialog box.
6. Click **Next**. The **Configuring Components** screen opens, and then the **Insert Disk** dialog box opens asking you to insert the Windows XP Professional CD in the CD-ROM drive.
7. Insert the Windows XP Professional CD, and click **OK** to return to the Configuring Components screen. A progress bar will display the advancement of the installation of the files as they are copied to the system.
8. After all of the files are copied onto the system, the **Completing the Windows Components Wizard** screen opens to inform you that the Wizard has successfully finished (**Figure 17-5**).
9. Click **Finish** to exit the Wizard.
10. Close the **Add or Remove Programs** window.
11. Open the **Administrative Tools** folder. Double-click Internet Information Services to open the **Internet Information** Services snap-in.
12. Expand the computer name node, the **Web Sites** folder and the **Default Web Site** node (**Figure 17-6**). This console tree represents the logical structure of your default Web site.
13. Close the Internet Information Services snap-in and the Administrative Tools folder.

tip

On a Windows XP Professional computer, you can create only one Web site, one FTP site, and one SMTP site.

Figure 17-5 Completing the Windows Components Wizard

Figure 17-6 Default Web Site node

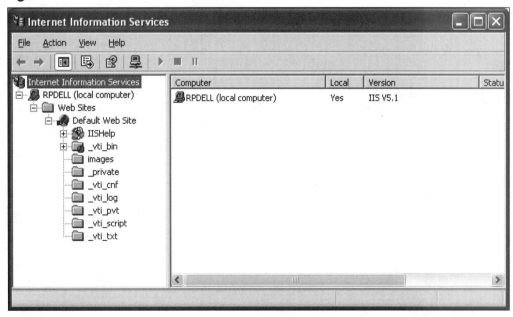